# THE NEW STARS OF TWENTY 20

*Making of India's Cricketing Tomorrow*

ARANI BASU

tara
India Research Press
Flat. 6, Khan Market, New Delhi - 110 003
Ph: 24694610; Fax: 24618637
www.indiaresearchpress.com
contact@indiaresearchpress.com

2022



ISBN 13: 978-81-8386-202-8

Printed and Bound in India

*To my parents,*

*Dipika Basu and Pankaj Kanti Basu,*

*and my wife Juhi Chakraborty*

# *FOREWORD*

A few decades ago, it was comparatively easy to predict where the maximum students would qualify from for the coveted Indian Institutes of Technology. Most of them would emerge from top schools in the major metros, a fair lot from the so called 'colony' towns like Jamshedpur and Bhilai and then a really small number from the rest of the country. The reason was simple – access to information, good teachers and a pedigree of students who had made it and showed a path to their juniors

The story was exactly the same in Indian cricket. Most international players would emerge from the traditional cricket 'gharanas' of Mumbai, Bangalore, Chennai and Delhi, teams that traditionally dominated the Ranji Trophy. Hyderabad and Punjab would occasionally provide a few excellent players and the rest of the country would contribute one or two outliers – a Debasis Mohanty from Odisha, a Gopal Sharma from UP.

Both institutions have changed beyond recognition. Today, while a good number of IITians come to polish their finishing skills in institutes in Kota, the students who study there are from every nook and corner in the country. And similarly, while a legendary coach like Tarak Sinha might have helped polish Rishabh Pant's skills at Sonnet Club in Delhi, Rishabh originally hails from Roorkee in Uttarakhand, definitely a backwater in Indian cricket.

He's not an exception. The current crop of young cricketers hail from every nook and corner in the country. And even though some of the players in this list are from the so called 'big cities,' they often hail from economic backgrounds not usually associated with the game.

These cricketers have stories to tell. And they need a voice that appreciates and understands their journey. Arani, himself a product of the tiny colony town of Burnpur in West Bengal who made it to a mainstream media giant, has taken it upon himself to document their incredible careers.

This book is not a result of a couple of zoom calls or post-match interviews. It's emerged from years of travelling to junior World Cups, unfashionable First-Class matches and spending time with these cricketers before they became darlings at the IPL auctions and later, household names.

The players you will meet in this journey are Rishabh Pant, Mohammad Siraj, Suryakumar Yadav, Prithvi Shaw, Shubman Gill, Washington Sundar, Shreyas Iyer, Deepak Chahar, Rahul Chahar, Avesh Khan, Ishan Kishan and Navdeep Saini. Each of them has a unique story to relate.

Do listen.

Joy Bhattacharjya

*Renowned sports commentator and quizzer*

# *INTRODUCTION*

There are certain images, over the last four decades, that define the evolution of Indian cricket as a powerhouse: Kapil Dev holding aloft the World Cup on the Lord's balcony on 25 June 1983, Sourav Ganguly hysterically waving his shirt at the same venue on 13 July 2002, S Sreesanth's catch of Misbah Ul Haq to claim the inaugural World T20 at Wanderers in 2007 and Mahendra Singh Dhoni depositing Nuwan Kulasekara into the stands to win the World Cup at Wankhede on 2 April 2011. The series wins in West Indies and England in 1971 make for the genesis of an enthralling journey that the sport took in the country.

These iconic images mark the eras of Indian cricket's nine-decade history.

Cut to January 2021, Rishabh Pant driving Australian fast bowler Josh Hazlewood for a boundary straight down the ground at the Gabba in Brisbane to complete a 2–1 win in the Test series Down Under screamed of the intimidating depths in Indian cricket.

At the turn of the twenty-first century, Indian cricket was rebranded under the captaincy of Ganguly. The path to that historic final win in the NatWest Series in the English summer of 2002 was methodically charted by Ganguly and then India coach John Wright.

Blooding in Yuvraj Singh and Zaheer Khan in the ICC Knockout Trophy in Nairobi in 2000, giving VVS Laxman the freedom to play the innings of a lifetime against Australia at Eden Gardens in 2001, trusting a beleaguered Harbhajan Singh to play the lead bowler, securing the enigmatic Virender Sehwag and backing the utility of Mohammad Kaif formed the base of a strong foundation.

Team India's 'fearless and in-your-face' brand of cricket was back in vogue after a tumultuous period in the '90s. In essence, 2002 was the foundation for the eventual triumph in 2011.

The World T20 triumph ensured India became the financial capital of the cricketing world through the successful launch of the Indian Premier League in 2008. India was *the* destination for cricket and the stocks went through the roof with the 2011 World Cup.

There were mild shocks around the corner though.

Indian cricket went through the throes of transition post 2011. Virat Kohli, Rohit Sharma, Ajinkya Rahane, Ishant Sharma and Cheteshwar Pujara have been the face of the new era in the last decade. For all the promise and individual records, major ICC trophies and Test series wins in SENA countries (South Africa, England, New Zealand and Australia) eluded Team India.

The Test series win in Australia in 2018–19 was special but the absence of Steve Smith and David Warner (serving bans for the infamous Sandpapergate ball-tampering scandal) took the sting out of the victory.

19 January 2021 became the watershed moment Indian cricket had been yearning for since 2 April 2011.

A team caged in a bio-bubble for three months in the times of the Covid-19 pandemic and ravaged by a spate of injuries to all the marquee players managed to pull off a victory against a full-strength Australian team and lifted the spirits of a nation that was writhing in pain amidst the pandemic. It's a heist for the history books.

Picture this: The team has just been bowled for 36 in Adelaide. It's down 0–1 in the series. Lead pacer Mohammad Shami suffers a fracture on his right elbow. The team's captain Virat Kohli flies back home on paternity leave. One senior player after another gets injured in the two following Tests and, yet, the team reaches Australian cricket's fortress in Brisbane with the score line reading 1–1.

When coach Ravi Shastri reached Brisbane, he had lost Kohli (on paternity leave) before Shami, Umesh Yadav, Jasprit Bumrah, Ravichandran Ashwin, KL Rahul and Ravindra Jadeja were felled by injuries. This is besides Ishant Sharma failing to get fit for the tour.

Right through the tour, every young player stepping into the team stepped up to the challenge. Pant, Shubman Gill, Mohammad Siraj, Navdeep Saini and Washington Sundar were now the face of new-age Indian cricket.

The tour marked the rich resources of Indian cricket. The 2020–21 international season threw up more names worthy of taking Indian cricket forward. The likes of Suryakumar Yadav, Prithvi Shaw, Rahul Chahar, Ishan Kishan, Shreyas Iyer and Avesh Khan have proved they are ready for the big league. It seemed like a given that every new player would deliver from the word go.

For most part of the last decade, the Indian Premier League (IPL) has been credited for India's rise as a cricketing superpower both financially and as a team.

The defining phase, however, started when the Board of Control for Cricket India (BCCI) decided to make Rahul Dravid the man-in-charge of India's developmental sides India 'A' and U-19s.

The cut-throat competition is scary. The IPL has been the stage that has ensured the spotlight is shared amongst a larger pool of players. Fame, money and exposure to international standard cricket added muscle to Indian cricket.

Yet, it needed streamlining. Too many options and an unstructured system doesn't really help in the expansion of the game. Dravid was now the caretaker of the supply line.

When Rishabh Pant and Washington Sundar were leading India's dash at the improbable 328-run target in Brisbane, they represented the next-gen which was nurtured by Dravid. Pant and Washington are a part of the first batch that Dravid coached. Shubman Gill and Prithvi Shaw make for his second batch.

Dravid's elevation to the post of India's men's team's head coach after the debacle in the T20 World Cup in November 2021 seems like an organic process. All the seeds that he had sown and nourished in his nursery, during his tenure with the National Cricket Academy and the developmental sides, are ready to bloom under his supervision at the highest level of cricket.

Dravid's trusted lieutenant and now accompanying him as Team India bowling coach, Paras Mhambrey, claims: 'It's extremely satisfying to know we have been on the right path with our processes for different players We wanted them to graduate to first-class cricket. Establish themselves then go on to international cricket.'

The revolution in the early 2000s was built on the principle of tapping raw talent from every corner of the country. The IPL offered a level-playing field for players outside the regular power centres of Indian cricket.

But this generation is bred on a T20 diet. The IPL offers instant fame and financial liberation. The gap between an IPL player and an India cricketer (in terms of both skills and financial stability) has narrowed down significantly over the years.

Every household can dream of breeding a cricketer now.

Cricket is a genuine career option at the moment. There are more families ready to make sacrifices.

A Rishabh Pant can move around like a vagabond across states in his teens in pursuit of his dream. Cousins Deepak and Rahul can give up school to solely focus on building a career in cricket. A Mohammad Siraj, brought up in a marginalised community of the society, can afford to live a dream. The Washington Sundars, Prithvi Shaws and Shubman Gills of this world have their fathers making sacrifices to groom them as cricketers from a tender age.

Over ten years in the field covering cricket, across all age-groups and formats, has reaffirmed my belief that if you have the talent, perseverance and are willing to make the sacrifices, the structure is too strong to let you go unnoticed.

Indian cricket is all about maximizing the diversity. The mindset has changed.

'As a coach, I realise I can't coach them as I was coached. I have to change. And that's the exciting part. I need to challenge my own thinking,' Dravid said during a conversation after returning from his first U-19 World Cup as coach in Bangladesh in 2016. He had just assumed the role of a mentor at Delhi Daredevils and we were chatting during a preparatory camp ahead of the IPL at the TERI Oval ground, a cute ground in the outskirts of Gurgaon.

'The good thing is the level of professionalism in the kids, the opportunities they get and the maturity level. The negative is that the pressure of competition has increased a lot. There are too many distractions for the kids compared to my time. Nowadays, it is very important to keep your head despite being successful early. The trappings of success come at a very early age,' he would sum up the situation.

Dravid would harp on the importance of having character.

But it's also about instilling enough confidence and imparting life skills.

Every young cricketer coming through the ranks, irrespective of their backgrounds, has a story. There are no short cuts to make it to the highest level. The glitz of Indian cricket is misleading. The challenges (psychological and physical) barely scratch the surface.

It is said it's tougher to sustain your position at the top because the air gets thinner. Rest assured, the breathing space in Indian cricket gets tighter three levels before the peak.

The stories of the twelve cricketers in this book are all inspirational in their own right. There's no option to renege once you set out on a path to make it as a cricketer.

The strength of Indian cricket is axiomatic. The stories are an effort to draw a picture of the journey full of curve balls and unexpected turns that make for a pool of cricketers primed to carry Indian cricket forward as world-beaters!

# *CHAPTER 1*

# RISHABH PANT: THE ENFORCER

## *Introduction to cricket*

If you visit the Sri Venkateswara College premises in south Delhi on the first weekend of May, you will see anxious parents, braving the brutal summer sun, thronging the ground. It's a month before the college throws open its doors for admissions. But this bunch of parents are about egging on their teenaged kids (some even in their pre-teens) to explore a career in cricket.

It's the time of the year when Sonnet Club, the most famous club in the city, founded by famed cricket coach late Tarak Sinha in 1969, organises trials to select fresh talent. Sinha, who passed away on 6 December 2021 after a prolonged illness, was the most prolific coach the city had ever been witness to. He always made it a point to personally train the players.

Manoj Prabhakar, Ashish Nehra, Aakash Chopra, Ajay Sharma, Atul Wassan and Raman Lamba happen to be Sinha's products who went on to represent India. There are countless number of players who have been giants in domestic cricket. If anything, just the Dronacharya Award eluded Sinha for years.

That Saturday, the summer trials in 2010 were as usual. Saroj Pant stood calmly in the crowd while a chubby twelve-year-old,

Rishabh, walked into the nets, hit the covers off the ball and came out.

'Rishabh was hitting the balls on to the roads,' recalls Devendra Sharma, Sinha's student-turned-colleague. Sinha and Sharma walked up to the mother and son duo on the second day of the trial.

'Where are you from?' Sinha shot the generic question.

'Roorkee,' replied the boy.

'Where are you putting up here?' was Sinha's expected follow-up.

'Mummy and I spent the night in the gurdwara on the other side of the road,' came the young boy's nonchalant reply.

Sinha and Devendra couldn't figure out how much exertion the mother and son must have gone through.

As the conversation went on, Sinha learnt that Saroj had packed a box of parathas, taken a state bus from Roorkee, which is 200 kilometres away from Delhi, in the wee hours of the morning, reached the venue in three hours just before sunrise and waited on a park bench before the trials began. Rishabh's father Rajendra was away at Roorkee, running his school.

This arrangement was followed for a while before things settled down for Rishabh in Delhi. Before he arrived in Delhi, Rishabh was into gymnastics and had some formal cricket coaching in Roorkee. But Delhi was where the opportunities were for him to grow as a cricketer.

Thus started Rishabh's strong relationship with cricket, Sonnet Club and a journey to remember!

## The early days: Delhi–Rajasthan–Delhi

Tarak Sinha moved to Rajasthan as director of the Rajasthan Cricket Association soon after Rishabh joined his academy.

Sinha built the core of Rajasthan cricket. This is when Devendra, a former Delhi wicketkeeper, was blown away by Rishabh's natural ability. Rishabh was thirteen or fourteen at the time.

'We were playing a tournament here at Venkateswara College. I had never seen a thirteen-year-old hit the ball so hard. He was single-handedly winning matches for us. I noticed how quickly he could pick up the length of the ball. He never looked hurried by any bowler. He had so much time,' Devendra recalls.

'I called up Tarak Sir in Jaipur and pleaded with him that this boy needed greater exposure.'

As the days went by, Devendra got eager to play Rishabh at a higher level quickly. So, he asked Rishabh to take up wicketkeeping. 'Keeping wickets and batting in the top order help to make it into senior teams quickly,' Devendra explains.

Sinha and Devendra had worked out that by the time Mahendra Singh Dhoni finished his career, Rishabh will be ready to make the grade. MS Dhoni's monopoly behind the stumps for nearly fifteen years would mean a dearth in wicketkeeping resources in the country.

Devendra makes sure he mentions that wicketkeeping wasn't just thrust upon the young boy. 'The idea of turning him into a wicketkeeper occurred to him after observing that Rishabh had really good hands while catching the ball. He barely dropped catches and could judge the flight of the ball really well.'

There was a seniors Delhi and District Cricket Association (DDCA) League match against LB Shastri Club, the other heavyweight club in Delhi, when Sonnet didn't have its first XI.

Devendra decided to field a fourteen-year-old Rishabh and asked Eklavya Dwivedi, who was already playing for Uttar Pradesh as a wicketkeeper then, to let the young boy keep wickets. The idea was to give him exposure to senior cricket. It was an important match for LB Shastri to stay alive in the tournament.

Rishabh was sent to open the batting and chased down the target with consummate ease. He won the match single-handedly with the bat!

It was time Rishabh played for a state side.

Sinha offered him to play for Rajasthan. Got him a domicile certificate in Alwar district. As Rishabh started churning out the performances in Under-16 cricket, discontent grew among the locals.

He made it to the list of shortlisted players for Rajasthan's U-16 team but was never picked to play. 'Outsider' was the label he began to live with.

'I felt so guilty. I brought him to Rajasthan and he lost a couple of years,' Sinha says. 'I had decided I had to make amends for this kid.'

Rishabh was back in Delhi. He had missed out on U-16 cricket. Sinha and Devendra swung into action.

It was almost impossible for Saroj to keep shuttling between Roorkee and Delhi.

The plan was to get him a place to stay and a school to study in Delhi. The place was a one-room apartment in Palam. Sinha and Devendra took care of everything, even provided him with a washing machine so that he didn't have to spend much time on washing clothes and other daily chores. On most days, Devendra would provide him food from his home. All of Rishabh's energy had to be driven towards cricket and studies.

'Tarak Sir is not like my father. He is my father,' Rishabh would maintain.

## The U-19 days and dogfight with Delhi cricket

By the time he had turned seventeen, Rishabh had become a bully on the cricket pitch. Himmat Singh, his mate from Sonnet

Club, was the hyped batsman. He has been leading Delhi U-16s and U-19s. Himmat notched up hundreds with ease but Rishabh was about demolishing opponents.

But it didn't come easy.

There was a time when he was about to get picked for Delhi U-19s. Selector Nikhil Chopra (former India off-spinner) called up Devendra at 12 noon and broke a tough news, 'We can't select Rishabh. He hasn't submitted the domicile certificates. The names have to be sent to Board of Control for Cricket in India tomorrow.'

Devendra called up Saroj in Roorkee and asked her to bring the papers by 5 p.m. at the Feroz Shah Kotla Stadium. 'His mother rushed from Roorkee but she got lost in the Kotla premises. I had to make a few phone calls to the selectors and the issue was resolved in the nick of time. Had he missed the bus that day, his career would have been pushed back by another few years,' Devendra recalls. You could sense the exhilarating hours as Devendra narrated the story.

Local umpires and ground-staff were in awe of Rishabh's approach towards the game.

Ankit Datta, chief curator at the Feroz Shah Kotla, says: 'He always had a retort ready for everything.'

His confidence could easily be mistaken for arrogance. His audacity was borderline scary. 'It was almost like he prided his confidence so much that he had decided that he will not let anyone even remotely think of damaging it,' Datta opines.

'*Mastikhor*' (extremely naughty), is the first thing that comes to the mind of people who have seen him grow. 'Rishabh never held himself back. He never got overawed by people but he never disrespected anyone,' Devendra says.

'His father was a disciplinarian. He would never have

Rishabh disrespect seniors. Tarak Sir too focuses on this aspect of a player,' Devendra claims.

Not for nothing does Rishabh refer to him as *bade bhaiyya.*

Even as he grew as a player, the Delhi selectors resisted his inclusion in the Ranji Trophy team in 2015 even as the first-choice wicketkeepers struggled for form. Rishabh was like a raging bull and putting a leash on him was almost impossible.

There are times when selectors do not want to pick a player from a particular club and push for someone else in exchange for favours. The situation with Rishabh's selection was somewhat similar.

Datta recalls an incident in 2015 when Rishabh was packing his bags after a practice session with the Delhi-23s at the Kotla. '*Bhaiya, kitne din mujhe nahin lenge? Itne* run *marunga lena hi padega* (How long will they not select me? I'll score so many runs that they will have to select me),' Rishabh told Datta.

He was talking about earning a place in the Delhi Ranji Trophy team.

'You will fall in love with that scary confidence,' Datta says with a smile.

## U-19 World Cup, Ranji debut and beginning of the rise

In October 2015, four games into the Ranji Trophy season, Rishabh had knocked down the door and was behind the stumps for a Delhi team that was led by Gautam Gambhir. He was already picked for a U-19 Challenger series that would determine India's pool for the U-19 World Cup in Bangladesh in another forty-five days.

In July 2015, Rahul Dravid had taken over as the caretaker of India's supply line. He was in charge of both the U-19 and

India 'A' teams. Dravid had identified Rishabh by September as he made a list of 45 players.

'Getting picked for Delhi's Ranji team would have firmed up his chances of making the U-19 World Cup team. We were on edge,' Devendra reckons.

'When he was named in the pool of 45 U-19 players in India, Ashish Nehra had come for practice and asked for Rishabh. He bowled to him for around 30 minutes and told us that he is a *bada* paise *ka* player (big-money player),' Devendra says, as he recounted one of the favourite incidents about his favourite ward.

The talent was visible. But like most successful players from Delhi, he was up against a system infamous for not backing it for long.

All Rishabh needed was a look in. And he got that. When you walked in at the Kotla on the first day of the match on 22 October 2015, it was difficult believe the boy behind the stumps with a floppy hat on and an erect shirt collar was an eighteen-year-old debutant.

He scored a 27, batting at No. 3, in the first innings in his Ranji debut against Bengal. But he stood out.

In the last innings of the match, on a turning Kotla pitch, Rishabh came out and hit veteran India left-arm spinner Pragyan Ojha for four sixes with four men patrolling the boundaries from long-on to deep square-leg. He had scored 57 but he had taken out two India bowlers in Ashok Dinda and Ojha. That knock of 57 has become a reference point in his career since.

Wriddhiman Saha, India's first-choice wicketkeeper in Test cricket at the time, was playing in the same match. The day Rishabh scored 27, he had slyly mentioned, 'There's something different about him.'

The 'something different' is best explained by former India wicketkeeper Vijay Dahiya, who was then the coach of the Delhi team. 'We didn't have much of a look at Rishabh when he first came in to the Ranji team. He came from U-19s and U-23s. But he looked like he meant business even as he was the naughty kid around. We were taken aback when he insisted that he would go out to bat at No. 3 even after keeping wickets for 136 overs. He loves to dictate the course of the game and believes he can do it. Gambhir was dismissed off the second ball of the innings and he walked out like a boss,' Dahiya recalls.

As destiny would have it, Rishabh had leapfrogged Saha to be India's first-choice wicketkeeper. We can come back to that later.

Forty-five days later, a man-of-the-series award in a U-19 International Triangular Tournament and a U-19 tour of Sri Lanka later, Rishabh was named the vice-captain of India's 2016 U-19 World Cup team.

A fortnight before leaving for the World Cup, he had claimed: 'I felt a bit let down when nobody took note that I was the highest scorer for the Delhi Under-19 team last year. It was my target to play Ranji Trophy before I went to play the U-19 World Cup. I dominated in the junior and lower levels of cricket. I would like to do so at the higher level too.'

As much as you were impressed by him, he loved keeping everyone around on edge.

As it turned out, he was the most-talked-about Indian player in the U-19 World Cup. Rishabh had scored the fastest half-century in youth cricket. It came against Nepal and off 18 balls before finishing with 78 off 24 balls.

'I was looking to break AB de Villiers' record of scoring a century off 31 balls,' he said, startling the media-persons after the game at the Sher-e-Bangla Stadium in Dhaka.

For the record, Nepal made it to the quarterfinals in that tournament and leg-spinner Sandeep Lamichhane was in their ranks.

India lost the final to West Indies in that World Cup but it surely was not the end of the world!

## The IPL break and the watershed Ranji season

As Rishabh was hammering a 96-ball 111 against Namibia in the U-19 World Cup quarterfinal at Fatullah Osmani Stadium, 50 kilometres away from the bustling Bangladesh capital of Dhaka, Delhi Daredevils (now Delhi Capitals) had purchased him for Rs 1.9 crore in the IPL auction.

He was the highest-paid U-19 player that year. He was the *bada aadmi* (money man) amongst the bunch of teenagers!

U-19 India coach Rahul Dravid was supposed to chart his progress as he joined Daredevils as head coach that year.

Devendra and Sinha did their bit too. Finding a high-end apartment and taking him to buy a car was thought to be necessary. Sinha works on a very simple philosophy: 'A player needs to feel good about himself first to dominate in the field.'

'We had moved him from Palam to a decent place in Chhatarpur when he played U-19s for Delhi. When he got this mega IPL deal, it was imperative he lived in an environment which could match his status. It doesn't mean he should lose his head. But he needed to feel really good about himself. So, we found him a high-end apartment on rent in a posh south Delhi locality,' Sinha says.

It was a steady debut IPL season for him in 2016. Right after he scored a 17-ball 20 on his IPL debut against the erstwhile Gujarat Lions in Delhi, South Africa all-rounder Chris Morris had said in the media conference: 'This Mr Pant is a serious player. He is going to be a big player for India.'

He scored a half-century while opening the innings against Gujarat Lions in Rajkot later in the tournament. This was followed by a match-winning partnership with Sanju Samson in a tricky chase against Sunrisers Hyderabad.

Five months later, Rishabh ran riot in the Ranji Trophy season. It was a defining season.

He started the season with 146 off just 124 balls against Assam.

And then came the defining knock that made people sit up and take notice of Rishabh. It was against Maharashtra at the Wankhede Stadium in Mumbai.

Swapnil Gugale and Ankit Bawne had scored unbeaten 351 and 258 runs respectively as Maharashtra declared at 635/2 in the last hour of second day.

The dressing room at Wankhede had a board. Rishabh had written 300 on it against his name after the second day's play. He had set a challenge for himself.

Pant was at the crease with Delhi at 135/3. What followed was awe-inspiring 90 overs of batting.

Rishabh Pant had scored 308 off 326 balls!

Delhi fell short of Maharashtra's 635 by just 45 runs. But the Indian cricket fraternity was buzzing.

Something else happened during the match that will stay with Rishabh forever. Sachin Tendulkar sent him a message and asked for the bat he used to score the triple century. A man arrived at Wankhede and Pant handed the bat over to him.

By late evening, the bat was back with him at the hotel. He flipped it around and found Tendulkar had signed it for him with a message wishing him the best for the future. That bat has not moved from a special corner of his home since.

He came back from the match and asserted: 'I am not a *todu* (a colloquial word for a mindless slogger). I would not have been able to score a triple century otherwise.'

Rishabh was not done with the season yet.

He followed it up by posting the fastest century in the Ranji Trophy. He brought up his century in just 48 balls against Jharkhand in Thiruvananthapuram. Rishabh was just backing up his 106-ball-117 knock in the first innings of the match.

By the time he finished with his 67-ball 135 in the second innings, he had hit 21 sixes in the match!

Rishabh eventually finished the season with 907 runs from eight matches at an average of 90 and a mind-boggling strike rate of 106.7.

The India cap wasn't far away!

## India debut and the tough year that followed

On 1 February 2017, Rishabh Pant was handed the India cap at Chinnaswamy Stadium in Bengaluru in the last of the three-T20I series against England. At the age of nineteen years and four months, he became the youngest men's cricketer to play a T20I for India. It was also the first anniversary of Pant registering the fastest half-century in U-19 cricket.

He didn't have much to do in that match. But when he did walk out to bat in the 19th over, there was MS Dhoni waiting to join him at the pitch. Here was a boy, hyped to be the successor to India's most prolific wicketkeeper-batsman, who actually had Dhoni's arm around his shoulders as he took guard for the first time in India colours. Stuff that one can only dream of!

Rishabh had just three balls to face, remained unbeaten on five, took a catch in the deep while India fielded and won the game rather easily by 75 runs.

He was soon made the captain of the Delhi state team in place of Gautam Gambhir for the Vijay Hazare Trophy. That did create some turmoil in the dressing room, but Rishabh held his own as a twenty-year-old boy leading a senior state team.

It was a smooth ride until this moment. The tough days were just around the corner.

Right at the start of the IPL season that year, Rishabh got a dreaded phone call at his team hotel in Delhi. His father had passed away following a cardiac arrest in Roorkee. He rushed to Roorkee that night, performed the final rites and decided to turn up in Bengaluru in a couple of days to play for Daredevils.

'I know my father would have wanted that,' Rishabh would insist. His mother and sister backed the boy who became the man of the family overnight. He scored a 36-ball 57. Daredevils lost the game but Rishabh had made his late father proud.

He had a decent IPL that year, scoring 366 runs. He did leave a highlight though.

Against Gujarat Lions, Rishabh hammered 97 off 43 balls at Feroz Shah Kotla as Daredevils chased down 209 with consummate ease. He had the cricket world buzzing again.

Sachin Tendulkar called that innings one of the best he had seen in the IPL till then. Dravid, in a post-match interview, went on to declare: 'Rishabh is going to be a very important player for India in the coming years.'

That raised the hope of making it to the Indian team for the Champions Trophy in England that followed the IPL. He remained a standby.

Rishabh was selected for a short tour of the West Indies. He got one T20I in Kingston and struggled to get going in his knock of 38 off 35 balls. India scored 190/5 which was easily chased down by West Indies.

The next India cap looked distant now.

The domestic season that followed was patchy. As he led Delhi to the Ranji Trophy final, a feat achieved by the team after ten years, Rishabh had a highest score of 99 that season.

The knives were out. His much-adored audacious brand of game was now referred to as lack of game sense in Indian cricket circles. He didn't have the highest score for the season. Which implies that he was inconsistent and did not score a single hundred that season, which means it was a below-par season. His flamboyancy in batting was widely criticised.

Rishabh was finding out playing with the big boys was not child's play!

## 2018: Breaking down the doors

Under Rishabh Pant's captaincy, Delhi had lost the Ranji Trophy final to Vidarbha on the last the day of 2017. The pressure was mounting on Rishabh. He was falling down in the pecking order for an India call-up.

The year 2018 started with the Syed Mushtaq Ali Trophy, India's domestic T20 tournament. Rishabh decided to open the batting for Delhi, going against the national selectors' advice to keep batting in the middle-order. The selectors wanted him to get used to the position he was most likely to play in. But Rishabh knew he needed game time.

Rishabh finished the tournament as the highest run-getter, plundering 411 runs in 10 matches at an average of 45.66 and an ominous strike rate of 195.71.

That tournament also saw him break another Indian record. Against Himachal Pradesh at the Kotla, Rishabh notched up the fastest T20 hundred by an Indian. He achieved the feat off just 32 balls. It was his first century in over a year.

Datta remembers Himachal's left-arm spinner Bipul Sharma, who has represented Kings XI Punjab in IPL, telling him on the boundary lines: '*Bhaiya, yeh kitna tez maar raha hain!* Ball *ko haath lagane se darr lag raha hain. Kissiko nahin dekha itna tez marte huye* (Bhaiya, he is hitting the ball so hard that I feel scared to lay my hand to his shots. Haven't seen anyone hit the ball so hard).'

Rishabh had unleashed his fury and he was in a zone where he felt he was in absolute control of his game.

'I thought I had faced many more balls in that innings than what I actually did. Every run was important for me at that moment,' Rishabh had said after the knock.

Rishabh had regained his mojo and he was on a manic bull run!

That run saw him being picked for the Nidahas Trophy, a T20I tri-series in Sri Lanka. Regular captain Virat Kohli and MS Dhoni opted out of the tournament. That opened up a spot in the batting line-up.

Rishabh managed just 30 runs in two matches as Dinesh Karthik re-emerged as Dhoni's back-up with an epic 8-ball 29 which clinched a thrilling final against Bangladesh.

But that was not going to slow down Rishabh.

Rishabh amassed 684 runs in the subsequent IPL. It included a thunderous century against the Sunrisers Hyderabad at Kotla. He scored an unbeaten 128 off 63 balls against an attack that had Bhuvneshwar Kumar, Rashid Khan and Shakib Al Hasan.

He had the India selectors under immense pressure now.

## The English summer and the big arrival

'Tarak Sir always said that he would not consider me an international player unless I played Test cricket,' Rishabh can keep telling you this on a loop.

On 18 August 2018, Rishabh Pant caught the attention of the international cricket community when he stepped out to England leg-spinner Adil Rashid and deposited him over the long-on boundary at Trent Bridge.

It was only the second ball he had faced in Test cricket! He scored 24 off 51 balls in challenging English conditions. But the twenty-year-old was already the new kid on the block.

He wasn't picked for the Test series initially. A thumb injury to Wriddhiman Saha and an out-of-place Dinesh Karthik opened up the opportunity for him in the third Test of the series.

Rishabh was sent with the India 'A' team to England for the white-ball leg of the tour following a stupendous IPL. The 'A' tour coincided with India's senior team's long tour of England.

A few match-winning knocks which helped India 'A' win the one-day series prompted coach Rahul Dravid to hold Rishabh back for the first-class leg of the tour. Rishabh curbed his game and scored a couple of fine half-centuries against England Lions and West Indies 'A'. Rishabh had consecutive scores of 67 not out, 61 and 58 in tough seaming conditions.

In Dravid's words, 'Rishabh has shown he can bat differently in longer formats.' The selectors were given the green signal by Dravid. And, thus, Rishabh realised his father-like coach's dream!

Barring winning that Trent Bridge Test, India copped a pasting in that series. Virat Kohli and pacers Ishant Sharma, Mohammad Shami and Jasprit Bumrah were the only ones giving the England team a fight consistently through the series.

On the last day of the tour, Rishabh offered hope to the Indian team management that he could indeed be a long-term wicketkeeping option.

Down 1–3 in the series, chasing an improbable target of 464

at the Oval, Rishabh joined an out-of-sorts KL Rahul at 121/5. The duo put on 204 runs together before Rahul fell for 149.

For a session and a half, it looked like a harmless innings from Rishabh before he changed gears and took on James Anderson, Stuart Broad, Sam Curran, Ben Stokes and Adil Rashid.

As he hit Rashid for a six to bring up his maiden Test hundred, the obvious parallels with Virender Sehwag were drawn. He fell for 114 off 146, trying to heave Rashid again.

India lost the match by 118 runs and the series by a 4–1 margin. But India finally got a wicketkeeper who scored a century in England.

'That I could play red-ball cricket too was important. If people tag me with any label, it doesn't mean I have to change immediately. I improve in my own way. The moment there was a vacancy, I ensured I was performing,' Rishabh had asserted upon his return from England.

Three weeks later, Tarak Sinha was honoured with the Dronacharya Award by the President of India.

Rishabh Pant had truly arrived!

## The high Down Under

Rishabh Pant was already the next big thing when Team India touched down on Australia for a Test series in December 2018. It was billed as India's best chance to win their first Test series in Australia as David Warner and Steve Smith were serving a one-year ban for ball tampering.

Retired from Test cricket for long, Dhoni was nearing the finishing line of his white-ball career's lap. Rishabh was the heir apparent to Dhoni's spot across all formats. At just twenty-one, he was already sprucing up India's fight on the field.

The records kept tumbling with Rishabh around. In the first

Test in Adelaide, he equalled the world record for most catches by a wicketkeeper in Test matches. He had taken 11 catches to complement Cheteshwar Pujara's gritty first-innings century and the rise of a formidable bowling attack. India had won the first Test.

India had the Australians on the mat by the end of the Boxing Day Test in Melbourne. They were 2–1 up.

Rishabh had scores of 25, 28, 36, 30, 39 and 33 in the first three Test matches. His chatter from behind the stumps, though, became the talk of the town.

Tim Paine, an inexperienced and rattled Australian captain, decided to aggravate this kid in Melbourne. The famous 'baby-sitter' comment was made while Rishabh was batting. 'I heard the big man MS is coming in for the ODIs. You may baby-sit my kids,' Paine was heard saying, implying that Rishabh might be jobless then. The idea was to rattle Rishabh.

Rishabh, in response, did click a picture holding his kids at a New Year's party thrown by the Australian prime minister. For all the team's achievements, that became the picture of that tour. Rishabh's brand of sledging on the field was up for debate anyway.

'If someone provokes me, I'll give it back,' he would say.

'I had a duty to do for my team. But I know my code of conduct. I remember my values. I have sledged and people have actually loved it. That my mother and sister enjoyed it makes me happy. The IPL has helped me get used to fame and money. But you have to know where you need to draw a line.'

Rishabh turned up at the Sydney Cricket Ground for the New Year's Test, scored an unbeaten 159, set up a platform for India to complete a 3–1 win.

Rain washed out the final day of the series. India had made history by winning a series in Australia 2–1.

Rishabh Pant returned to India after becoming the only Indian wicketkeeper to have scored centuries in England and Australia.

## The World Cup blow and a tough year

Things started to wobble for Rishabh Pant once the IPL started in 2019. He started blowing hot and cold. But his stocks remained high as the selection for the subsequent World Cup loomed.

Being sent back from Australia after the Test century may have disrupted his run. He played a couple of ODIs against Australia in India. He didn't really set the stage on fire with the bat, and a couple of blemishes behind the stumps had the Mohali crowd chanting Dhoni's name to taunt Rishabh.

That he was not finishing off matches for the Delhi Capitals wasn't sitting pretty with the Indian team management.

The national selectors met to pick the team for the World Cup midway through the IPL. Rishabh Pant was missing from the squad. It was partly his fluctuating form coupled with the fact that he had played only five ODIs at the time.

Former India captain Sourav Ganguly and former Australia captain Ricky Ponting, both in mentorship roles at Capitals in 2019, kept harping about India missing a trick by not picking Rishabh.

The non-selection did sting the youngster.

'I take criticism positively. Finishing matches is important. I will learn to do it consistently,' Rishabh made a humble statement days after he was left out of the India's World Cup squad.

'Things don't change overnight. I am just twenty-one. It's difficult to think like a thirty-year-old man. In due course, my mind will be stronger and there will be a lot of maturity. You need to give it time.'

He literally threw a challenge to the world.

There on, he took it upon himself to finish matches for Capitals in the latter half of the IPL, literally single-handedly ensuring the team finished third in the tournament.

It took an unfortunate injury to in-form Shikhar Dhawan's hand for Rishabh to be flown over to England as his replacement two weeks into the World Cup.

Soon Vijay Shankar returned home with a broken toe.

Rishabh Pant was out there in the middle, batting at No. 4 against tournament hosts and favourites England in Birmingham.

He did his bit in three matches as a red-hot Indian team made the semi-final. Chasing a modest 240 in Manchester, New Zealand blew away India's prima donnas in the top order. Rohit Sharma, Virat Kohli, KL Rahul and Dinesh Karthik were gone in 30 minutes.

Rishabh soldiered on and looked assured till he got to 32. He decided to slog left-arm spinner Mitchell Santner and was caught in the deep.

India lost by 18 runs despite Ravindra Jadeja's valiant 59-ball 77 and MS Dhoni's 72-ball 50.

That shot was going to haunt Rishabh for a while.

Things started unravelling after the World Cup. Though Dhoni didn't announce his retirement, his absence from the game was a fair indication that he would never play for India again.

Rishabh seemed to wilt under the baggage of having to carry forward Dhoni's legacy. The runs dried up post the World Cup. Questions were raised on his wicketkeeping ability and shot selection. Wriddhiman Saha was preferred for Test matches in India.

Sinha reckoned that Rishabh was getting confused when people started believing he should ape Dhoni's way of batting in limited-overs cricket. And that impacted that free-flowing bat swing.

In December 2019, before a three-ODI series against West Indies, Sinha had tried to get that bat swing. Delhi was struggling to breathe as pollution from farm fires engulfed the Capital city. Pant turned up at his alma mater, Sonnet Club. Sinha, who was on assignment with the Jharkhand State team then, and Devendra opened up the field to him and asked to just keep hitting big. Incessant hitting for seven hours through a weekend ensured his bat swing was back. It translated into a score of 71 in Chennai. But soon he lost his place in the playing XI.

At the start of 2020, Rishabh was just warming the benches in the Indian team's dressing room across formats. He wasn't played in any of the T20Is and ODIs in New Zealand. The mediocre two-Test series didn't help.

A spot in the playing XI suddenly looked a fair distance away!

## Resurgence post lockdown: Becoming undisputed match-winner

'I believe the lockdown was a blessing for me mentally. I was starting to feel the pressure before that. There were self-doubts creeping in.'

Rishabh Pant had decided to address his inner demons and 'stay happy', as he puts it. As the Covid-19 virus went on a rampage and brought the world to a standstill, Rishabh went back to his native place in Roorkee. It was about clearing the cobwebs in his mind.

It wasn't the easiest thing to do though. By his own admission, there were far too many awkward silences at home. 'I knew I could not show my family and close ones that I was getting worried. Even I sensed they were a bit disturbed but we would never talk about it. It was a strange time,' he would concede.

But as Indian cricket resumed with the IPL in the UAE, Rishabh had showed up at the Delhi Capitals rusty.

His fitness became the talking point in the tournament even as he went searching for some form through the tournament. Capitals made it to the IPL final for the first time in their history but Rishabh had an average by his standards. A run score of 343 doesn't justify his talent.

Another jolt came when the selectors dropped him from the T20I and ODI teams for the tour of Australia. He was retained as the second wicketkeeper for the Test series.

In a matter of three months (two during the IPL and one in Australia), Rishabh had shed at least 10 kilograms. He was put on a strict diet and was given a gruelling fitness routine. Sinha and Devendra kept counselling him from India and asked him to wipe off all the negative thoughts from his mind. 'Staying happy' in the face of adversity was the mantra.

The results followed soon.

Rishabh was brought into the Indian playing XI after the team was bowled for 36 in the first Test in Adelaide. The spark in the team was there to see. His breezy 29 in the Boxing Day Test changed the momentum of the Test. Stand-in skipper Ajinkya Rahane scored a century and set up a series-levelling win.

India's fairy-tale run gathered steam in the next Test in Sydney.

Looking down the barrel at 102/3 while chasing an improbable target of 407 on the last day, Rishabh dished out a master-class in counterattack. Off-spinner Nathan Lyon, Australia's trump card, was bludgeoned to all parts of the ground. It was reminiscent of his onslaught against Ojha on his First-Class debut five years earlier.

It was almost impossible to make out that he was on sedatives and had taken multiple injections to bat through the pain of copping a Pat Cummins bouncer on his left elbow in the first innings.

Rishabh went for the glory shot and eventually fell short of his hundred by three runs to Lyon. His 97 off 118 runs had rattled the Australians by tea.

Ravichandran Ashwin (with a bad back) and Hanuma Vihari (boasting a torn hamstring) put up a heroic partnership in the last session to save the Test for India.

Team India reached Brisbane for the final Test with a team literally on its last legs. Injuries had ravaged the squad. A mauling at Australia's fortress Gabba was in the offing.

Rishabh Pant had another special left in his bank. This time it was going to be etched in history.

This time he produced another counter-attacking unbeaten 89-run innings of on the final day of the tour to chase down 328. The final-day drama uplifted the mood of the entire nation which was at the time healing from the scars of first wave of the Covid-19 pandemic.

'Rishabh always believed we could chase the target and win,' Rahane had said after the win.

'Winning is always the better option. The mindset was that I had to win the series for my team and not just play for a draw. The two innings in Sydney and Brisbane is just the beginning of a long innings.'

Rishabh was never one to renege on his innate look-in-the-eye-of-challenge, fearless approach. He revels in intimidating oppositions on the field.

'When I got out in the 2019 World Cup semi-final, it was a very disheartening moment for me. It was a big opportunity to do something special for India. I didn't know when such a big moment would come again. I have always dreamt of winning matches from tough situations and doing something which is unbelievable,' he put things in perspective.

His batting prowess aside, doubts lingered on about his wicketkeeping abilities on raging turners in India. He fixed that too in the four Tests against England at home as India came back to win the series 3–1 after losing the first Test in Chennai.

The first quarter of 2021 in Indian cricket was all about Rishabh Pant.

He finished the Test season with a match-winning, series-clinching hundred against England in the fourth Test in Ahmedabad. He had scarred a veteran fast bowler in James Anderson by reverse-sweeping him over the slip cordon.

Rishabh had scored 544 runs in seven Tests in the season. His glovework behind the stumps looked exemplary and the naysayers soon couldn't get tired of praising Pant.

'Turners *pe* keeping *karne ka mazaa hi alag hain*,' a beaming Pant would now say. 'I can sense the opponents fear me. *Bada mazaa aya jab first* Test *mein* England declaration delay *kar rahe thhe itne acche* position *mein rehne ke bawajud* (I enjoyed the fact that England delayed their declaration in the first Test despite being in a strong position). I knew it was because of me.'

He won his place back in India's T20I and ODI teams for the series against England in March and capped off a stellar international season with another match-winning 78 against England in the last ODI in Pune on March 28.

During the ODI series, Shreyas Iyer dislocated his shoulder while fielding. A week later, Rishabh Pant assumed duty as captain of the Delhi Capitals.

Rishabh Pant is the toast of world cricket. And now he has established that he is an undisputed match-winner!

# CHAPTER 2

# MOHAMMED SIRAJ: A BEAST WHO IS ALL HEART

## *An aimless beginning*

First Lancer, an ex-servicemen colony in Telangana located near the Masab Tank and at the foothill of Banjara Hills in Hyderabad, is an area where the population is largely consumed by the daily struggle to make ends meet.

The Eidgah Maidan is the face of First Lancer. It is said to be one of the country's largest *eidgahs*. A dusty ground with loose gravel and not an inch of grass in sight, it was not meant to breed sporting dreams until Mohammed Siraj scripted a fairy tale for himself and offered some hope to his own people.

You will find two-wheelers and autorickshaws jostling for space in the busy lanes of First Lancer, but they are not wide enough to let in any heavy vehicles on four wheels.

Siraj's journey is fascinating and inspiring. It's hair-raising and heart-wrenching. It's more than just another rags-to-riches story. It's a story steeped in the overwhelming emotions of a rather marginalised class of population that could barely afford to dream of having a lavish life.

Mohammed Ghaus was caught in the hustle of earning a living for his wife and two sons, Ismail and Siraj. Driving an autorickshaw around the city, he could sustain his family in a tiny rented house in Khaja Nagar. The house was literally on a rock. The conditions that Siraj was born in wasn't the most hospitable.

Ismail, driven to bring stability to his family, would put his head down and study hard. Siraj was the restless one and would spend most of his time at the Eidgah Maidan, where tennis-ball cricket was the way of life.

Mohammed Shafi has been Siraj's closest friend since his childhood. He paints a picture of the circumstances in First Lancer.

'Playing cricket was all about gully cricket. *Aagey badhne ka toh koi* chance *hi nahin thha* (There was no scope of making it big in cricket). Tennis-ball tournaments were the only big thing,' Shafi says.

'*Koi dekhne wala aur poochne wala nahin thha* (There was no one to look at us or even care for our kind of cricket). We used to only play as a pastime. *Bas* ground *jana aur khelna* (Life was all about going to the ground and playing). But nobody even thought of playing for India. India *aur* IPL *toh door ki baat hain*, Ranji Trophy *bhi nahin sochte thhe* (Even playing Ranji Trophy didn't ever cross our minds; playing for India and the IPL was not even a dream, distant or otherwise).'

From 2009, when Siraj was only fifteen, he and Shafi started spending most of their time at the Eidgah Maidan, playing matches after matches with the tennis ball.

'Siraj was a little kid when he used to come and bowl in matches. He bowled so much that his pace increased dramatically. *Khelte khelte* Siraj *ek dum* Hyderabad *mein sabse tez* bowler *ban gaya thha* tennis-ball cricket *mein* (As he played more and more matches, Siraj became the fastest bowler in tennis-ball cricket in Hyderabad),' Shafi recalls.

*Khep* cricket is one of the most intriguing colloquial forms of cricket. Local tennis ball tournaments would draw sponsors and pretty handsome prizes (both in cash and kind). Siraj was now a hot property in and around Hyderabad.

Siraj didn't just come across as regular good tennis-ball player though. He was different and he could draw eyeballs to a cricket field with his bowling. A soft-spoken genial persona would be overshadowed by the beast with the ball in his hand on the field.

'When he started out playing tennis-ball cricket, he was like any other player playing with us. In two years, there were noticeable changes in him. Once he started bowling quick in tennis-ball tournaments, he got opportunities to play tennis-ball cricket in the districts in Telangana. He started getting a lot of offers. He became the fastest bowler in Hyderabad and Telangana,' Shafi narrates.

The passion to keep playing tennis-ball cricket was unmissable. Siraj was hooked on to it. '*Theek thaak* match fees *mil jaata thha* (He started earning decent match fees),' Shafi explains.

Shafi claims Ghaus cared about both Siraj and him a lot. Ghaus used to call up Shafi to ask about Siraj's whereabouts.

'College *ke liye nikalta thha par jata nahin thha* (He used to leave home for college but would never reach college). He didn't even write his exams for tennis-ball tournaments. He once skipped his final exams just to play a semi-final for us,' Shafi remembers.

Siraj had little time for anything else outside tennis-ball cricket. He would become a vagabond in and around Hyderabad and Telangana.

'*Hafte mein* do ya teen districts *mein* tournament *khelte thhe* (We used to play tournaments in two or three districts in a week).

The matches would be eight-overs, 10-overs or 12-overs a side. Those were ten- or fifteen-day tournaments. The prize money would vary from Rs 30,000 to Rs 1 lakh for winning teams. A team usually had to play at least six matches to make to the final of each tournament,' Shafi says.

For all the attention Siraj was getting, having a career in professional cricket still never occurred to him.

'Ranji players would come to give away trophies at tennis-ball tournaments. We used to be overjoyed seeing them. Clicking a photo with a Ranji player was big for us,' Shafi talks about the mindset that governed Siraj's actions.

As Siraj went about tormenting batsmen around Telangana in tennis-ball cricket, the ones seeing him from close quarters couldn't believe that this talent was going to remain untapped.

Shafi remembers when Siraj was coaxed to play with the *deuce ball* (colloquial word for leather cricket balls) and life took a turn.

'Telangana used to have many tournaments in the districts. *Log ussko* tennis ball *mein dekhte dekhte bole,* 'Tennis ball *kyu khel raha?* Deuce ball *khel'* (People who observed his talent for a while told him he should play with the leather ball and not restrict himself to just a tennis ball),' Shafi recalls the enthralling journey.

One of Siraj's maternal uncles was part of running a team which played with leather balls in local one-day tournaments. 'His *mamu* (uncle) insisted he play for his team. Siraj returned with 9 wickets in the first match he played. He got on a roll there too,' Shafi says.

'Somebody told him that don't waste your time on playing one-day tournaments. He was advised to play two-day league matches in Hyderabad where selectors take note.'

Professional cricket and the system were now waiting to embrace Siraj. It was up to Siraj to garner enough confidence and conviction to venture into the unknown.

## Foray into the professional leather-ball set-up

Siraj was now eighteen and oblivious of his life goals. He lived for the day and was satisfied by the appreciation he got for his exploits in tennis-ball cricket.

His teammates at First Lancer started believing he could do well for himself and break away from the daily struggles of life in their area.

Kaleem was one such friend. Kaleem sold vegetables for a living but hoped for a professional career in cricket. He would turn up at Charminar Cricket Club to grow as a cricketer.

Kaleem felt that the club could use and nurture Siraj well. He went to Charminar Cricket Club's secretary Mahboob Ahmad and informed him about Siraj.

'There was one boy named Kaleem who was Siraj's friend. He was a vegetable vendor,' Ahmad remembers the first instance he learnt about Siraj. '*Mere paas mein khelta thha bachcha* (Kaleem used to play for us). He told me '*Yeh bachcha* (Siraj*) bahut achcha* bowling *dalta hain. Aap issko* please *dekho* (He told me that this kid, Siraj, bowls very well. You please have a look).'

There used to be practice games at the club. Siraj bowled in those matches and grew in confidence. He used to produce impressive performances in every match.

'*Ladke mein dum dikha. Maine mere* club *se ussko khilaya* (I noticed grit and power in the boy. I started playing him for my club in Hyderabad Cricket Association's two-day league),' Ahmed proudly declares.

Yet, growing as a bowler in leather-ball cricket wasn't going to be a cakewalk.

The first hurdle in front of Siraj was Siraj himself with a regimented mind which refused to see a world beyond tennis-ball cricket.

'*Yeh khelna hi nahin chahta thha. Issko* tennis ball *hi khelna thha.* Timepass *hi karna thha* (He didn't want to play. He only cared about tennis-ball cricket. He was wasting his time),' Ahmad claims.

It was difficult to convince Siraj. He wasn't going to play with the leather ball unless there were immediate incentives.

'I told him you can earn money from here, try to understand,' Ahmad tried to lay out the prospects. But it had very little effect on Siraj.

'He agreed to play only when we spoke about bearing his expenses. Only if I paid for his expenses, he would come and play for us,' Ahmad recounts. '*Jaise hi* paise *milne lage, woh khelna chalu kar diya* (The moment he received money, he started playing). We got him to play club matches with the leather ball.'

The club provided him with the kit which included basic gear like running shoes, bowling spikes and clothes.

Next up was understanding the basics of the game. Rudimentary lessons in how the leather ball behaves couldn't be bypassed.

'He learnt to bowl with the leather ball (outswing and inswing) from our coaches at our club. He learnt the nuances like how to release the ball from his hand. After he started playing with the leather ball, it took him around three years to really get it to talk,' Ahmad says.

'He used to play at least three tennis-ball and leather-ball matches a day. Usually, when young boys practice, they do it in enclosed nets. Here, he was honing his skills in match conditions,' the secretary talked about the unusual ways to keep Siraj interested in leather-ball cricket and simultaneously grooming him.

All this while, though, Ahmad had an unwavering belief that Siraj had the potential to do special things at a higher level of cricket.

'He took a fiver in a two-day match in his initial days. I believed he could go the distance. I have been in cricket since I was twelve, and I am fifty-two now. I had 100 per cent belief that Siraj would become a big name,' Ahmad declares.

Three years on, Siraj was now knocking on the doors of the Hyderabad selectors.

## Breaking into the system and adjustment pangs

The Siraj journey had found wheels at Charminar Cricket Club.

The fear he could instil within the batsmen facing him spurred him on. He loved intimidating batsmen with the leather ball, and skittling out oppositions wasn't much of a task for him.

Professional cricket wasn't ever going to be limited to just dominating batsmen in local leagues. Siraj had to learn the art of setting up batsmen. The searing short balls weren't going to take him to the next level.

'He used to bowl a lot of short-pitch deliveries. Ball *ko bas patakta thha* (He would just bang the ball short). We taught him unless you get the batsman to play, you won't get wickets. If you bowl too wide, you will be wasting your energy. Then he got convinced that he should bowl just one short ball in an over and that should not be a wasted delivery,' Ahmad recounts the days of grooming Siraj.

Producing stand-out performances seemed like just a formality for Siraj in the two-day league matches. Much of it had to do with the uncluttered approach he had towards the game.

He was never weighed down by any expectation and neither did any anxiety creep in to excel in the sport.

'*Apun toh bas aise hi dalta hain* (I just bowl this way),' Ahmad remembers Siraj's punchline to anyone who asked him about his bowling.

'He was very friendly and uncomplicated,' Ahmed reckons.

The first season he played in the two-day league, the forces in HCA started taking note of him.

Former India off-spinner Arshad Ayub was a strongman at HCA who would go on to become the state association's president in a year. Ayub was really interested in Siraj and named him in thc probables for the U-23 Hyderabad team. Shafi remembers Siraj taking 5 wickets in his first trial match. Ayub was impressed.

The first match Siraj was slated to play for Hyderabad was against Saurashtra in the U-23 CK Nayudu Trophy. It was an away match. The debut didn't come without drama.

Siraj contracted severe diarrhoea three days before the U-23 team was supposed to leave for Saurashtra.

'He was admitted in Gandhi hospital. He was on drips. He could barely get up on his feet,' Shafi makes a revelation.

Nobody in HCA circles could have known about Siraj's sickness. 'If Siraj had informed the selectors about his sickness, he would have been dropped. He decided to hide his sickness,' Shafi says.

Not turning up at training would have made everyone suspicious. Thus, Siraj ran out of the hospital without informing anyone and went for practice sessions.

His father went around in the city, looking for his son missing from the hospital, before he found Siraj practising at Gymkhana ground.

'*Kya re? Tera tabiyat kharab hain* (What are you doing? You are sick),' the worried father asked the son.

'Papa, *main* practice *mein nahin aata toh* (If I didn't come for practice), I would have been removed from the list of probables. It would have been difficult to come back,' Siraj offered an explanation with a straight face.

The drama didn't end here.

Siraj barely had enough money for his expenses while he was with the team. The BCCI pays the players' match fees at the end of the season and the local state associations sanction the dearness allowances after a few matches after the player raises an invoice.

'When he was first going to play for Hyderabad, he didn't have any money for his expenses. His father didn't have a fixed income. Daily *ka kamate thhe* (His earnings varied each day). His father borrowed money from people and arranged Rs 3000 for Siraj's expenses,' Shafi recalls the anxious moments.

The excitement about a new life soon overshadowed the anxiety. A future, which Siraj had never imagined, beckoned.

Shafi narrates with an unmistakable smile: 'We used to hang out near his home only. When he first received his fight ticket, he came to us and showed us. He was elated that he would be boarding a plane. He also sent me a photo where he posed with the aircraft. He was so happy that he would be flying.

'When he reached Saurashtra, he said people told him that he was staying at a hotel owned by Ravindra Jadeja. He was so awestruck.'

Siraj bowled well there as well. He went to Rajasthan next and did well there too. Hyderabad qualified for the knockouts before they lost in the semi-finals. By then, Siraj had made rapid progress.

This is when, according to Shafi, Siraj started believing he could play Ranji Trophy.

The Ranji Trophy cap wasn't coming that easily in an association that has been perennially plagued by controversies. In the 2015–16 season, the senior Hyderabad team had Sudeep Tyagi, a fast bowler who had represented India in four ODIs in 2009–10 and then migrated from Uttar Pradesh, a U-19 World Cupper Chama Milind and a seasoned Ravi Kiran to lead the pace attack.

Siraj had picked up 53 wickets in the HCA league that season. Yet, he couldn't find a place in the Hyderabad side.

'When he took 53 wickets, HCA was still ignoring him for Ranji matches. *Main bahut lada uss* time *pe* (I had to fight a lot for him at the time),' Ahmad says.

Ahmad remembers a pre-Ranji season incident which hurt Siraj's chances. This was in the lead up to his Ranji debut that season.

'There was a medical camp at HCA. Players were made to run and tested. Professionals from Apollo Hospitals were conducting the camp. Siraj used to skip sessions. They had expelled him from the camp,' Ahmad recalls.

The letter issued against Siraj was damaging. 'He was handed a letter too which said he was an indisciplined boy. It said Siraj was not good enough to play at a higher level,' Ahmad reveals.

'I went to Arshad Ayub and John Manoj (then HCA secretary) and pleaded with them that Siraj should be given a chance to play in the state team. I then went to Siraj and did some counselling. *Phir wapas* team *mein lekar aya thha* (Only then was he drafted in the Hyderabad squad).'

Five matches into the Ranji Trophy season, Hyderabad failed to register a single win in a group which is played between relegated sides from the previous season. They had no chances of qualifying for the quarterfinals.

Sudeep Tyagi was dropped from the team for their sixth match against Services at the Air Force Ground in Delhi. Siraj made his First-Class debut under Hanuma Vihari's captaincy on 15 November 2015.

Siraj had a rough game. He went wicketless in his 26 overs in the first innings and managed just one wicket in the eight overs he bowled in the second. He was dropped for the last two matches.

Ahmad spoke to Ayub and Manoj again. He pleaded that Siraj be given a run for three–four games. But Siraj had to wait for the next season.

Siraj had a forgettable outing in First-Class cricket. But he got an idea what cricket could do for him.

'Once he got selected for Hyderabad, he got accommodation in five-star hotels. He realised life could be like this. *Wahan se woh* change *ho gaya* (He transformed from that point),' Ahmad says.

Ahmad remembers Siraj himself was pleasantly shocked when he first played Ranji Trophy.

'*Main yeh* level *pe bhi khel sakta hoon* (I am good enough to play at this level),' Siraj's beaming confidence declared to the world.

## Big Ranji season and life-altering IPL deal

In 2016, Anil Kumble had replaced Ravi Shastri as the head coach of the Indian team and bowling coach Bharat Arun too was relieved of his duties with the national team.

It turned out to be a blessing for Siraj. The Hyderabad Cricket Association (HCA) had roped in Arun as the head coach for the 2016–17 season.

'Bharat Arun turned him around. He played a big role behind his development,' Ahmad states.

Arun had first seen him as a net bowler in Hyderabad during the IPL's previous season when he was an assistant coach with the Royal Challengers Bangalore.

Arun had enquired about Siraj with the mentor of the Sunrisers Hyderabad, VVS Laxman. He had even asked if Laxman planned on playing him.

When Arun assumed charge of the Hyderabad state team, Siraj was not on the radar of the selectors.

In a show on Ravichandran Ashwin's YouTube channel, Arun recounted his first objective was to get Siraj playing for Hyderabad.

'I had thought it was a one-time thing with this pace and aggression that I saw in the nets. When I went as Hyderabad coach, I called up Siraj. He was not even in the probables then. When I saw him bowling again, he was even more impressive. I asked him what happened, and he said, 'They didn't select me, but I'm ready to give my life'.

'He had the same passion and intent, and he bowled exactly the way I had seen him do so earlier. When I went to Hyderabad as a coach, they gave me full power. So, I told them that this kid should definitely play.'

Siraj repaid Arun with a sterling Ranji Trophy season. He finished as the third highest wicket-taker with 41 wickets in nine matches. His wickets came at an average of 18.92 while dismissing a batsman every 39.5 balls. Hyderabad had made it to the quarterfinals largely because of Siraj's bowling prowess.

'Another striking feature with Siraj is, if we tell him to do something, he will do it exactly the way he has been asked to. Of course, he will try his own experimentations, and I will shout at him when he does it. It's not to hurt him, but just to make him understand, I will shout at him. He likes it when I shout at him. He absolutely likes it, and when I shout at him, he'll smile and say, 'OK, I'll do it',' Arun tells Ashwin on the show.

Siraj's name was now buzzing in Indian cricket circles when the IPL auctions for 2017 came around on 20 February.

It was going to be a life-altering day for Siraj's family. The expectations were not pegged at a big amount. He just wanted to be a part of the IPL which could subsequently open up a world of opportunities for him.

Siraj went to Shafi's house to watch the auction. The anxiety was palpable.

'*Gyarah se ek baje tak baithe rahe hum log* (We waited from 11 a.m. to 1 p.m.). Siraj was very nervous,' Shafi recounts the drama that played out that day.

'His name didn't come up for the bids till lunch. *Hum uthke chale gaye* (We got up and left). We went for a joy ride. Siraj then insisted that we go back and watch it again,' Shafi says.

At 2.30 p.m., Siraj's name was called for bidding.

'There were no bids for him for 15 seconds,' Shafi narrates the most intense five minutes of his best friend's life.

Soon, the Royal Challengers Bangalore started bidding for him and then the Sunrisers Hyderabad got into the bid.

The price at the bottom of the screen kept ticking like the meter on his father's autorickshaw. Siraj was now billed at Rs 2.6 crore.

The Royal Challengers Bangalore had exhausted their money. Siraj went to the Sunrisers Hyderabad to become the story of the IPL auctions that year. The events of the day were overwhelming for the entire neighbourhood, let alone his family.

'Siraj *ka ek hi khwab thha usse* base price Rs 20 lakh *bhi mil gaya toh kaafi hain* (Siraj had only one dream: To be sold at his base price of Rs 20 lakh and that would have sufficed). He just wanted to be in the IPL. When people started bidding for him, he broke into tears,' Shafi's voice chokes as he remembers the momentous day.

Once his bid was done, Siraj walked back to his home which was two minutes from Shafi's place.

'He went up to his mother and broke the news. Both of them hugged each other and started crying,' Shafi says of the emotional moment. 'He has seen very tough days. He didn't even have shoes. Neither did he have a kit bag. His first kit bag was provided by Charminar Cricket Club. *Har cheez dusre log dilaye usse* (Everything was provided to him by someone else outside his family).'

'I will buy a decent house first. I will see what else can be done later,' was Siraj's humble first reaction after the auctions.

'When he got the IPL deal, I spoke to him over phone. He kept saying his life had changed and '*Aapka mere pe bahut ehsaan hain* (I will remain forever indebted to you)',' an emotional Ahmad says.

'When his brother's wedding was fixed, they had booked a marriage hall for Rs 13,000. Once Siraj came back from the IPL, they decided to book a banquet which cost them Rs 7 lakh. It was so heartening to see that family so happy,' Ahmad adds.

Siraj took his friends to buy his first car. It was a Corolla. 'IPL *ke time hum usske gaadi mein usse chhodne jaate thhe* hotel (We used to drop him back at the team hotel in his car during the IPL) when he used to visit his home. He gave us tickets for all matches in Hyderabad,' Shafi fondly remembers.

This was also the year when the Sunrisers Hyderabad had formed a lethal bowling attack comprising Bhuvneshwar Kumar, Afghanistan's Rashid Khan, Siddarth Kaul and a veteran Ashish Nehra. It was difficult for Siraj to get a long run.

He got six games to take 10 wickets. The economy rate of 9.21 didn't help his cause to make the playing XI in the business end of the tournament as the Sunrisers Hyderabad finished third in the tournament.

Siraj was now in the big league and on a learning curve.

## Learning on the road and an indifferent India debut

Chairman of national selection committee MSK Prasad had heard and seen enough of Siraj. This was also the phase when the selection committee was invested in creating a pool of fast bowlers for the national team.

Prasad picked him for the Board President's XI game against the touring Australian team in February 2017. Siraj didn't get to play the game but the selectors had made up their minds to invest in him.

'He was athletic, agile and enthusiastic. He will not mind even if you bowl him for 40 overs,' Prasad noted the attributes that impressed the selectors.

Soon after the IPL, Siraj was going to fly out of the country for the first time. He was picked for the India 'A' team which was touring South Africa. It was time to go through the finishing school under the supervision of Rahul Dravid.

This was unfamiliar territory again. From First Lancer to Pretoria, it was a massive leap for him.

He calls Shafi every day to share his feelings. Shafi is his go-to person.

'*Woh bolta thha bahut mushkil ho rahi hain* (He used to say he was struggling to adjust to the environment). He couldn't mingle with anyone. He would say everyone was senior to him,' Shafi says.

'He was always a good athlete. He is a shy person but you could see the fire in his eyes. The hunger was obvious,' Abhay Sharma, the fielding coach in Dravid's team of support staff, talks about the first impression he had of Siraj.

Abhay says, looking at Siraj, you got the feeling that he believed that '*Mere paas ek hi raasta hain aur issi pe chalna hain* (This is the only path for me and I can't deviate from it).'

'He was not distracted,' Abhay states while adding: 'Humble is the one word that best describes Siraj.'

There was a plenty of work that needed to be done on Siraj though.

'You knew he was skilful, but he was raw. He didn't know how to maximise his skills,' reckons Abhay.

The India 'A' management led by bowling coach Paras Mhambrey first identified the strengths in Siraj's bowling.

'If you observe him closely, he isn't express quick. His strength is that his deliveries skid off the surface. It's similar to Mohammad Shami. They don't seem that quick through the air, but they are lethal off the pitch. They impart backspin during release. Even Kapil Dev had that. You can't teach that to anyone. That comes naturally,' Abhay explains.

Before the coaches got down to working on him, it was imperative that Siraj was made comfortable in an environment which he had no idea about.

'Once you come through Ranji Trophy, you get exposed to five-star accommodations these days. But India 'A' is different because you are very close to international cricket. You are provided everything which the senior Indian team gets. It's not that we organise lengthy lectures, but we definitely speak to them. Rahul Dravid plays a big role,' Abhay gives an idea about how they handle cricketers coming from humble backgrounds.

That India 'A' team had Navdeep Saini in it. Saini too walked a similar path till this point. He too had spent his teens playing amateur tennis-ball cricket. Both Saini and Siraj were on their first trip overseas.

'Siraj and I used to stay together and be in a corner. For us, it was like we were in a goldmine of cricketing knowledge. Our motto was to speak as less as possible and lap up every bit of information on bowling. We would blindly follow what was asked of us,' Saini says.

'All he understood was that he had to just bowl and bowl well. What makes for a good bowler, he learnt it on the road,' Abhay says.

A raw, enthusiastic Siraj showed enough promise with the ball on the tour. Five wickets in three one-day matches were followed by an incisive spell of 4/61 in the only First-Class match he played on tour.

Indian cricket was now eager to see Siraj make the grade.

In another two months, the home international season was due to start. The veteran Ashish Nehra was due to retire after a farewell T20I match against New Zealand at his home ground, Feroz Shah Kotla. Mohammed Shami and Umesh Yadav were struggling to be consistent white-ball bowlers.

The selectors turned to Siraj as the back-up option to Bhuvneshwar Kumar and Jasprit Bumrah.

Siraj's family was bubbling with excitement. Their son was going to put the ignored community of First Lancer on the map of Indian cricket. His elder brother even flew over to Delhi for the first T20I match of the series. Siraj didn't get a game as Nehra drew the curtains on his long and agonising career.

Siraj was standing with the Indian playing XI for the first time as the national anthem went off in the next T20I in Rajkot on 4 November 2017. National anthems at sporting events are usually hair-raising. And here was a guy who broke into tears once the anthem was done. Bharat Arun was back as India's bowling coach in the dressing room.

Shafi remembers Siraj was 'extremely nervous' leading to the game.

The journey from being a part of the ignored class in the society to standing along with the elite sportsmen of the country, Siraj had broken the glass ceiling.

The occasion was too overwhelming for a twenty-three-year-old boy who mostly spent his childhood in oblivion without formal training until he was eighteen.

The pictures were bound to be moving.

He was still getting used to the aura of the event by the time Martin Guptill and Colin Munro feasted on his inexperience. The figures of 1/53 in four overs were nothing close to what he had even remotely experienced in the five years of professional cricket. The dream turned into a nightmare in a matter of an hour.

In the other two T20Is he played against Sri Lanka in Mumbai and Bangladesh in Colombo, he conceded 45 and 50 runs respectively. He was now left with the tags of being 'erratic' and 'wayward'.

Ashish Nehra had seen enough of him to realise his potential though. Nehra moved to the Royal Challengers Bangalore as an assistant coach for IPL 2018. He had picked two raw pacers to work with. One was Saini and the other one was Siraj. The Royal Challengers Bangalore paid Rs 2.6 crore to get Siraj from the Sunrisers Hyderabad.

Eleven wickets in 11 IPL games with an economy rate of close to nine runs an over didn't help him shed the 'erratic' tag.

MSK Prasad and his committee weren't going to give up on him though. Dravid too knew there could be something really special in Siraj.

Siraj was now a regular feature in the India 'A' teams. He was mostly picked to play First-Class games for India 'A'.

'Initially he was wayward,' Prasad concedes. 'But you couldn't ignore him for sheer consistency. He had picked up several five-wicket hauls for India 'A' in England, South Africa and at home against Australia 'A'. His speciality is that he has the knack for getting five-wicket hauls,' he explains the rationale behind persisting with Siraj.

There needed to be some fine-tuning done to how Siraj approached the game. It was just about making him comfortable and bringing in a sense of calm in his game while playing at the highest level.

'Siraj is one guy you don't have to tell much. All you have to say is just focus and don't get too excited because his energy level is very high. It just needs to be channelised,' reckons Prasad.

Abhay concurs. Channelising his lava-like energy was one of the delicate tasks the India 'A' management had.

Abhay says: '*Ussko kuchh bhi bolo* (You ask him anything to do), he is always ready. Once he is done with bowling, if you ask him to go through fielding drills, he would do it. He will never make excuses and ask for rest. We had to tell him that he needed rest. It's important to keep them (the fast bowlers) fresh and work on them properly. Workload management is so important. We had to guard against burn out.'

The wickets started to come on tours of England and New Zealand besides the home 'A' series against Australia in 2018.

He was the highest wicket-taker in the two First-Class matches in England. And a spell of 8/59 against Australia 'A' in Bengaluru was building a solid reputation for Siraj.

Abhay picks out a couple of his spells that convinced that Siraj was ready for the highest level. One was in New Zealand and the other in England.

'Those were long spells. He was bowling against the wind. He was bowling sharp all through the spell. It's one thing that the ball's travelling quickly. But the other important thing is how your approach is in your run-up. If you have the same intensity in the tenth over of your spell, that takes mental strength. It shows character,' Abhay remarks.

India 'A' team bowling coach Paras Mhambrey had devised the bowling-against-the-wind plan. The sole objective of the developmental teams under Dravid's supervision is to keep players outside their comfort zones while in the field.

Abhay explains: 'When you first make it to the highest level, there will be senior bowlers in the team. Senior bowlers get the option to choose the ends. Most captains would try to give you options but you don't necessarily get your choice. Siraj learnt how to bowl against the wind and to manage the workload while bowling against the wind all day.'

Siraj's progress was heartening for the caretakers of Indian cricket.

At the same time, it was imperative he was not to burn out while he was playing matches on the bounce in the India 'A' and domestic circuit. Educating him about NCA's workload management was the crucial task now.

Mhambrey narrates once such incident: 'Everyone including Rahul (Dravid) sits with the players to put it in terms of the stats and data that is available about the number of balls they bowled even in practice. You educate them saying that generally players tend to get injured two or three weeks from this point. In 2017–18, Siraj bowled a lot and picked up a lot of wickets. There was a game in Bangalore that we were playing against South Africa 'A'. The trainers felt this was a good time to pull him back. Any player who's in form and picking wickets, he wants to build on it because obviously opportunity gets created play for the Indian team. We explained to him why we are doing it and this was in his interest. We had to win his trust and he finally got convinced.'

'He picked 8 wickets in an innings in Bengaluru. It was a fantastic spell to watch. That's when I felt this fellow belongs to a different league,' Prasad claims.

'Navdeep got quick attention because he did well in white-ball cricket and had that magical Ranji semi-final. Performance wise, Siraj had better ones. Navdeep didn't have many five-wicket hauls. Siraj has performed against every opposition on 'A' tours,' Prasad proudly states.

There was just one last step left to make a name for himself.

## Road to the emotional Test debut

For all the strides he was making with India 'A', Siraj was yet to perform when the spotlight was on him.

His figures of 0/76 on his ODI debut against Australia in Adelaide in 29 January was not a reflection of his progress. Seven wickets in nine IPL matches in 2019 while conceding runs at 9.55 an over did nothing to shed the 'erratic' tag. If only, it was now stamped next to his name.

Even as the Indian selectors went about inducting fresh faces in the senior Indian team after the 2019 World Cup, Siraj's underwhelming performances on high-pressure stages went against him.

He was back to the grind with India 'A' and Hyderabad. The likes of Saini, Shardul Thakur, Khaleel Ahmed and Deepak Chahar had zoomed past him.

'I always believed he was a better bowler with red ball,' chief selector Prasad insisted.

It was time to hit the reset button and clear his head. The not-getting-ahead-of-himself cliché was in force. It was time for an overhaul in his regime.

Nehra reckons Siraj always had great skills but was not aware how to excel at the highest level. His natural athletic physique had brought him to this level. But he really started putting in the hard yards (like having a strict fitness regime, doing special high intensity gym sessions) from 2019.

Biryani, his staple diet, had to be done away with. It became just a cheat meal. Spice went missing from his food. Siraj had endured many a hardship in his life but it was time to sacrifice big little joys of his life. The bigger picture was clear to him. He wanted a taste of success and it could come through by giving up his indulgences.

Indian cricket, by the 2019–20 international season, had a fair number of pacers jostling for places in the Indian team. Siraj had fallen behind in the pecking order.

The scenario was clear to Siraj. It had to be the sheer volume of consistent performances that could win him back his place in the Indian team.

'He never got anxious about selection. He would never come and badger the selectors about why he wasn't getting picked for India,' Prasad reveals.

Covid-19 hit humanity and the world was not the same again. The lockdown gave Siraj some breathing space. And when Indian cricket resumed with the IPL in the UAE in September

2020, Siraj turned up a mature bowler, a clear departure from is erratic days.

Midway through the tournament, Siraj had warmed up nicely and was in his element. It required skipper Virat Kohli's hunch for Siraj to translate his form into a stellar performance.

In a game against the Kolkata Knight Riders in Abu Dhabi, Kohli deviated from his usual plan of opening the bowling with Washington Sundar's accurate off-spinners. Just when the batsman was marking his guard at the beginning of the second over of the match, Kohli took the ball out of Washington's hand, screamed '*Miyan*, ready *ho jao!*' and lobbed the ball to Siraj.

Anyone who has spent a decent amount of time with Siraj knows that a little bit of faith in him is all he needs to get charged up.

Siraj extracted every little bit of help the pitch had in it for seamers and exhibited a spell of immaculate pace, swing and seam. Under the night sky and inside an empty stadium, Siraj was breathing fire. 4–2–8–3 are figures that define the turnaround of Siraj.

The selectors had no second thoughts while naming him in the squad for the subsequent tour of Australia.

Happy days? Not quite.

Siraj was fighting an anxious battle in his mind. His father Ghaus was ill and admitted in the hospital for most part of the IPL.

Making video calls from the UAE every day was the only way he could be at peace. Moments after each match finished in the UAE, Siraj would rush back to his room and call to see his dad.

The family did everything to ensure Siraj wasn't bogged down by his father's health. They understood Siraj was in a critical phase of career when opportunities don't come easy.

'His father kept assuring him that he was doing well. His father loved Siraj more than his elder brother,' Shafi says.

'When he used to be done talking to his family, he would call me up and check if they were lying to him. If I told him he was doing well, his eyes would light up. But if any day his father struggled, he used to get very depressed. *Khana nahin khata thha. Bahut rota thha* (He would stop eating and keep crying). His mother would console him and say just keep praying and don't worry too much,' Shafi recalls the testing days.

Siraj boarded the flight to Australia from Dubai.

Barely five days into the tour, the dreaded news reached Siraj in Sydney. His father had passed away.

It seemed the world around Siraj had come crashing down. He insisted that he returned and the BCCI had even offered travel arrangements.

Shafi recalls Siraj's mother's words: '*Tere* papa *ka sapna thha ki tu* India *ke liye khele.* Fulfil his dream. Anyway, you won't be able to come in time for the final rites.'

Siraj would call up Shafi and say what Kohli would tell him. 'Virat bhai *bolte thhe tere* Papa *kya bolte?* India *khelna ya ghar aa jana? Tera kya khwahish hain* (Virat would ask me would his father have wanted him to come back or play for India. What is your dream)?'

Siraj was eventually convinced by his mother and Kohli that he should fulfil his father's dreams. After all, in 2006, an eighteen-year-old Kohli too had turned up for Delhi to save a Ranji match on the morning of his father's demise.

Coming to terms with the loss was going to take longer. The quarantine rules made the grieving process all the more tough on Siraj.

'It took him a week to get a grip on himself. *Barabar baat nahin karna. Rote rehna* (He wouldn't speak properly and keep sobbing). He was in quarantine. He was all by himself in his room. It was very difficult. Nobody could meet him. That week was torturous for him,' Shafi recalls.

Hanuma Vihari, Siraj's first captain in Hyderabad, would make video calls from his room in the same hotel.

The big boost came when coach Ravi Shastri walked up to him, wrapped his arm around his shoulders and declared: 'You will take a five-wicket haul by the end of this tour.'

The team management could sense the scary passion in Siraj. They would later claim they had a premonition that Siraj would roll out a special performance on the tour.

Shastri's words would turn out to be prophetic in a couple of months' time.

By the time the Boxing Day Test in Melbourne arrived, India had lost Mohammad Shami to an injury. Ishant Sharma didn't make it to the tour due to fitness issues. And India was recovering after being bowled out for 36 in the first Test in Adelaide.

Siraj pipped Saini for his Test debut and to be the third pacer at the Melbourne Cricket Ground (MCG). He clicked straight away picking up 2/40 in the first innings.

In the second innings, he assumed greater responsibility when Umesh Yadav limped off the ground after bowling 3.3 overs. Siraj responded to the call and returned figures of 3/37 set up a comeback win for India.

The Indian team reached Sydney next to play the New Year's Test. As the Australian batsmen were running the Indian attack rugged in the second innings of the match, the historically hostile Australian crowd had turned nasty.

Siraj, fielding on the boundary lines, was subjected to racial abuse. 'Monkey' and 'brown dog' was what Siraj was referred to. Siraj immediately walked up to the umpires and his captain Ajinkya Rahane. Play was stopped for a while and the umpires even offered the Indian team to leave the ground.

Siraj's reaction to racism was hailed. The awareness that Rahul Dravid tried to instil in his players on 'A' tours was yielding results.

'He didn't say anything about racism to us. We read it in the newspapers. We called to check with him if he was doing OK. He used to say that he only wanted to focus on his game,' Shafi says.

'They are doing this to distract me. I am trying to ignore them,' is all Siraj would tell Shafi.

India staved off a miraculous draw in Sydney and flew to Brisbane for the final Test. Jasprit Bumrah was now ruled out of the Test due to an abdominal injury.

Siraj, in his third Test match, was now the leader of the attack with his mate from India 'A' days Navdeep Saini playing his second Test. Shardul Thakur had bowled just 10 balls in Test cricket before the match.

'Siraj and I got talking on the eve of the match. We just decided to do whatever we have been doing over the last three years and blindly follow the team management's plans,' Saini fondly remembers the little chat he had with his buddy.

The leader in Siraj stepped up in the second innings. He removed Steve Smith and Marnus Labuschagne, two of the most prolific batsmen in the Australian line-up, to break the back of the middle-order and ensure the hosts didn't run away with the game.

When Josh Hazlewood top-edged a ramp shot to Shardul Thakur, Shastri's words came true. Siraj had figures of 5/73. Australia's lead was restricted to 327 runs, leaving Indian 328 to chase on the final day of thc tour.

'He was over the moon after taking 5 wickets in Brisbane. He would take fivers frequently in two-day, one-day and Ranji matches. *Sapna thha* Test match *mein* 5 wickets *le* (It was a dream to get a five-wicket haul in Test cricket),' Shafi shares the euphoria of his friend's success.

Siraj's fairy tale journey was capped off by Shubman Gill's 91, Cheteshwar Pujara's 56 and Rishabh Pant's unbeaten 89 that sealed a memorable series win.

## A trailblazer who is all heart

Siraj is all heart. It reflects in his cricketing journey.

'He may not be the most fluent of the guys while talking. But he knows the demands of the game and what it takes to exhibit in pressure situations. He played T20 corporate tournaments after tours. Even if he gets a break, he will come to Hyderabad and play club cricket or corporate tournaments,' MSK Prasad highlights. 'All those who have come from tennis-ball cricket – Javagal Srinath, David Johnson, Jasprit Bumrah – require a lot of strength and accuracy. In order to fox the batsman, you have to be very smart. And Siraj certainly has that,' he adds.

'Siraj is a soft-natured boy. *Ussko kuchh samjhado* (If you make him understand properly), he will go after that only,' Ahmad points out his greatest attribute.

Abhay Sharma likes to stress on the need to win his trust so that he could share his problems. 'He wants to share his feelings. He had once shared something very personal with me. I can't reveal it. But I was left choked and teary-eyed. I had to console him and assure him that everything will be fine. He turned up a lighter person the next day,' Abhay says.

Siraj was bathing in glory and fame when he returned from Australia. But his heart still lies at the Eidgah Maidan in First Lancer. His mates from his childhood days form the core of his life.

'He used to play tennis ball even after playing Ranji Trophy,' Shafi says with a childish smile.

Shafi sums up Siraj the star of Indian cricket:

'*Aate hi humein* call *karta hain. Hum hi* airport *se leke aate hain. Humare saath hi rehta hain. Humein bahut* help *karta hain.* Paisa *ho ya naya* shoes *raha ho. Kapde bhi dilata. Bolta hain kabhi bhi koi bhi cheez ki zaroorat ho toh sharmana nahin* (Whenever he returns from a tour, he calls us up. We go to receive him at the airport. He helps us a lot financially. He buys us clothes and shoes too. He insists that we should never be shy about asking for help).'

'He will still hang around in First Lancer ground for 3–4 hours. *Bastiwale roz dekhne wale hote hain toh utni bheed nahin hoti. Baahar se log aa jate hain ki* Siraj Hyderabad *wala idhar hi baithta hain* (The people in the neighbourhood have seen him every day for years. So, they don't crowd around him. But people from other parts of Hyderabad come after knowing that Siraj usually hangs around here). People from other districts come to just click photos with Siraj.'

Siraj has beaten anonymity and classism and turned Eidgah in First Lancer into a celebrity corner.

Yet, people who know him will tell you Siraj doesn't get satiated easily!

## *CHAPTER 3*

# PRITHVI SHAW: THE BORN SHOWSTOPPER

## *Overnight teen sensation*

The third week of November 2013 was an emotional one for Indian cricket. Sachin Tendulkar was playing for the last time for India. Between 14 and 16 November, everything was about Tendulkar. That India wrapped up a Test match against the West Indies within three days in Mumbai only seemed like a formality bartered for a grand farewell for a man who had been the face of Indian cricket for the last twenty-four years.

There was delirium while celebrating a fabled career. There was nostalgia that swept everyone who took even the slightest interest in cricket. There were persisting withdrawal symptoms. Imagining cricket after Sachin Tendulkar was going to be tough for a country that has been obsessed with the brand called Sachin Tendulkar.

Four days after Tendulkar was done with his cricket, Mumbai was still recovering from one of the most emotional farewell speeches in India's sporting history at the Wankhede Stadium.

Around the time some news trickled in from the storied Azad Maidan – three kilometres from Wankhede. A fourteen-year-old-boy named Prithvi Shaw had scored 546 runs for Rizvi

Springfield School in a Harris Shield inter-school match. It was a record in minor league cricket. A number that will forever stay with Prithvi.

It's the same tournament where Tendulkar and Vinod Kambli had put on an epic 664-run partnership thirty years ago.

The frenzy that followed Prithvi's knock was reminiscent of what Tendulkar and Kambli had received three decades earlier.

Mumbai cricket, forever obsessed with producing heavy-scoring batsmen, had found its latest prodigy. It found its next 'wonderkid'!

At fourteen, Prithvi Shaw had become national news.

It's no secret that the media in Mumbai loves going to town with every player that shows a glimpse of potential.

Young Prithvi was about to find out.

'Our coach just asked me to concentrate on every ball. The only plan was to score as many runs as we could. I wasn't thinking of a record, but it feels good,' an innocent Prithvi said with a straight face when a mob of reporters hounded him after the game.

The 'Tendulkar wave' was still strong and the parallels were drawn immediately. 'It's too far ahead. For now, I am happy playing at this level and scoring the runs. Tendulkar is my idol in cricket and one thing I try to pick up from him is how he carries himself in a humble manner.'

Young Prithvi had hit 85 fours and five sixes off the 330 balls he had faced in the innings. But minutes later, he was fending off awkward questions from the media with a poise beyond his years.

The blinding spotlight that day was just an indication of the unrelenting media attention on his evolution that has stayed with him since.

## Early days and the build up to the 546

All Prithvi had in the name of family was his father Pankaj. He had lost his mother when he was four.

Pankaj ran a small readymade garment business in Virar, a suburb 65 kilometres from Mumbai. To put it very bluntly, Pankaj struggled to make ends meet.

The money that Pankaj earned was never going to be enough for Prithvi's education and cricket. There was a spark in Prithvi when he held a cricket bat when he was a toddler. Prithvi would captivate local crowds in his neighbourhood in Virar as he disdainfully hit older boys bowling at him. Pankaj had identified the potential but was helpless to do anything about it as affording the means to tap it was beyond him.

Prithvi was barely eight years old when Pankaj decided to take him to Rizvi Springfield School in mainland Mumbai. The Rizvi Sports consortium includes the Springfield High School, Rizvi College and Rizvi Sports Club.

An admission in Springfield High School based on his game could have ensured a scholarship.

Raju Pathak, a revered coach in Mumbai cricket circles, remembers the first interaction with Prithvi. '*Bahut hi chanchal bachcha thha. Bahut hi chhota thha* (He was a very restless kid. And he was a very, very young kid). He was barely seven or eight years old at the time but looked like six. Someone I know in Virar had told me about this kid. So I met his father,' Pathak says.

As is the usual drill, Pathak asked him to pad up and go into the nets to bat.

Just when Prithvi was about to go into the designated nets, he stopped and said: 'Put me in the nets with older boys. I want to play with bigger boys.'

Pathak had assigned him the nets meant for kids up to the age of twelve.

'You will have to bat here first and then graduate to the next level,' Pathak explained to Prithvi. Prithvi rebelled.

'He kept insisting he wanted to play with the bigger boys,' Pathak recalls. 'He was almost on the verge of throwing a tantrum.'

After a few minutes of argument, Pathak managed to convince him by literally pleading with the kid: '*Pehle iss mein toh jaa* (First try here). I will soon move you to the nets with the senior boys.'

It took Prithvi to face just four balls for Pathak to interject and ask him to move to the Under-14 nets. 'The way he struck those four balls – the power and timing behind the shots – were such that I knew this boy was a God's gift to cricket,' Pathak claims.

The scholarship was Prithvi's. Pankaj did not need to worry about his basic education anymore.

'Prithvi's father's financial situation was not very sound. The school gave him free education. We provided his clothes and whatever gear he needed to play cricket in,' Pathak says.

Prithvi's cricket training was supposed to happen at MIG Cricket Club ground in Bandra, the very turf where Sachin Tendulkar had started his cricketing journey.

The dream journey had begun.

If there was a hurdle in his way, it was travelling from Virar for one hour and 45 minutes every day. For over a year, Prithvi and Pankaj's day started at 4.30 in the morning and went deep into the evening post training and school.

Pankaj couldn't let such a young boy cover such a distance all by himself. He decided to shut down his garment business. All his energy now went into Prithvi honing his talent as a cricketer.

Sachin Tendulkar's son Arjun was also training with Prithvi

at MIG Cricket Club ground. Pathak remembers an instance when Sachin came to the ground to watch his son play, but left impressed by Prithvi. Tendulkar gifted him a bat.

'When I was eight years old, he (Tendulkar) came to MIG. That's all I remember. He was watching from somewhere but I didn't know till he said something. When he gave me the bat, I was very emotional. He wished me good luck and said 'I hope you score tons of runs with this bat'.' This was all Prithvi could recall of the moment while speaking during an interview last year.

By the time Prithvi had turned ten, he began being talked about in Mumbai's cricket circles. Nilesh Kulkarni, former India left-arm spinner and a stalwart in Mumbai cricket, was impressed by this kid. Kulkarni had already started a sports management company and, in 2010, he signed up Prithvi for a contract worth Rs 3 lakh a year.

That was the year when life started getting easier for the Shaws. Local corporator, and now a Shiv Sena MLA, Sanjay Potnis came up in support of the father and son. Potnis had watched the kid play at MIG and was touched by his struggle. He arranged an apartment for Prithvi and Pankaj in Santacruz East and its location cut down the travel time by 70 minutes.

Potnis had become Prithvi's godfather.

As things started falling into place and the Shaws didn't have to worry about their survival, the Rizvi stable was breeding three batting prodigies together – Sarfaraz Khan, Arman Jaffer and Prithvi Shaw.

These three kids had set the grounds in Mumbai on fire. Sarfaraz had set a record in Harris Shield cricket by scoring 439 runs in 2009 at the age of twelve. Armaan, nephew of former India opener Wasim Jaffer, outdid Sarfaraz the following year. Armaan created history in school cricket when he hammered

498 in the Under-14 Giles Shield tournament. He too was twelve at the time.

Sarfaraz, Armaan and Prithvi were scoring centuries for fun. By 2013, the trio had conjured up 120 centuries between them in three seasons.

Sarfaraz was close to a spot in India's U-19 team for the 2014 World Cup in the UAE. Armaan and Prithvi were dominating players in the U-16 Mumbai team. Kulkarni sponsored a trip to England for a school exchange programme when Prithvi was just twelve.

Before Prithvi had broken the record for the highest score in the Harris Shield in November 2013, he was already captaining the Mumbai U-16 team. But a major record eluded him.

'When three young batsmen grow together, ego becomes a big factor. Prithvi was fourteen, and it was his last year in high school cricket. He didn't even come close to matching Sarfaraz and Armaan's scores,' Pathak remembers the days leading to Prithvi's first big record.

'He used to throw his wicket away after scoring 150s, 200s and 250s,' Pathak says.

'Throwing your wicket' are harsh words for a boy who consistently scored double centuries in his early teens. 'That's what the standards are in Mumbai cricket. The competition between batsmen is so cut-throat,' Pathak reasons.

'Prithvi was getting anxious to play an innings that would be defining and remembered for long. I asked him to put his head down and keep batting for as long as he could. The Harris Shield matches are three-day, four-day matches. I asked him to not rush.'

The result followed soon. The 546 happened. It was as much a redemption as a statement for Prithvi. He got an innings that will forever be talked about whenever his name is discussed!

## Life after 546: Shielding from attention and a big deal

Within months of Prithvi scoring the record-breaking 546, Sarfaraz had played in the U-19 World Cup in 2014. Sarfaraz was just sixteen. Two years later, Armaan was scoring so heavily in Cooch Behar Trophy, India's domestic U-19 tournament, that he too made it to India's U-19 World Cup team under coach Rahul Dravid in Bangladesh. Armaan made it when he was seventeen. Armaan and Sarfaraz played together in the 2016 World Cup where India finished runners-up.

Sarfaraz had already been grabbing headlines for the two years with his street smart and audacious game for the Royal Challengers Bangalore in the IPL. Armaan was in senior Mumbai teams which played the touring New Zealand team in warm-up matches in 2016.

While Sarfaraz and Armaan were hogging the limelight, the caretakers of Indian cricket had an eye on Prithvi.

Post the 546, the first thing that Prithvi's mentors had to guard against was his overexposure to media. There was a conscious effort to shield this teenager from the world's vulturous hunger to cover him.

Pankaj would take most calls from media persons and answer for Prithvi. This way Prithvi was barely exposed to media interactions.

'The first thing we all wanted was to ensure that he kept his head. *Paer zameen mein rakhne ka* (One should always remain grounded).' In Pathak's words, it was drilled into the kid's head.

The apartment offered by Sanjay Potnis was his safehouse. The Air India ground in Santa Cruz was his place of practice in the mornings.

In effect, the lives of the Shaws revolved around Potnis. An influential man in his own right, Potnis had the wherewithal to shape Prithvi's career. His wife made up for the void in Prithvi's life created by the death of his mother. He was now an integral part of the Potnis family.

Prithvi called Potnis *kaka* and he could blindly trust what his *kaka* had planned for him. Potnis had taken charge of everything, be it personally monitoring Prithvi's day's schedule or the kind of friend circle he must move in, or the people who got to meet him, besides pushing him harder for bigger goals by offering gifts as incentives.

The National Cricket Academy (NCA) and zonal cricket academies (ZCA) became a constant feature of Prithvi's calendar. He was now officially part of the BCCI's system.

The hype around him may have faded in a year but the interest in him remained as strong in the cricket circles.

Prithvi's evolution was closely followed by Makarand Waingankar. Waingankar has been a cricket administrator and a scout for a few decades. The idea of a talent resource development wing (TRDW) was first introduced in Indian cricket by Waingankar. He had started this wing in Karnataka in 2001. The programme dealt with tapping talent from remote districts in the state.

The BCCI was so impressed with the results that it started its own TRDW and appointed former India captain Dilip Vengsarkar as its head. As history will always remember, the TRDW unearthed a certain MS Dhoni which was followed by the likes of S Sreesanth, Suresh Raina and Irfan Pathan, to name a few.

Now back to Prithvi. Waingankar was convinced this kid was made for great things and understood he needed financial stability to solely focus on his cricket. In September 2014, he cracked a once-in-a-lifetime deal for Prithvi with cricket equipment giants Sanspareils Greenlands (commonly known as SG).

The sponsorship deal was worth Rs 36 lakh. For a fourteen-year-old to land such a hefty deal was unheard of. As news of the deal broke, Prithvi was back in the limelight.

'We learnt that he belongs to a modest background. Our association with him will provide him the support that he needs. Besides getting to use our world-class equipment, he won't have to worry about travelling and coaching expenses. We believe he has the potential to play for India. That's why we wanted to sign him on a long-term basis,' SG's marketing director Paras Anand was quoted as saying in the *Times of India* on 18 September 2014.

Now, Indian cricket waited with bated breath to see Prithvi Shaw arrive on the big stage!

## Rapid rise to First-Class cricket and announcing himself

In October 2016, eight months after the U-19 World Cup in Bangladesh, Rahul Dravid got down to preparing his next batch of U-19 cricketers. The next U-19 World Cup was still a good fourteen months away.

Dravid was not preparing for the next World Cup. His idea was to strengthen India's pool of cricketers. So he wanted to try out a lot of players who wouldn't make it to the U-19 World Cup in 2018 as they would be overage by the time the World Cup came around.

Prithvi made it to the U-19 Indian team which was supposed to play in an Asia Cup in Sri Lanka in December 2016. His talent was unmistakable. India won the tournament but Prithvi had an average tournament. He had scores of 39, 22, 36, 89 and 5. The 89 came against Malaysia, a cricketing nation which falls under the category of Associates as per the International Cricket Council.

His average scores notwithstanding, Dravid was bewildered by the talent Prithvi had for a seventeen-year-old.

A week after the India U-19 team came back from the Asia Cup, Mumbai selector Milind Rege was tempted to pick Prithvi for the Ranji Trophy semi-final against Tamil Nadu. Rege too had followed Prithvi's evolution in the *maidans* of Mumbai. Handing him a First-Class debut in a Ranji Trophy semi-final was going to be a huge call.

Unsure of himself, Rege called Dravid for his feedback. Dravid highlighted his strong backfoot game and his urge to be on an overdrive besides having a good technique. Dravid believed it was a good idea to pick him.

On 1 January 2017, at the age of seventeen, Prithvi Shaw became a First-Class cricketer for Mumbai. He was picked to open the batting against a consistent Tamil Nadu attack on a rather unusually seamer-friendly pitch in Rajkot. On the eve of the match, Sachin Tendulkar sent a message to Mumbai coach Chandrakant Pandit which read: 'Ask him (Prithvi) to play the way he likes to play.'

Tamil Nadu had posted 305 batting first. Prithvi took strike for Mumbai in the first over of the reply. He creamed Aswin Crist through the covers to get off the mark with a boundary. But he perished in the next ball trying to repeat the expansive cover drive and was caught behind for four.

Was it too early to blood him in? The Mumbai selectors were on edge.

On the last day of the match, Tamil Nadu set a target of 251 for Mumbai. Over the next 61 overs, for the first time on live television, the world got a glimpse of what Prithvi Shaw was all about.

On a wearing fifth-day track, a seasoned Tamil Nadu bowling line-up was bullied by a baby-faced teenager. Prithvi's flashing cuts and thunderous drives left the Tamil Nadu team ravaged. Like Tendulkar did when he was fifteen, Prithvi too scored a hundred on Ranji debut. He became the second youngest centurion for Mumbai.

The innings of 120 runs off 175 balls, consisting 13 boundaries and one six, finished 10 runs before Mumbai eventually knocked off the target in the next over after his dismissal.

'He played quite fearless cricket. It was a brilliant innings. He played some rash shots too, but got away with it. But he lived by his sword and credit to him,' Abhinav Mukund, captaining Tamil Nadu, said of Prithvi after the game.

All the skill with the willow aside, a 'fearless' mindset has always been Prithvi's virtue. 'Prithvi would never get overawed, let alone being intimidated, by any senior cricketer. He always believed he belongs to where he is playing. For him, the ball delivered at him mattered more than the one delivering it from the other end,' Pathak says.

The action moved to Indore in five days. Mumbai, who had been champions for forty-one times, were playing their 46th Ranji Trophy final. Gujarat, under Parthiv Patel, made it this far in the tournament after 66 years. They were the classic underdogs story. Yet, Prithvi's presence in the match threatened to overshadow the occasion for Gujarat.

The first morning of the match proved why. Prithvi had raced to 71 off 93 balls in the first 34 overs with the wily veteran left-arm pacer RP Singh extracting every bit of bounce and movement from the pitch to unsettle the batsmen at the other end.

The ominous innings was cut short through a run out. Mumbai were bowled out for 228; Gujarat scored 328 in reply. Prithvi came out in the second innings in a hurry to wipe off the 100-run deficit. Yet again, he raced to 44 off 35 before nicking one off Chintan Gaja to Parthiv behind the stumps.

Mumbai set a challenging target of 312 but Parthiv, once a teenage sensation fifteen years earlier, backed up his first innings score of 90 with a superlative 143 to chase down the target with 5 wickets in hand.

Gujarat had made history, winning their maiden Ranji Trophy title. It was a long grind for Gujarat cricket to reach this far.

Indian cricket was excited for a whole other reason though. Prithvi Shaw just showed that First-Class cricket was child's play for him!

## 'Unusual' road to U-19 World Cup

The 239 runs that he scored in the Ranji Trophy semi-final and final was evidence enough that 'Boy Wonder' Prithvi was ready for full-fledged men's cricket at the age of seventeen.

Not much was read into the total of 50 runs he managed in four matches in the subsequent Vijay Hazare Trophy. Everyone in the cricketing ecosystem in India was obsessed with charting an absolute roadmap to groom this talent. Rahul Dravid was at the forefront of it.

The India U-19 team travelled to England for a month-long tour in July–August in 2017. They were supposed to play two four-day Youth Tests and five Youth ODIs. Prithvi was named captain for the Youth ODI team.

Prithvi was the highest run-getter in the Youth Tests. He scored three half-centuries, the highest being 86, to conjure 250 runs at an average of 62.50 and strike rate of 90.90. In the Youth ODIs, he was the second highest scorer. In the five matches he played, he scored 160 runs at an average of 32 and a strike rate of 100.62. India U-19s had won every match of the tour.

'Prithvi is fearless, dominating and confident. He has a special ability to get runs quickly. In another two years, he will find out a way on how to be aggressive consistently for longer periods of time,' former India opener WV Raman, a coach on the tour, had opined about Prithvi in the *Times of India* after the tour.

Clearly, U-19 cricket wasn't going to pose much of a challenge!

Post the England tour, Dravid had six months to finalise a team for the U-19 World Cup scheduled to be played in New Zealand in January–February 2018. Keeping the sensational initiation in First-Class cricket in mind, Dravid didn't want Prithvi to get stuck at the U-19 level for long.

A bold decision was taken. Prithvi was asked to skip the U-19 Asia Cup in September and advised to play in the Duleep Trophy instead.

There was another First-Class record waiting to be broken here. The national selectors slotted Prithvi in the India Red team. The zonal teams were done away with the previous year. Duleep Trophy was played between India Red, Blue and Green.

MSK Prasad, the chairman of national senior selection committee at the time, doesn't shy away from conceding how eager he was to pick Prithvi. 'We all knew this special young boy was coming through the ranks. We eagerly wanted to blood him into senior cricket. And the opportunity came through the Duleep Trophy,' Prasad says.

Prithvi was played only in the final against India Blue. It was played with the pink ball and was a day-night fixture. Prithvi lit up the final on a sluggish, turning pitch in Lucknow with a mesmerising 154 off 249 balls.

At seventeen, Shaw now became the youngest player to score a century on Duleep Trophy debut, a record previously held by Sachin Tendulkar. He threatened to score heavily again in the second innings before he was run out for 31 off 33 balls. India Red had comfortably won by 163 runs.

There was a reason why Prithvi was only played in the final and not in the previous two matches. There was a chance he could have missed the entire tournament.

'Prithvi had come into the tournament with jaundice,' Prasad says. At the start of the tournament, Prasad was stunned by an audacious request. 'He came up to me and kept insisting that he be played in the first two matches despite the jaundice. It took a lot of convincing. I even had to tell him that if he went in with this state of health, he may collapse in the field and the selectors will be sued,' Prasad recalls.

The incident takes you back to the day when a seven-year-old Prithvi, on his first day at Springfield, argued with his coach Raju Pathak to bat in the nets where senior players played.

Prasad goes on to add: 'But the innings that he played when he came back was mind-boggling. He was still weak. The pitch was slow and taking a prodigious turn from the first over of the match. I remember spinners opened the bowling in the match. But he was scoring so freely and hitting them with so much ease that he stood out from the rest.'

The Duleep Trophy success created suspense over the possibility of Prithvi skipping the U-19 World Cup in four months' time.

During an interaction with Dravid around the same time, he talked about his vision. 'One of the things I realised when I took over the U-19 team was people stay on and play too much of U-19s. They want to keep on playing U-19 cricket which is very dangerous. So we took a decision of not allowing players to play two U-19 World Cups.'

Dravid further elaborated the core of his plan for the young players coming to him for finishing school.

'Age-group cricket has a purpose to solve but it's only a limited purpose. Then on they have to go and play men's cricket. That's what we decided with Prithvi as well. At the moment, we definitely want him to be a part of the World Cup team. It's also important to represent your country at the junior level. As and when he had the opportunity to play for Mumbai and the success he'd had in Duleep Trophy meant we could give him the leeway,' Dravid had stated.

The statement dispelled all the suspense.

Prithvi Shaw was going to the U-19 World Cup as the captain of the Indian team!

## U-19 World Cup high, IPL and Test debut

In a tournament where teenagers arrive to make a name, Prithvi reached New Zealand in January to play the 2018 U-19 World Cup with a big reputation.

The fireworks opened with the team's first match against Australia U-19s. A sublime 94 off 100 balls from Prithvi's blade deflated the young Australians. Prithvi made a statement that he was leading a team that is going to dominate the tournament.

That knock and the 100-run win set the template for the India U-19s in the tournament. That bunch of kids appeared to be ahead of the rest of the teams in the tournament by a country mile.

A day after the quarterfinal against Bangladesh, these kids were going under the hammer in the IPL auctions. Prithvi was getting starts in each of the matches but the big score eluded him. His reputation, though, was enough for Delhi Daredevils (now Delhi Capitals) to buy him for Rs 1.2 crore.

The big runs may not have come but Prithvi was moving around in the grounds of New Zealand like a boss. Every innings that he played pushed the opponents on the back foot.

Literally unchallenged, India won the U-19 World Cup with consummate ease. Prithvi finished ninth in the list of run-getters in the tournament. That 94 in the opening match stayed his highest score but every single run of his 261 was awe-inspiring. His runs came at an average of 65 and a strike rate of 95.

Prithvi's bat didn't really take the tournament by storm but he left the shores of New Zealand as a World Cup-winning captain. His stocks kept growing.

'We have spent two years preparing for it. There will be emotions when we say goodbye. Even if we don't go on to be a part of a senior World Cup-winning team, we will have this to remember,' Prithvi said after lifting the trophy.

This was only a step towards bigger things that awaited him. And they were not far away.

It was IPL season in a couple of months. If anything, Prithvi's inability to convert the pretty starts in limited-overs cricket was becoming a bit of a concern.

Raju Pathak, as every protective childhood coach does, warned Prithvi. 'I had to drill it into his head that he has so many strokes for every kind of ball that he doesn't have to rush. He got out for 29 in the U-19 World Cup final and I told him he can't be doing this. He has to keep his head with fame coming to him,' Pathak says.

After returning from the U-19 World Cup, he played a couple of matches for India 'A' in the Deodhar Trophy (a 50-over tournament played between India 'A', India 'B' and the winners of Vijay Hazare Trophy). He managed a 28 and a 40. There was hardly a bowler who looked to fluster him but he found a way to get out.

The IPL debut came midway through the tournament. Pravin Amre, a former India batsman and a Mumbai legend, was the assistant coach of the Daredevils. He got working on Prithvi to prepare him for the big league.

In a low-scoring game, which Daredevils lost by four runs while chasing 143 set by Kings XI Punjab, Prithvi smacked 22 off just 10 balls. The short stay on his debut screamed to the world that he was the real deal. An eighteen-year-old scoring 245 runs from nine games at a strike rate of 153 in his debut season had got Daredevils' head coach Ricky Ponting excited.

It felt like it was a matter of time before he was picked for the Indian team.

It was formality on the national selectors' part to send Prithvi with the India 'A' team for a full tour of England in the summer of 2018. The tour overlapped with the Indian senior team's tour of England. He turned out to be the highest run-getter in the two First-Class games, scoring 250 runs at an average of 62.50. More than the runs scored, the annihilation of full-grown First-Class attacks of West Indies 'A' and England Lions in bowler-friendly English conditions stood out. He scored those runs at a strike rate of 98.42.

His highest score of 188 against West Indies 'A' came off just 169 balls. The likes of Chris Woakes, Dom Bess and Jack Leach featured in the England Lions attack. And a century in a List A match earlier on the tour was strengthening his chances for an international break.

During the same summer, India opener Murali Vijay was dropped after the second Test at Lord's. India were down 0–2 in the five-Test series. Shikhar Dhawan, too, was put on notice. The selectors felt that was the right time to get Prithvi inside the Indian team's dressing room. He was made the back-up opener to Dhawan and KL Rahul.

India eventually suffered a 1–4 drubbing. It was time to revisit their combinations.

A month later, India were to host West Indies for a two-Test series. It was kind of a trial run before the tough tour to Australia in November 2018.

MSK Prasad's selection committee had to make a controversial decision. Mayank Agarwal, scoring heaps of runs in domestic and

India 'A' cricket for years, was ignored and Prithvi was tipped to open the batting in the first Test in Rajkot.

'That was one of the toughest calls we had to make in our four-year tenure,' Prasad recalls. 'Mayank had scored 2200 runs in the previous domestic season. But Prithvi looked special. The team management had seen him in the nets in England. Everyone felt it was the right time to blood him in.'

On 4 October 2018, Prithvi Shaw was a Test cricketer for India. And he was 36 days shy of turning nineteen.

The controversy was put to rest in the first 90 minutes of the Test match. Prithvi reached his half century in just 56 balls. And in another 43 balls, he was raising his bat to the dressing room to celebrate his hundred.

Prithvi Shaw, like he has done on each of his Ranji and Duleep Trophy debuts, eviscerated the West Indies attack to score a hundred on Test debut.

The pitch at Rajkot is historically a flat one but his range of shots during his knock of 134 off 154, during which he peppered the boundary from cover to backward point, was a hair-raising session to watch.

His dismissal was against the run of play when he offered a simple caught and bowled to leg-spinner Devendra Bishoo.

At day end, he was asked about the team management picking him ahead of Agarwal. A beaming Prithvi, with his innate confidence, replied: 'It's up to the coach and Virat Kohli *bhai* to decide on when to play me. But I was ready for the England series as well.'

Prithvi meant business.

The days of hardship weren't too far behind and he did acknowledge it. 'I want to dedicate this hundred to my dad, he has made a lot of sacrifices for me, he is still doing it. He has been very helpful throughout my journey. He has always been there, whenever I have been nervous or have gotten out early. I can't list it out all but he has done a lot.'

India wrapped up the match by an innings without much of a fuss.

In the following Test in Hyderabad, Prithvi put up another show with a 53-ball 70 and an unbeaten 33 off 45 balls as India claimed the series 2–0.

Kohli and coach Ravi Shastri were smitten by the teenager's talent.

'Prithvi is a special talent. He looks like he will nick off a ball anytime but he middles them all the time,' Kohli said of Prithvi.

Shastri's praise is one for the history books. 'There's a bit of Tendulkar, Sehwag and Lara in Prithvi.'

One could not wait to watch Prithvi bat in Australia in a month's time.

## Tough times: Injury, dope ban, comeback

The hype around Prithvi gathered steam as he landed in Australia in November 2018. The Australian public, forever crushing over Sachin Tendulkar since he scored the twin hundreds on their turf as an eighteen-year-old, was eager to see if this nineteen-year-old could repeat it against Pat Cummins, Mitchell Starc and Josh Hazlewood.

The smattering of crowd at the Sydney Cricket Ground got a first-hand experience of this prodigy during India's warm-up match against Cricket Australia XI. The punches off the backfoot, the cracking square-cuts and his trademark drives through the covers echoed around the arena as Prithvi scored 66. It was all building up for a fascinating Aussie summer.

And then the next day, Prithvi was carried off the field after he twisted his left ankle while taking a catch at the long-leg boundary. A few hours later, he was walking with crutches. His tour was over.

As if all the hype, buzz and excitement around him were too good to be true!

Prithvi came back to India, went through a rehab programme at the National Cricket Academy (NCA) in Bengaluru and was back on the field for Mumbai in the Syed Mushtaq Ali T20 Trophy. He was bound to be rusty and the performances said so. He scored just 134 runs in eight matches.

Soon, he was back in his elements as the IPL 2019 came around – 353 runs in 16 matches at a strike rate of 133 (when they played seven matches on a slow pitch at Feroz Shah Kotla in Delhi) were good signs. A 99 off 55 while chasing 186 against the Kolkata Knight Riders was the highlight. He was finally getting his white-ball game in place.

Again, it was all too good to be true.

On 30 July, a press release from Board of Control for Cricket in India (BCCI) announced that Prithvi Shaw failed a dope test and was being suspended from playing in any competition till 15 November 2019.

He was found guilty of consuming terbutaline, a prohibited substance as per the World Anti-Doping Agency (WADA).

It was on the day of a Syed Mushtaq Ali match against Punjab in Indore on 22 February that Prithvi felt sick. He had a sore throat and felt a bit feverish. Advised by his father over the phone, he bought a cough syrup over the counter. The cough syrup contained the prohibited substance.

Since he consumed the substance inadvertently, it went in his favour as he was handed a lenient punishment.

Things went from being rosy to midnight dark in a matter of months.

Chief national selector MSK Prasad recalls that he rather saw a fire in Prithvi during that period. 'I remember he went to England when he was suspended. He wanted to be away from all this negativity. But he spoke frequently with me over the phone and talked about his game. He would even send me videos of his batting,' Prasad says.

There's no denying that Prithvi is flamboyant. It started reflecting in his lifestyle. The incident also triggered speculations about his lifestyle. He still fights them.

The caretakers of Indian cricket now had to make sure he didn't lose his way. Sachin Tendulkar had special sessions with him. Rahul Dravid always had an eye fixed on him. Prasad recalls: 'We asked Jatin Paranjpe, our selector from the West zone, to talk more to him since Jatin also hailed from Mumbai. Sachin and Dravid spent a lot of time on him. Then we felt that he should spend less time in Mumbai and be at NCA so that he doesn't get distracted.'

The Mumbai team included Prithvi for the Syed Mushtaq Ali Trophy in November 2019. It didn't matter that he was not eligible to play for half of the tournament.

On 16 November, a day after his suspension ended, Prithvi was back opening the batting for Mumbai against Assam at the Wankhede Stadium. He smacked 63 off 39 balls which included six boundaries and three sixes. The knock was so unassuming that it never looked like he was away from the game.

When he reached his half-century, he turned towards the TV cameras, pointed at his bat and gestured that it was his bat that was doing the talking.

He had made a statement! That was the fire Prasad had noticed in him a few months earlier.

The Syed Mushtaq Ali Trophy yielded 240 runs in five matches with three half-centuries. That was just a prelude to the destruction that was to be caused.

Prithvi opened the Ranji Trophy that year against Baroda with a 62-ball 66 only to demolish them in the second innings with his maiden First-Class double century. His 202 came in just 179 balls.

The selectors didn't want to waste any time. A couple of Ranji matches later, Prithvi was on the plane to New Zealand where India 'A' was playing in a shadow tour in January 2020 before the Indian senior team reached there for a full tour.

Shikhar Dhawan missed the tour due to an injury. Rohit Sharma flew back after the T20I series. A half-century in three List A games was good enough for the selectors to pick Prithvi for the ODI series in New Zealand.

He made his ODI debut at Hamilton and scored 84 runs in the three games.

The Test series arrived. Both Tests were played on pitches with so much of grass cover that they could barely be distinguished from the lush green outfield. Tim Southee, Trent Boult and Neil Wagner were always going to be more than a handful on those surfaces.

Prithvi scored a counter-attacking half-century in the first innings of the series and then the form started to fade. Scores of 14, 0 and 4 followed as India returned home having suffered a 0-2 defeat.

Still early days for Prithvi in international cricket!

## Loss of form and a comeback statement

The pandemic and lockdown hit and Prithvi couldn't consolidate his form he had struck upon his return from the doping ban.

For a while, it didn't seem like the lockdown had affected Prithvi when cricket resumed with the IPL in the UAE in September 2020. He raced to 182 runs in the first five matches of the tournament. There were two half-centuries.

And then things went south. Just 46 runs in the next eight matches meant he was dropped from the playing XI of the Delhi Capitals as the business end approached. Capitals made the final but Prithvi wasn't played in the three most crucial matches in the back end of the tournament.

India travelled to Australia for four Test matches after the IPL 2020. Prithvi retained his place as the first-choice opener. It was obvious he was not in the best of shape.

Capitals coach Ricky Ponting was on air on the first day of the Test series in Adelaide. As Mitchell Starc prepared to run in with the new pink ball, Ponting went on about how Prithvi leaves a gap between his bat and pad when the ball swings back into him from a left-armer.

As Ponting finished his monologue, Starc swung one back in to Prithvi and rattled his stumps. He was gone for naught off the second ball of the series.

In the second innings, it took Cummins four balls to sneak one in between his bat and pad. Gone for four!

India were bowled out for 36. India were down 0–1 in the series and Prithvi was dropped. His fitness and lack of concentration during a match were marked as his drawbacks.

For the rest of the tour, he watched from the sidelines as India found new young heroes to script a historic 2–1 series win.

By the time he landed in India in late January 2021, his name went missing from the India squad which was supposed to play four Tests against England at home.

Hurting, he went back to the drawing board in Mumbai. The

Delhi Capitals had brought back Pravin Amre in its coaching staff after a gap of one year. Amre was tasked to work on Prithvi and iron out the flaws in his technique.

The back lift was rectified and the cluttered mind was cleaned. Mumbai selectors backed its prodigy and handed him the captaincy of a struggling team for the Vijay Hazare Trophy in February–March

The results came immediately.

He finished the tournament as the highest run-getter. By amassing four centuries and 827 runs in just eight matches at an average of 165.40 and strike rate of 138.29, Prithvi led Mumbai to the title. You could smell vengeance in his marauding stroke play.

Happy days!

The IPL started in a month. He was on a roll – 308 runs came off his blade at a strike rate of 146 in the eight matches Capitals played before the tournament was indefinitely postponed due to the second wave of the Covid-19 pandemic.

Prithvi had declared to the world he is not going anywhere anytime soon. Every time he was sent back to play domestic cricket, he proved he is too good for that level of cricket.

International cricket is yet to see the best of Prithvi Shaw!

## *CHAPTER 4*

# SHUBMAN GILL: THE QUIET ROCKSTAR

## *A father chasing a dream with his son*

Shubman Gill comes across as the quintessential lovable boy in his early twenties. The tall structure, the broad shoulders and the sharp features aside, the boy from Punjab is mellow, and the composed demeanour is a departure from the in-your-face breed of 21st century Indian cricketers. He moves around the crease against the best of fast bowlers as if he owns the turf though.

Much of his rise to the league of playing with the best needs to be traced back to a bold decision taken by his family in 2007.

Lakhwinder Singh Gill has been a cricket fanatic for most of his life. A regular farmer from Chak Khere Wala, a village in Fazilka district, which is some 350 kilometres from Chandigarh, Lakhwinder and his family were doing just fine with their work of investing in and tending to crops. Lakhwinder's wish to become a cricketer in a remote village was next to impossible. He had moved on with his life and cricket had become more of a pastime.

Lakhwinder's outlook towards the game started to change when his son Shubman got hooked to cricket. A three-year-old Shubman had absolutely no interest in toys. All he yearned for were a bat and a ball.

Toddler Shubman's interest in the sport had got Lakhwinder excited. As Shubman started growing, Lakhwinder took it upon himself to sharpen the boy's skills.

The father made Shubman play 500–700 balls a day. Lakhwinder had decided to push his boy harder. A six-year-old Shubman was made to face balls which bounced off a *manji* (charpoy). The balls travel faster after bouncing on the charpoy. It was done to sharpen his reflexes against quick bowling. Lakhwinder would also make Shubman bat with a stump.

All that training notwithstanding, Lakhwinder realised that Shubman needed formal coaching, guidance and opportunities to bloom as a cricketer. It was not possible in Fazilka.

Chandigarh was the destination for the Gills. Lakhwinder didn't want his son's dreams getting nipped in the bud like it happened with him in his younger days due to lack of facilities and support from family.

'My father saw a spark in me when I was seven and then it was decided that I should go to Chandigarh. They made a lot of adjustments by shifting to Chandigarh,' Shubman invariably gets emotional talking about his parents' sacrifice.

The Gills had to start from scratch in Chandigarh. Their family was left behind in Fazilka. Adjusting to the ways of a city was not going to be easy.

For Shubman, though, the inspiration to become a cricketer came in 2007. The images of the Indian team lifting the World T20 trophy left a lasting impression on him.

He clearly represents the face of the Gen Next of Indian cricket. The transition from a regimented text-book era of cricket to a generation which is bred on a T20 diet seems complete with the emergence of this generation.

The earliest impression of cricket was watching Sachin

Tendulkar drive straight down the ground. 'I don't remember much but I do recall the straight drive Sachin sir used to play. I was fascinated by it,' Shubman says.

Upon reaching Chandigarh, academics was nowhere near being a priority. The father and son were chasing a dream!

## Catching the attention

Mohali was Shubman's place of training. He joined a local academy. Lakhwinder would never take his eye off his son. He would be at the ground, watching his son practice. There wasn't going to be any let-up in the effort put in.

Three years went by. Shubman turned ten. The plan was a usual one. Take part in trials and graduate through the ranks in age-group cricket in Punjab.

But things started happening rather quickly for Shubman. It happened through an unexpected turn of events.

'*Main 11–12 saal ka thha tab mujhe* Punjab Cricket Association (PCA) *ke* nets *mein* bat *karne bola gaya thha. Sab* U-19 *aur* state bowlers *thhe. Maine achhi* batting *ki thhi* (When I was around eleven or twelve years of age, I was asked to bat in the PCA nets. There were senior U-19 and state bowlers. I batted well),' Shubman, during an interaction in 2019, very humbly describes his first major break.

The session in the nets that he was talking about wasn't any regular session at the PCA Stadium in Mohali. Not for nothing did this incident become one of the most inspiring stories in Punjab cricket in the last decade.

Back in 2010, the Board of Control for Cricket in India (BCCI) had roped in former India fast bowler Karsan Ghavri to run a pace bowler's academy to create a pool of future fast bowlers for the country. The Mohali surface was considered the fastest pitch in India for a long time.

Ghavri was going through the routine drills with the young fast bowlers for the first three days. That batch had Sidharth Kaul, a U-19 World Cup winner in 2008, and Sandeep Sharma, who had already played in the U-19 World Cup in 2010 and would later go on to win the trophy in 2012.

Just the routine drills were not enough for Ghavri. He wanted batsmen in the nets to simulate match conditions for the raw bowlers. Once when he went out for a casual stroll in Mohali, he stopped at a local ground to watch a few kids playing. There he observed little Shubman playing some technically sound shots. He walked up to a man watching from the sidelines. It was Lakhwinder.

Ghavri extended an offer to Lakhwinder to send his son to the PCA Stadium. He also assured Lakhwinder that Shubman will be provided with good facilities. It was an offer Lakhwinder could not turn down.

Over the next few days, Shubman never looked out of place playing bowlers who were nearly twice his age. Ghavri informed the senior officials at PCA that boy needed to be immediately drafted in the Punjab Under-14 team.

Daljit Singh, the man credited for changing the look of grounds and pitches in India, gives an account of how special this boy was. One may be reminded that Daljit had played Ranji Trophy for Bihar, Delhi, Northern Punjab and Services from 1961–1979. He had since coached Punjab teams across age groups. He is one of the most respected and revered figures in Punjab cricket.

'There was an academy not far from the PCA in Mohali. I used to drop by frequently and saw this boy tirelessly batting in the nets. He batted on cemented pitches as well as turf ones. He seemed to have great ball sense. His father, despite his limitations in technical knowledge, worked really hard on this boy,' Daljit recalls.

Shubman had started to score heavily in the U-14 district matches. 'He was a special talent. We allowed him to practice at the PCA. Special nets were reserved for him. We even allowed him to bring his friends from his academy to bowl at him. His father's eyes were fixed on him; so was his mother's. In fact, it was his homemaker mother who, despite taking care of his food and domestic needs, was very involved on the field too and would visit the PCA Stadium to watch him play. All decisions related to cricket would be made by his father. The parents and the kid were extremely devoted towards his cricketing dreams. As he started scoring heavily in district and state matches, the special nets became a permanent fixture. Every time he went for major tournaments or trials like the India U-19s, we would prepare special pitches for him to practice. We made sure he got the truest pitches to bat on since we didn't want him to get hurt while batting on rough pitches. It continues even after he has played India 'A' and India. He would get the kind of surfaces he thought would prepare him best for an upcoming tour,' Daljit says.

Talking about the important innings in his life, Shubman promptly mentions a triple century in a U-16 district match and double century in another U-16 match. For the record, he had hammered 351 in a U-16 inter-district match and then followed it up with an unbeaten double century on his U-16 debut for Punjab.

By the time he had turned fifteen, he had set the junior cricket scene in India on fire. He won the award for BCCI's best junior cricketer of the year for two consecutive years: 2013–14 and 2014–15.

Shubman Gill's rise in Punjab coincided with Prithvi Shaw's emergence in Mumbai.

Abhay Sharma had just become a part of the National Cricket Academy's core coaching staff in 2014–15. He would later go on to be one of Rahul Dravid's trusted lieutenants when Dravid took charge of the India U-19 and India 'A' teams in 2015.

Abhay recalls his first sight of Shubman. 'I had seen this boy during his U-16 days. He was barely fourteen. I was in Mohali conducting a coaching programme when I noticed him. He was playing at the other stadium in Mohali. He had already hit some six–seven centuries in inter-district matches. I was amazed looking at the boy bat. He was batting in a different league. I didn't interact with him but had asked around. The name Shubman Gill got registered in my mind.'

The next season he was at the NCA U-16 camp. 'Both Prithvi and Shubman had come for the U-16 camp. Everybody knew about Prithvi and was excited about him since he was making the headlines and he was much-hyped in Mumbai. But when I saw Shubman, I immediately recognised him. I wasn't as close to Rahul at that time, but I had mentioned Shubman's name to him. I had told him we need to keep an eye on this boy.'

At fifteen, Prithvi had grabbed the headlines and Shubman had caught the attention of the men who matter.

Exciting times lay ahead!

## Playing with stars in Punjab team and U-19 days

Months after the 2016 U-19 World Cup, Rahul Dravid was still growing into his role of India U-19 and India 'A' coach. That's when Shubman arrived at the NCA for the U-19 camp. The next U-19 World Cup was a good sixteen months away.

'We had decided that we will identify the core of the U-19 team which will play the U-19 World Cup in 2018. We saw Shubman in the NCA camp. Rahul was aware of Shubman's exploits in junior cricket and was following his game. He was in the first list of probables and we decided to stick with him,' Abhay Sharma says.

The first two series that he played for India U-19s, he was outscoring Prithvi. His 148 runs in two matches helped India win the U-19 Asia Cup in Sri Lanka in December 2016. Over the next month, a touring U-19 England team had to face the wrath of Shubman. The scores in the four Youth ODI matches he played read: 29, 24, 138 (not out) and 160. The 138 and 160 came when Prithvi was moved down to No. 3 and Shubman was made to open.

While he was hammering 160 off 120 balls in the fourth match, Prithvi had smacked 105 off 89 as the two batting prodigies ran the English boys ragged under the warm winter sun in Mumbai. That was the first time Shubman and Prithvi combined.

The Punjab selectors, itching to play him in the senior team for a while, wasted no time and drafted Shubman into the state team for the Vijay Hazare Trophy. Shubman and Prithvi, both seventeen, had made it to their respective senior state teams.

At the age of seventeen, Shubman was in a Punjab team that had Harbhajan Singh and Yuvraj Singh in the dressing room – heroes of 'that' 2007 World T20 campaign which inspired him to become a cricketer.

After he was run out for 11 in his List A debut against Vidarbha at the Feroz Shah Kotla in Delhi, Harbhajan, in a passing remark, said: 'Watch out for this boy. He has presence at the crease which says he will become a big player.'

One would understand the next day what Harbhajan meant.

On a nippy February morning, Punjab were down 3/19 in the third over against Assam. Mandeep Singh and Yuvraj were back in the pavilion by the sixth over of the match with the ball jagging around prodigiously.

Young Shubman got about resurrecting the innings and scored 121 off 129 even as Gurkeerat Mann, another player who had already played for India, played second fiddle with a 58 off

102. Punjab could only manage 243 before Assam chased down the target when the pitch flattened out under the afternoon sun.

Shubman had shown his class.

He finished with 220 runs in six games, the second highest for his team, even as Punjab crashed out of the tournament.

Five months after his Punjab debut, the India U-19 team flew over to England for a full tour.

This was the time Shubman was coming into his own. He had found his core.

'There are times when you know that everything has clicked for a cricketer. That England tour was one such time when you could see Shubman had peaked to a different level,' Abhay remembers.

'I particularly remember a couple of matches in Brighton and Bristol. Rahul Dravid was not on that tour. At that time, there was a lot of discussion around Shubman's batting position. Prithvi was opening the batting and we had other players who were specialist openers. I told Rahul that I wanted to use him at No. 3. He had the technique to play the new ball and could also build an innings. His game in the V (straight down the ground between long-off and long-on) is so strong that he could play long and pace an innings.

'The first things you have to do with U-19 cricketers is to teach them how to play out all 50 overs and pace an innings. You need someone who can bat long. Shubman had all those qualities. In the match in Brighton, he scored 147 off 120 balls in chilly and windy conditions. He was toying with the bowling. I remember, we felt like he could score a double hundred. He got out when six overs were left. That innings confirmed he had the ability to go places in international cricket. I remember Rahul asking me how he went, and I said that this boy was ready for the next level.'

Shubman was the highest run-getter in the Y-ODIs with 278 runs in four matches at a strike rate of 100.36. In the two Youth Tests, he had scored 178 runs at an average of 43.5 which included a score of 102.

Abhay wasn't off the mark with his assessment on that tour.

Ajay Ratra, a former India wicketkeeper, was appointed as the coach of the Punjab state team for the 2017–18 domestic season. Ratra was Yuvraj's teammate in the victorious U-19 World Cup campaign in 1999. He also happened to be the first Indian wicketkeeper to score a Test century in West Indies.

The major thing that happened in his tenure was Shubman Gill getting selected to play in the Ranji Trophy in the middle of the season. 'I had first seen him in the NCA U-16 camp. But in three years he had grown so much as a player. Punjab is a big team where big names play and it's very difficult to break in for a teenager. But both Yuvraj and Harbhajan had endorsed Shubman's inclusion. And Shubman was doing so well in the U-19s that it didn't make sense to keep him waiting. He earned his place,' Ratra recalls.

'The first time when he batted against experienced pacers like Sidharth Kaul, Sandeep Sharma, Barinder Sran and Manpreet Gony in the nets, he looked so comfortable. He had so much time to play the deliveries. You need to have a strong backfoot game to succeed at the international level. He seemed to have mastered that already,' Ratra elaborates Shubman's initial days of rubbing shoulders with the big names in Indian cricket.

'I tried to not get overawed by them. They were very helpful,' Shubman would say of his heroes Yuvraj and Harbhajan.

That would be an understatement.

It was obvious he was cagey while facing Harbhajan in the nets. He had confided in the coaches that he feared hurting Harbhajan if he charged him and hit aggressive shots in the nets.

Both Harbhajan and Yuvraj were twice his age. Shubman wasn't born when Harbhajan made his international debut and he was barely a year old when Yuvraj first played for India. Here were two people who had made their India debuts in their teens.

Ratra explains the emotional roller coaster that Shubman went through. 'It happens. There are bound to be nerves when you come into a team which has legends like Harbhajan and Yuvraj. When you get into the nets in your early days, you think of the reputation of the bowler. He looked so calm and composed from a distance, but he must have been feeling the nerves.

'He may not have played too many shots against Harbhajan but when we had conversations and he mingled with the team, he opened up. Harbhajan and Yuvraj spoke to him a lot. They made him comfortable. And as he got used to the team environment, he started showing his range of shots in the nets too.'

The conversations that Yuvraj had with Shubman were not restricted to cricket. Yuvraj would go on to be his mentor. So much so that Yuvraj arranged sessions with Sachin Tendulkar before Shubman went for his first Test tour in Australia in November 2020.

'Yuvi *paaji* is my inspiration. His journey, his struggles with his health (Yuvraj had overcome a rare cell cancer in his lungs after winning the 2011 World Cup) and the way he looks at the game is so inspirational. That has helped me so much to get ready for top-grade cricket,' Shubman proudly states.

On 17 November, an eighteen-year-old Shubman was making his First-Class debut against Bengal one chilly morning in Amritsar.

He couldn't have expected a tougher initiation in First-Class cricket. He was opening the batting on the first morning of the match in conditions that aided seam and swing against a Bengal attack that had the veteran and a Ranji giant in Ashok Dinda.

As the Punjab batting crumbled around him, Shubman stood tall with a 63 off 102 balls. Punjab were bowled out for 147 and no other batsman could score even 20. Eventually, Punjab lost the match by an innings.

A week later, in similar conditions at the same venue, Shubman dished out a masterclass in batting. He knocked the wind out of an ordinary Services bowling attack and scored 129 off 142 on the first day of the match. It set up a huge victory for Punjab.

Ratra recounts the two innings. 'Batting in the morning in northern India in winters is very difficult. The ball jags around a lot. I remember he was scoring so freely on his debut while everyone else struggled around him. And in the second game, he nearly completed his hundred before lunch. That could have been a record. Those two innings showed he could bat in any conditions.'

Those were the only two matches Shubman played that season. It was time to prepare for the U-19 World Cup, which was fifty days away.

It was time for the world to see his talent on live television.

## U-19 World Cup glory and big IPL deal

Prithvi Shaw and Shubman Gill were the two marquee players in the Indian U-19 team that reached New Zealand to play the U-19 World Cup in January 2018. Prithvi, already popular in media, was the captain and Shubman was named his deputy for the tournament.

Shubman was identified to bat at No. 3. The first match against Australia, his first on live television, had the world sit up and take notice. An authoritative 63 off 54 balls was just a marker to what was coming.

The Indian team was thrashing opponents as if it was mere formality to turn up for the matches. The cameras preferred having Prithvi in the frame but Shubman was slowly taking up more space.

The 63 in the opening was followed up with a 90 off 59 balls against Zimbabwe before he cranked it up when India made it to the knockout stage of the tournament.

The quarterfinal against Bangladesh saw him score 86 off 94 balls. It was a couple of days ahead of the IPL auctions.

The tension in the Indian camp was palpable even after brushing aside Bangladesh by 134 runs. The Indian team's ruthless run so far in the tournament had raised hopes of a few boys going for big money in the auction.

It did happen. Shubman Gill, along with fast bowlers Kamlesh Nagarkoti and Shivam Mavi, were the face of Kolkata Knight Riders' big investment in youth. Shubman landed a deal of Rs 1.8 crore.

Dravid and his team had a complementary job to do besides just preparing these bunch of boys to win a U-19 World Cup.

Abhay offers an insight. 'We had learnt our lessons during the 2016 U-19 World Cup after seeing the changes in some of the boys after the auction. A generic talk was not going to be enough. We started working on these boys well before the auctions. We decided to have one-on-one chats with every boy in the team. There had to be an environment where there were no over-the-moon celebrations if someone got a big deal and the ones who didn't get a deal should not be sulking. It's easy to just say that the eventual goal should be to play for India irrespective of IPL deals but to implement it is very tough. But this set of boys responded really well.'

A day after the two-day IPL auctions, the Boys in Blue were about to play a big semi-final against Pakistan. This was the first big high-pressure, emotionally charged match that these teenagers were playing. Much of the tournament's TRPs hinged on this draw.

Shubman Gill rose to the occasion. He was touted as the most complete batsman in this bunch. For over a year, he was earmarked as the batsman to anchor and pace the innings. Every aspect of his talent and training culminated into a perfect match on 29 January in Christchurch.

Batting at No. 3, Shubman anchored a stuttering innings before taking off in the death overs. He brought up his hundred off the last ball of the innings. In his knock of an unbeaten 102 of 94 balls, he had nullified the threat of exciting left-arm pacer Shaheen Shah Afridi besides helping India post a 272/9.

This was his sixth consecutive score of fifty or more in Youth ODIs. Yet, it qualified as his first complete innings with composure, temperament and flourishing stroke play, all in the right balance.

As the Indian bowlers were completing a 203-run rout in the match, Shubman pulled off a stunning catch at long-off. Pakistan U-19 captain Hassan Khan had miscued a slog off Riyan Parag. Shubman turned around at mid-off and set off on a sprint towards the boundary, flung his body and snared the ball that was going away from him.

He was in a happy zone and it was time to strut his stuff. He was a rockstar amidst a bunch of future stars.

'Shubman was always very quick on the turn. He stood out from the rest. We used to time him and we realised that he could turn and run faster than the best in the business. He may give the impression that he is an easy-going and laid-back boy. But he is extremely agile and fit. We communicated it with him, and he understood why he was the best fielder to field at mid-off and mid-on,' Abhay says.

'Shubman is very honest with his training and had great work ethics for a teenager. Rahul had given us a free hand in pushing the boys hard. We would give them throwdowns and deliveries very quick, targeted at the helmet. He wore them on the helmet and the knuckles but never complained. Best thing about Shubman is he will not follow instructions blindly. He will ask questions and try to understand how a certain drill is going to benefit him. That shows how much the kid is thinking about his game.'

The match-winning century against Pakistan made him a celebrity overnight. He may have been oblivious of the fact that he was a rage back home in the other hemisphere.

His wristy cover drives against spinners were compared to Virat Kohli. A backfoot punch off a fast bowler for nearly a six-over mid-wicket was reminiscent of Kohli punching Chris Woakes into mid-wicket stand a year ago. The boss-like presence at the crease and ability to pace an innings was again compared to Kohli.

Kohli has been his idol. The adulation only grew when he had shared the stage with Kohli at BCCI's annual prize ceremony to collect the award for the best junior cricketer of the year for two years in a row – 2014 and 2015.

For all his adulation for Kohli, Shubman did make sure he set a record straight. 'I have my role models. I try to follow the work ethics of Virat *bhaiyya*, but I know every player is different and you can't copy anyone,' he insists.

He didn't have much to do in the final against Australia four days later. Chasing a modest target of 217, opener Manjot Kalra did the bulk of the scoring, staying unbeaten at 101 and Shubman chipped in with a 31 off 30 balls to ensure India reached home with 8 wickets in hand, and the U-19 World Cup Trophy was regained after six years.

His score: 372 runs in five innings, an average of 124, three half-centuries, one century and a strike-rate of 112.38 – Shubman Gill was the player of the tournament and talk of the cricket town!

## IPL high, deluge of runs and pushing for India selection

Indian cricket could not wait to see more of Shubman Gill once he returned from the victorious U-19 World Cup campaign.

A couple of months later, he joined the Kolkata Knight Riders camp at the Eden Gardens. Coach Jacques Kallis didn't waste much time and played Shubman early in the tournament. The Kolkata Knight Riders, with a new captain in Dinesh Karthik, were figuring out a balanced batting line-up.

Karthik brought consistency, Andre Russell instilled fear in opponents, Nitish Rana played the supporting act but young Shubman brought stability to the batting line-up. He wasn't given one certain position in the batting order but he did his job floating around in the line-up.

The Kolkata Knight Riders made the play-offs. Shubman played 13 out of the 16 games and scored 203 runs, mostly batting down the order, at an average of 33.83 and strike rate of 146.04.

A boy who had batted up the order during his formative years was now finishing games with aplomb. The unbeaten 36-ball 57 to chase down 178 against eventual champions Chennai Super Kings at a throbbing Eden Gardens propelled him up as the next big thing in Indian cricket alongside Prithvi Shaw.

The boy was in vogue now.

Taking the field with his collar up, the red handkerchief tucked in his trousers while batting, the hunk-like walk and wielding the willow like a master make for a flamboyant Punjabi boy.

Shubman is every bit different from his on-field persona.

In Abhay's words he is a 'quiet and emotional boy'. 'That doesn't mean he is shy. He mingles with everyone and is funny in his own way. He has a great sense of humour and he does it unassumingly. He pulled pranks on his teammates but never bullied any of them. The best thing is that he could take jokes about himself very sportingly.'

Abhay recounts one of Shubman's funny acts. 'We were in Bristol with the U-19 team in 2017. India's women's team was playing the World Cup final against England that day. Shubman was sitting quietly in the dressing room. There was tension in the air. The boys were also invested in the game.

'We kept checking scores. So somebody came and said, 'Veda Krishnamurthy out *ho gayi* (Veda Krishnamurthy just got out).' And Shubman replied with a poker face: '*Kya? Teeno ek saath out ho gaye* (What? All three of them got out together)?' I can't tell you how everyone in the dressing cracked up. He knows how to cut the tension in the air. Even today when we meet, he brings that up.'

As for the handkerchief dangling from his waist, it's more of a superstition than a fashion statement. 'Once I was going through an indifferent phase when I was playing U-16 cricket. Then one day I scored a hundred and when I came back to the changing room, I found a white handkerchief in my pocket. I carried a handkerchief while batting in the next match and I scored a hundred. It became a habit from there,' he clarified in 2019.

Three weeks after the IPL was over, the national selectors were supposed to pick an India 'A' team for a tour of England. By that time, the pool of players had become strong enough. To fit Shubman in the India 'A' team ahead of strong performers from the preceding Ranji Trophy season was very tough. Shubman hadn't played one full domestic season yet. One must remember that even Rishabh Pant was not selected for Duleep Trophy six months post his successful U-19 World Cup campaign citing that he hadn't played a full First-Class season. It became a reference point.

Shubman's Punjab teammate Anmolpreet Singh had amassed 753 runs in five Ranji Trophy matches. The selectors were clear in their minds to reward Anmolpreet.

This time, however, Rahul Dravid decided to intervene. Dravid usually never questions or interferes in the selectors' job. This was the first time he extended a formal request to the selectors. It was for Shubman.

Dravid opined that Shubman was too good a talent to be left in the cold storage and wasn't far off from being ready to play for India.

Shubman didn't disappoint. He grew stronger with every exposure – 187 runs in four one-day matches of a tri-series in England wasn't a bad return.

He started the following domestic season with 418 runs in seven Vijay Hazare matches, and followed it up with 168 runs in three Deodhar Trophy matches. He played a Ranji Trophy match, scored a half-century, flew to New Zealand for an India 'A' series, scored 62 in two List A matches and came back to play the Ranji Trophy.

It was like he was just working up his appetite for a deluge of runs in the following year. This is when he was about to take India domestic cricket by storm.

Shubman set foot at the PCA Stadium in Mohali to play a Ranji Trophy match against Tamil Nadu, literally, immediately after disembarking from the plane from New Zealand. Replying to Tamil Nadu's first innings score of 215, Shubman tore into the Tamil Nadu bowling attack like a tornado and walked off scoring 268 off just 328 balls, leaving the visiting side ravaged.

Daljit Singh, an integral part of Indian domestic cricket for fifty years, reckons that the innings proved Shubman was too good for domestic cricket.

A week later, he nearly single-handedly pulled off a win against Hyderabad. Chasing a target of 338 in two sessions on the last day, Shubman toyed with the Hyderabad bowling attack led by Mohammad Siraj to score 148 off 154 balls. For most part of the last session, it appeared that Shubman would walk past the target.

It required a fiery late burst from Siraj for Hyderabad to avoid shock defeat. Punjab fell 14 short of the target and the match ended in a draw.

Shubman played just five Ranji matches that season but ended up as Punjab's highest run-getter with 728 runs at an average of 104.

Shubman Gill was now a *dada* player (a colloquial word for dominating) in domestic cricket. He was close to getting into the Indian dressing room.

The opportunity came a month later under some unfortunate circumstances. Hardik Pandya and KL Rahul were found guilty of making misogynistic comments on a talk show hosted by Bollywood director Karan Johar. BCCI suspended them from playing for India in a five-match ODI and three-match T20I series in New Zealand in January–February 2019.

Prithvi Shaw was still nursing an ankle injury he sustained in Australia and that meant Gill was on the plane to New Zealand.

Shubman's arrival came on the back of the emergence of Rishabh Pant and Prithvi. After a couple of nets sessions, India captain Virat Kohli was blown away. 'Thc talent these boys have is mind-boggling. At their age, I wasn't even 10 or 20 per cent of what they are,' Kohli says.

Shubman got his first international cap in the fourth ODI of the series in Hamilton on 31 January 2019. He managed to score a nine and seven in his first two ODIs against the wily New Zealand seamers.

These two scores were no proof of his talent. Shubman was about to crank it up a lot more!

## Big runs and battling frustration

The underwhelming international debut notwithstanding, Shubman Gill was still a rage. The excitement around him barely ebbed.

The IPL 2019 was the audition for the World Cup in England. Making it into the Indian team was always going to be a stretch.

The Kolkata Knight Riders had a captain in Dinesh Karthik who was himself pushing hard to find a place in the Indian squad that was going to travel to England a fortnight after the IPL. None of the Indian batsmen in the Kolkata Knight Riders set-up was in contention for a spot in the Indian team. Shubman was the only other Indian in the team who was closest to having an India career in the near future.

The campaign hit rough waters for the Kolkata Knight Riders. The batting line-up was tinkered with, and Shubman had no definite number to bat at. The journey of Kolkata Knight Riders went from sublime to substandard in the back end of the tournament and they failed to make the play-offs. Despite all the uncertainties in the gameplan of the Kolkata Knight Riders, Shubman managed to score 296 runs in 14 games at an average of 32.88 while striking at 124.36.

Karthik made the cut for the World Cup as the second wicketkeeper to MS Dhoni ahead of the red-hot Rishabh Pant.

But Shubman had grown into a reliable force in the Kolkata Knight Riders set-up.

Post the heartbreak in the World Cup semi-final against New Zealand in Manchester, Indian cricket had to carry out a transition. It was time to move on from MS Dhoni, Dinesh Karthik and phasing out Kedar Jadhav. It was also the time to groom players as back-up for the ageing Rohit Sharma and Shikhar Dhawan.

The selectors were supposed to pick an India 'A' team for a tour of West Indies in July–August before they named the senior India team which would travel to Caribbean for a full tour in August–September.

Shubman, expectedly, was picked for the 'A' tour. His appetite for runs and the aspiration to be back in the India team knew no bounds.

Daljit Singh recounts Shubman's preparation in Mohali for the 'A' tour. 'It was the onset of monsoons. Preparing pitches in the stadium was difficult. And it's usually the off-season. We curators repair and renovate the pitches during this season. But he insisted upon proper practice facilities. So, we prepared the indoor nets at the PCA Stadium. He had asked for bouncy pitches but also ones that aided seam movement. There were cement pitches as well. He would call his fast-bowling friends, his father would accompany him, and the PCA coaches would always be around. He practised on those hard pitches for hours. After the bowlers left, his father would feed him bouncers on the cement pitches.'

He had done his homework on the pitches in West Indies. That season, the pitches in the islands offered a lot of pace, bounce and lateral movement.

That 'A' tour turned out to be whirlwind. He was the highest run-getter in both formats of the tour. But the best was reserved for the last innings of the tour.

In the third unofficial Test of the tour in Tarouba, the India 'A' team were in dire straits in the second innings at 14/3, when Shubman walked in to bat. Soon, they were 50/4 and in danger of collapsing to a loss. With a steady, seasoned Hanuma Vihari at the other end, Shubman launched a brutal counter-attack on the Windies bowlers.

After 72 overs, Shubman brought up his double hundred. Vihari, captaining the team, calmly watched this nineteen-year-old score an unbeaten 204 off 248 balls as he himself remained not out on 118 off 221 balls. At 365/4, Vihari declared the innings.

The quality of that knock raised the teenager's stock manifold.

But the call to be part of the Indian team for the corresponding Test series in the Caribbean still evaded him. A month shy of his twentieth birthday, Shubman expressed his disappointment at not being picked.

Devang Gandhi, a national selector at the time, remembers that tricky phase in Shubman's career. 'That knock was special. I remember our colleague Jatin Paranjpe was at the venue and I was travelling with the senior India team in the Caribbean. He called me and talked about that knock.

'Shubman is a very polite and well-mannered boy. He let the frustration get the better of him. We understood his disappointment. We spoke to him and told him we couldn't pick him since there was no vacancy. Rohit Sharma was not getting a place in the playing XI in Tests at that time. He understood our position too.'

Gandhi also likes to point out the no-nonsense side of this otherwise genial boy. 'He will ask questions. Don't go by his soft-spoken and polite demeanour. He knows when he needs to assert himself. He always preferred opening the batting but the competition in Indian cricket is such that he adjusted to batting in the middle order.'

Upon his return from West Indies, Shubman did talk about getting anxious to break into the Indian team. 'It does cross my mind sometimes, but I am playing so much cricket around the year that it doesn't allow me to think about it constantly. And the 'A' tours have helped me be ready to make the transition as an India player,' he would steer away from controversy.

'I fall back on my father whenever I feel uncomfortable although I don't get much time to share everything. He keeps a tab on the money I earn. He ensures that I don't get carried away or distracted by the fame and money I have already got because of IPL.'

In October of 2019, though, Shubman Gill was named in the Test squad for a three-Test series against South Africa. Chief selector MSK Prasad declared his ability to both open the innings and bat in the middle overs which went in his favour.

Rohit Sharma assuming the role of an opener meant Shubman didn't get a game. But he was firmly in the scheme of things.

The runs kept coming in the Syed Mushtaq Ali tournament but the pressure and anxiety to cement a place at the highest level showed during a Ranji Trophy match against Delhi in Mohali in the first week of 2020.

The umpire had given him a caught-behind out while he was batting on 10 in the first morning of the game. Unhappy with the decision, he stood his ground and hurled abuses at the umpire. After a heated argument, the decision was overturned. Play was halted for 10 minutes. He didn't last long and got out for 23. Reprimanded for his action, he fell for four in the second innings. He stood his ground even in the second innings but managed to drag himself off the field.

He was supposed to tour New Zealand for an India 'A' series in a couple of weeks. That gave him time to unwind and come back afresh. He did. Shubman was at his dominating best in New Zealand.

A marauding unbeaten 204 in the first unofficial Test won him the opening slot for the next game. He cracked another 136. Shubman Gill was back as a reserve opener for India for the subsequent two-Test series in New Zealand.

Rohit was injured. But Prithvi's exploits in Test cricket and good form meant he was opening with Mayank Agarwal in both Tests.

It had been a year and Shubman Gill was in the same country where he had last worn the India cap. Shubman's turn was in sniffing distance.

India returned from New Zealand and were supposed to play a three-ODI series against South Africa at home within a week.

The team reached Dharamsala for the first ODI. Shubman was slated play in the XI. Rain washed away the game and then the pandemic-induced lockdown got the series cancelled. Shubman's wait got longer!

## The big arrival

It took six months for Indian cricket to resume in the post-Covid world. The IPL was the stage and the UAE the venue. Shubman Gill wasted no time in resuming his business.

The opening slot at the Kolkata Knight Riders now belonged to him. The unbeaten 70 to tame the Sunrisers Hyderabad in the second game of the tournament screamed of his growth as a batsman. The Kolkata Knight Riders struggled with leadership through the tournament, and Eoin Morgan replaced Dinesh Karthik as the captain midway.

Amidst all the turmoil in the Kolkata Knight Riders camp, Shubman was the lone constant. He grew as the lead batsman and finished the tournament with 440 runs in 14 matches as the

Kolkata Knight Riders narrowly missed out on a spot in the play-offs.

He was now a part of ODI and Test squads that were travelling to Australia in November 2020.

Rohit Sharma was nursing a hamstring injury which he picked up during the IPL. He was only supposed to join the squad for the last two Tests of the tour. That opened up a spot to partner Shikhar Dhawan at the top. Mayank Agarwal was preferred ahead of Shubman.

After India suffered a mauling in the first two ODIs of the tour in Sydney, Shubman was given a look in. The 33 off 39 on his international comeback game indicated he was in sublime touch. Shubman was on the verge of earning a Test cap now.

In the warm-up match that India played at the Sydney Cricket Ground (SCG), his delectable, crisp and clean stroke play was amplifying the pressure on a Prithvi Shaw struggling for form.

The Indian team management went with Prithvi for the first Test in Adelaide. He failed, India collapsed to 36 all out and it was time for an overhaul.

Shubman Gill was handed the Test cap on 26 December 2020 for the Boxing Day Test match at the Melbourne Cricket Ground. He did reveal he went numb when coach Ravi Shastri handed him the Test cap. Shubman was going to open in place of Prithvi.

'I was waiting for my Test debut for a while. I had been travelling with the team for three–four series. My parents and I would wake up early in the morning to watch Test cricket in Australia on TV. Now, it was my turn. I was numb when Ravi bhai handed me the cap and gave a speech,' Shubman said in an interview to KKR TV.

In Shubman's words, he was both excited and nervous walking out to bat for the first time through the hallowed corridors of the MCG on to the field with the intimidating structure looking down upon him. He described the feeling as 'going to war'.

Collar up, chest thrust out, ambition in his eyes and an unwavering resolve, Shubman took guard against the most potent fast-bowling attack (comprising Pat Cummins, Mitchell Starc and Josh Hazlewood) in their own den. Cummins, Starc and Hazlewood were fresh from inflicting deep scars a week ago in Adelaide.

Shubman's nonchalant presence at the crease took the sting out of the red-hot trio. A 45 on debut calmed the nerves of an edgy Indian dressing room. It set the tone for a revival which would go down in the history books in another three weeks.

Shubman screamed to the world he belonged here. Ravichandran in his YouTube channel summarised his unfettered attitude. 'Australia were seven down and about 45 runs ahead in the second innings on the third day and there was around an hour of play left. Shubman came up to me from the boundary rope and said, 'Ash bhai *jaldi khatam karo. Main aaj hi* 5–6 overs *mein* runs *maar dunga* (Ash, finish off the tail quickly and I will knock off the runs in 5–6 overs).'

On the fourth morning, he ensured he was there at the end when India chased down the 70-run target.

It seemed Shubman was in his comfort zone. He provided a solid start in the next Test at SCG, scoring 50 and 31 as India drew the Test and stayed alive in the series.

India reached Brisbane for the final Test with seven players injured. The Gabba is called Australia's fortress and their fast bowlers have been ruthlessly hunting down opponents for three decades at the venue.

Set 328 to chase on the final day. Cummins, Starc and Hazlewood were ready for one last burst in the gruelling series. But Shubman reserved a masterclass in how to play fast bowling.

All those years of his father hurling balls at his body was going to culminate into a beautiful story at Gabba.

He wore off the pacers in the first session before taking them on after lunch. The disdainful pulls, hooks, square-cuts and backfoot punches surely hurt the ego of the Australians.

An expansive drive outside the off-stump off off-spinner Nathan Lyon ended his charge at 91. He later claimed: 'I was really disappointed when I got out for 91. I really wanted to show my real game after I reached my century.'

But he had laid the platform and initiated the tempo for his 'hero in the team' Rishabh Pant to complete a memorable series win with an unbeaten 89 in the last session of the series.

Shastri and stand-in captain Ajinkya Rahane would not get tired of praising Shubman.

Shubman Gill was the real deal now.

The subsequent four-Test series against England, however, was tough for him. The experience of James Anderson and the skill of Jofra Archer stifled him.

That's bound to happen once you are in the limelight. That's when teams start to strategize against you.

The world watched Shubman Gill as he boarded the plane to England to play the inaugural World Test Championship final against New Zealand as the undisputed first-choice opener for Team India.

# CHAPTER 5

# SURYAKUMAR YADAV: THE UN-MUMBAIYA *KHADOOS*

## *Humble beginnings*

Bhabha Atomic Research Centre (BARC) colony in Mumbai is a hub comprising the service class. Cricket at BARC colony is only a form of recreation. Even though the postal address has Mumbai in it, it's nowhere close to the realms of competitive Mumbai cricket, the kind we are more conversant with.

At the turn of the century, Ashok Yadav was still settling down in his job at the BARC, which is cut off from the rush of mainland Mumbai, as an electrical engineer after moving from Bihar.

Cricket coach Ashok Aswalkar had just started a cricket coaching academy in the locality. Ashok Yadav decided to enrol his son Suryakumar in the academy with no other motive than cricket being an extra-curricular activity for his ten-year-old son.

Here started one of the remarkable tales of perseverance in Indian cricket.

Young Surya's enthusiasm for the game was unmistakable.

'We had very few kids at the ground because we had just got started with the academy. Surya was just another ten-year-old kid in the small group. But he would not leave the ground easily. The coaching used to start at 3 p.m. in the afternoon. He would hang around in the ground till 7.30 p.m. *Nikalta hi nahin thha* (He would just not go home from the ground),' Aswalkar recalls.

'He was a new kid. But whenever there used to be a match at the ground, he would come to watch the match and stay on beyond the match,' he adds.

There was something about Surya that could not miss the attention of his coach. The power he generated in his shots would draw eyeballs.

'He was a natural hitter. He could hit the ball very hard and long at a tender age. His game needed to be streamlined. *Woh achcha khasa* fast bowling *bhi karta thha* (He was a pretty decent fast bowler too). But since batting was his stronger suit, it was decided he rather paid more attention to batting,' Aswalkar says.

The grooming of a cricketer in Mumbai usually happens through the strong school and club cricket culture in the city. Those tournaments are springboards to enter the system.

Surya was far from it. BARC colony was not a part of the robust Mumbai cricket system. There was no scope of playing the fabled U-16 Harris Shield and U-14 Giles Shield tournaments.

'Cricket wasn't very strong in our area. Harris Shield and Giles Shield was played by reputed schools,' Aswalkar says.

Two years went by when Mumbai Cricket Association (MCA) had set up a camp for U-14 cricketers at the BARC Colony ground. Aswalkar saw an opening to get Surya a platform to get noticed.

The camp is held for around 45 days during the summer vacations. Kids make it to the camp only after a thorough screening process by the MCA.

By this time, Aswalkar was smitten by the power Surya could

generate in his shots. '*Hitting power achcha thha* (His power-hitting was really good),' Aswalkar would literally say on a loop right through any discussion on Surya.

'He had already trained with us for two years. We had our eyes on him. I felt he was playing well. *Hitting power achcha thha. Khelna theek se nahin aata thha par achcha marta thha* (He wasn't polished but could strike the ball really well),' the coach would insist.

Aswalkar was consumed by the idea of getting Surya into the MCA camp.

'Coaches came from different parts of Mumbai. I used to be there. I wanted to check out what would happen if he was in the camp. I knew he wouldn't fulfil the criteria. He was very young for a U-14 camp. He was not even twelve,' Aswalkar remembers.

'I told him one day that the camp is here and he should go to the camp.'

'*Theek hain main jata hoon* (Fine, I am going to the camp),' pat came the reply from Surya. The confidence in his response had brought a smile on Aswalkar's face.

Aswalkar's colleague Ashok Kamath was the MCA coach. Kamath had told Aswalkar that Surya was playing well, but he was too young.

'*Apna bachcha hain. Issi* colony *ka hain. Baahar wala hota toh nikaal dete* (He is one of our own kids who belongs to the colony. Had he been an outsider, he would have been rejected,' Aswalkar would implore and insist on including Surya in the camp. 'I said just keep him in the camp,' he would say with a smile.

And Surya did find a place in the camp.

Getting him into the camp was not the only hurdle. Aswalkar understood that it was imperative Surya's parents were on board with the idea of pursuing a career in cricket.

'The mentality in our area is that irrespective of how talented a kid is or how well he plays, parents would divert him towards studies once they reach eighth or ninth standard. Engineering side *mein jana hain bas* (A career in engineering was preferred),' Aswalkar talks of the regimented mindset in populations living in BARC colony.

Surya's parents knew Aswalkar on a personal level. The coach decided to have a heart-to-heart with the parents. It was about presenting the scenario.

'*Aap usske (*Surya*) aur humare upar kitna* faith *rakhte ho* (How much faith do you have in your son and us)?' Aswalkar laid the ground for the conversation with the parents.

'Daring *toh karna padega na agar* result *chahiye toh* (You have to go out of the way and be daring enough if you want good results),' Aswalkar followed up, leaving no room for ambiguity.

'What do you make of the potential Surya has?' senior Yadav cross-questioned.

'He is playing really well, *aur mere hisaab se aagey chala jayega* (According to me, he will go the distance),' Aswalkar responded with utmost conviction.

'*Kya karna hain phir* (So, what do you want to do)?' the coach left the ball in the parents' court.

The response from the parents lifted a huge weight off Aswalkar's shoulders.

'The parents said if you believe so, *aap bindaas kaam karo uss par* (You work on him without any worries). Once I got the green light from that end, I started giving him my full attention,' Aswalkar fondly remembers the conversation.

It was time for the thankless single-minded training. Aswalkar says the two MCA camps he attended in two years were a bonus for Surya.

'He only believed in hitting the ball hard. The MCA camp taught him about technique. The MCA camp has kids selected only from trials. *Yeh taiyyar ho gaya do saal mein* (He was ready in two years). He got selected for the camp in the third year,' Aswalkar says.

According to Aswalkar, there were two things working for Surya. One, he had a refreshingly positive approach towards the game. Two, he was not a *Bambaiyya* (not the quintessential Mumbaikar). He would not put himself under any undue pressure playing the game.

'He got used to every challenge and he was on the field all the time. *Jab chhota thha tab* (When he was a little kid) there were very good players in the senior age-groups at our academy. He used to train with the seniors. When a kid mingles with the seniors it becomes easier for him,' Aswalkar claims.

Aswalkar's perseverance ensured Surya was now officially in the registers of Mumbai cricket. It was now up to Surya to build on it.

## Steady rise through the ranks

Every cricketer has one performance that defines his career. Surya's moment came while playing in an Under-16 tournament in the fabled Cross Maidan in Mumbai. There were glimpses of his talent when he was regularly scoring 50s and 60s but there wasn't one noteworthy innings.

It came in the final of the tournament. According to Aswalkar, Surya scored some 140 runs in about 40–45 balls. The knock has stayed with Aswalkar since.

'The Mumbai selectors had asked him how he could hit so high and far. Surya very casually replied '*Main aisa hi marta hoon* (I usually bat like this),' a smile breaks out on Aswalkar's face while recalling the innings. 'Our ground had 65-yard boundaries. From his U-14 days, he used to clear the field very easily. He had that much power,' the coach remembers fondly.

'The selectors took note. He peaked from there. *Chalu ho gaya*. Limelight *mein aa gaya* (He was on a roll and was in the limelight),' Aswalkar reckons.

Surya was now into high-performance training, and the BARC ground was the back-up.

'He was then practising less at our ground. Once you are in the MCA set-up, you have to go through their coaching,' Aswalkar mentions.

The stalwarts of Mumbai cricket were meant to monitor his growth.

This is when Chandrakant Pandit happened to him. Pandit, a former India wicketkeeper and a hard taskmaster in Mumbai circles, could barely tear his eyes away from Surya when he batted. Surya was just graduating to U-19 cricket when Pandit was appointed the director of the MCA.

'He was just promoted from U-16 to U-19. He was in the probables of both teams. I saw him in a practice session and thought he had enough talent to excel,' Pandit recounts his first impression of Surya.

'I had seen Prithvi Shaw when he was fourteen. These were the players we were focusing on. There was this fearless approach and he looked confident while batting,' Pandit adds.

At the same time Dilip Vengsarkar had seen him train at his Elf Academy. Vengsarkar offered him to play for Dadar Union. Some jaw-dropping knocks later, Pandit was smitten by his potential.

Then again, those big scores, which define a batting prodigy in Mumbai circles, were missing. He was nowhere close to playing for India U-19s.

Yet, his potential couldn't be left untapped. Surya was drafted into the Mumbai Ranji Trophy squad in 2010–11. The Mumbai team had a raging, young Rohit Sharma, the veteran Wasim Jaffer and a seasoned India cricketer, Ajit Agarkar.

His First-Class debut in the last league match of the tournament was against Delhi at the Roshanara Club in Delhi. The opposing team had a Virat Kohli, Shikhar Dhawan, Mithun Manhas and the up-and-coming Unmukt Chand.

Delhi vs Mumbai has been the marquee event in Ranji Trophy cricket for decades.

Surya walked out and smacked a counter-attacking 73 off just 89 balls when Mumbai were bowled out for 267. He managed another seven runs in the second innings. The match ended in a draw. Mumbai were in the quarter-finals. Surya didn't find a place in the XI in the quarter-final against Rajasthan.

Rajasthan beat Mumbai on a first-innings lead. Surya had to wait another year to leave his impression on the Mumbai team.

Next year, Surya got a match in the third game of the season against Karnataka. He made a 23 but that was enough to retain his place for the next match against Odisha in Cuttack.

He came out to bat when the scoreboard said 200/3 in 60 overs. Mumbai needed to go hard at the bowlers to push their bid for a win.

Surya counterattacked and finished with a 200 off just 232 balls. That was only his third First-Class match. He finished the season with 754 runs in nine matches at an average of 68.54 and strike rate of 85 as Mumbai's campaign got over in the semi-final stage. An IPL contract from the Mumbai Indians also came his way.

The next season, he struggled. He could muster only 73 runs in the entire season and then started to fade away.

The turning point in his career came when Pandit was made the chairman of the national junior selection committee in 2012. BCCI had tasked his committee with selecting U-23 and India 'A' teams in 2013.

The India U-23 team was supposed to travel to Singapore to play Asian Cricket Council Emerging Teams Cup in August 2013.

'Considering his ability and approach, I thought he was capable of going on that tour,' Pandit says.

Just selecting Surya for the tournament wasn't the end of it. 'For that U-23 tournament, we decided to make him captain of India,' Pandit says of the bold decision he made as a national selector.

The decision couldn't have been a straightforward one. That India U-23 team had the likes of KL Rahul, Unmukt Chand and a host of players who had represented India in the previous two U-19 World Cups.

Unmukt was the hot property in Indian cricket, having led India to a U-19 World Cup victory in 2012. Rahul was just evolving as a batsman of repute. Unmukt was already captaining India 'A' teams which had Yuvraj Singh and Suresh Raina in them. Making Surya captain was a big call.

'Every player doesn't show the spark and climb the ladder through age-group cricket. There are players who take one or two years more to mature,' Pandit explains.

India U-23s did beat Pakistan in the final to be the champions. But Surya had a quiet tournament. He managed just 44 runs in four games. A realisation dawned on Surya. He had a fair way to go to be taken seriously for the highest level.

## Impressive stint at Kolkata Knight Riders and turbulence in Mumbai

Surya went back to the drawing board. The focus shifted to fitness and hardcore training to elevate his game at the First-Class level.

He was looking a different player when the 2013–14 Ranji Trophy season started. He got eight matches in the season. The 529 runs at an average of 40.69 was dotted with some crucial knocks which helped Mumbai make it to the quarter-finals of the tournament that year.

Surya was still far from the limelight. But the Kolkata Knight Riders had an eye on him which fetched him a Rs 70 lakh contract in 2014.

Former India wicketkeeper Vijay Dahiya, assistant coach at the Kolkata Knight Riders at the time, explains the reason behind bidding for him: 'We had seen him in the domestic circuit. Surya was very unorthodox and could hit the ball in unusual areas in the field. He was not a typical Mumbai batsman.'

The Kolkata Knight Riders' punt on him seemed to work straightaway as the team under Gautam Gambhir hurtled towards the IPL title.

There were no big runs from Surya's bat. Yet, his 20s and 30s while batting down the order in crunch situations made the difference to the Kolkata Knight Riders' campaign. Each of his 164 runs in the 16 matches he played had an impact. He was now the finisher in the ranks.

'His self-confidence was next level. What happens sometimes is that when you are not a big name and you consistently get out playing shots, people call you an average player. But playing unconventional cricket is Surya's strength,' Dahiya reckons.

Dahiya goes on to elaborate the role Surya was given by Gambhir and him.

'For KKR, he was still figuring it out and establishing himself. One needs to remember that the pitch at our home ground Eden Gardens was very slow and challenging. It was more so for those who batted in the lower middle order. If you remember 110 150 was a par score that year. He consistently played those crucial knocks to take us over the line and that's why he caught the eye of people.

'You give players like him more responsibility. He was groomed as a leader and he was announced the vice-captain of the KKR for some matches in the following seasons,' Dahiya states. This is a hack to get the most out of Surya, and this is something that is corroborated by all his mentors.

Suryakumar was now a celebrity. The swagger made him a popular figure. When the 2014–15 Ranji Trophy season arrived, the wise people running Mumbai cricket believed it was time to carry out a transition and the young player be made the leader of the team. The Mumbai captaincy came to Surya. It was a season where Mumbai cricket was willing to punt on players untested in extreme pressure situations. Shreyas Iyer, with his unorthodox technique, was also picked in the side.

The Mumbai captaincy came with turbulence. Mumbai lost their opening game of the season at Wankhede Stadium, their den, to Jammu and Kashmir.

It rattled the egos of the pioneers of Mumbai's rich cricketing history. The pressure was about to hit the ceiling.

The Mumbai team travelled to play Railways at the Karnail Singh Stadium in Delhi. And there was more misery waiting for Surya and his team. Railways posted 242 and then rolled over Mumbai for 101 in the chill of Delhi winter.

Mumbai's campaign, already in tatters, was hit by unseasonal rain. Their only chance of a jailbreak was to get a full game and force a result.

The torrential rain early on the third morning of the match would wash out the entire day's play. Surya was not going down without a fight.

He grabbed a bucket, rolled up his trouser and got down to clearing the puddles in the outfield. The desperation to make a name for himself was for everyone to see. He did not want to lose any game time. He continued for a good couple of hours before play was officially called off.

Mumbai were in choppy waters and twenty-four-year-old Surya was at the wheel to steer them out of it.

Shreyas Iyer triggered a revival with counter-attacking knocks in the following matches. Surya too was slowly regaining his form. And then, another controversy hit the Mumbai camp.

Surya got into an on-field altercation with teammate Shardul Thakur during the season. And the rumours and allegations started flying. There were complaints of him being hot-headed. Then there were reports of infighting and indiscipline.

Within a year, his career went from finding wings to be on a freefall. Two matches remaining in the league stage, he decided to step down from captaincy at a time when Mumbai were on the verge of completing a turnaround and making it to the quarter-finals.

The only thing going Surya's way was that he was back in the runs. Mumbai's campaign ended in the semi-final against Karnataka. Surya had finished the season with 690 runs at an average of 43.12 with two centuries and three half-centuries.

'I knew something was happening there in the Mumbai camp. There were speculations about his attitude. At that time his cricket was perfect. I didn't talk much about cricket with him. I only asked him about how he was going in the MCA and how his behaviour was,' Aswalkar, aware of the fact that his ward had a different outlook than a typical Mumbai cricketer, says.

It's not just Aswalkar. Dahiya too concurs with him.

'Surya is unlike a Mumbai cricketer. He is different. There may have been issues but when you perceive someone as different in a bunch then you tend to start seeing attitude issues in him. If you look at his personality, he is more like an in-your-face Delhi cricketer,' Dahiya explains

'The game teaches you so much. You need to realise a lot of things while playing for a big state which has contributed so much for the national side. He needed somebody who believed in him,' Dahiya sums up the situation.

It was time to look in the mirror and turn things around!

## Turning a corner

Twenty-four is considered the age for a player to really flourish in domestic cricket and give the national selectors sleepless nights. For all the popularity won through his stylish cameos in the 2014 IPL, Surya was nowhere close to be considered for a place in the Indian team.

The controversies in Mumbai refused to leave him alone. He was still fighting for absolute acceptance in the Mumbai set-up.

'Once you reach the higher level of cricket, there's going to be groupism. Our area of cricket (BARC Colony) is cut off from Mumbai. Mumbai cricket is very strong. *Ek* side *mein chalta hain* (It goes on in one corner of the city). When someone from that area gets into the Mumbai set-up, it pricks people to see someone who is an outsider,' Aswalkar gives an idea about the dynamics in Mumbai cricket.

'*Na koi* school cricket *hain na kuchh hain* (There's no kind of high-profile school cricket tournaments). On the other side, kids are in the limelight from a tender age in Mumbai. Now Surya got the limelight. It was bound to upset people in the system,' was all Aswalkar could make of the issues Surya was facing.

Yet, the coach couldn't turn a blind eye when it came to his ward's attitude.

Aswalkar recounts an incident that shook him.

'Surya has always been a flamboyant boy. Once I got to know that he went for a Mumbai selection with dyed hair and he had also got tattoos. Some selector said it to his face, '*Tu* cricket *khelne aya hain ki hero banne aya hain* (Have you come here to play cricket or become a movie star)?' He had the right to say so.'

It was time to have a man-to-man chat with Surya. Aswalkar would shudder to even think that his favourite ward was running the risk of fading away from the scene. Aswalkar sat Surya down for a chat.

'*Tere ko kahan pe jaana hain* (Where do you want to reach as a cricketer)?' Aswalkar was not about to waste any time, and got straight to the point. It was time for the tough talk. 'You are a professional cricketer and aspire to play at a higher level, you have to decide if you want that,' Aswalkar remembers the conversation.

The coach had his reason to be cynical. He explains: 'When you get the money and limelight all of a sudden, people lose their way.'

The chat ended with a piece of advice from Aswalkar: 'If you fix your aim then even I would not have to tell you how you can achieve that.'

It was drilled into Surya's mind that he could barely afford to have any distractions.

Dahiya talks about the importance of the environment when it comes to extracting the best out of characters like Surya. The management of the Kolkata Knight Riders was about providing him with just that.

The Kolkata Knight Riders struggled in IPL 2015 and so did Surya. Batting lower down the order, he scored just 157 runs in 13 matches. But the management, in no way, was going to lose faith in him.

'If any set-up gives him freedom, Surya will flourish. You just need to give him an environment where he could feel he could go out there and be himself. You need to strike a chord with him. He wants to believe in you. And if you reciprocate, he will do anything for you,' Dahiya opines.

The absolute environment that Dahiya harps on could be only provided by one of his trusted people. And it happened when Chandrakant Pandit was appointed as the coach of the Mumbai team.

Surya was battling a battle and most of it was in the mind. A flamboyant stroke-maker like him is often conveniently labelled as one with the inadequate technique.

Pandit worked on a basic principle: Never tinker with innate batting technique. For a man who has been bred in the regimented 'Bombay school of batting', Pandit developed a rather open mind.

'As the game evolves, new generation shows positivity in the game. As a coach I had to accept it,' Pandit would say.

'I don't think anybody really fiddled with his technique. You ought to retain the natural flair. It was about the temperament. It is true for every player,' Pandit elaborates.

Surya was stamped with the 'un-Mumbai batsman' tag. He had to work around it. And for Pandit, it was more about getting him into a mental space where he had an uncluttered mind.

'Player like him in a Mumbai team is a bonus,' Pandit asserts. 'He had the ability to change the game at any given time. I always encouraged that. But he had to understand the situation.'

'Even when the team is struggling, he is not one to stay down. He would counterattack with a 70. I backed him for that. There's no point in having batsman after batsman going in and struggling to score. Dilip Vengsarkar and Sanjay Manjrekar said let batsmen like Surya and Shreyas Iyer do it their way. Gavaskar and Vengsarkar had the in-born quality to bat for longer durations. These boys are innately positive and fearless.'

Pandit had a plan laid out for Surya. And it started to click during the Ranji Trophy season of 2015–16.

While Shreyas Iyer was batting on a different plane in domestic cricket, Surya was playing the perfect support role. Eleven matches and 788 runs with an average of 46.35 and three centuries was a fair result in the victorious campaign.

'Thinking about scoring big hundreds could put undue pressure unless you have ability of the likes of Amol Mazumdar, Jatin Paranjpe and Dilip Vengsarkar, who had patience. Surya was like the Australian batsmen in early 2000s. He would just get on with the game,' Pandit talks about his gameplan.

'When I became coach of Mumbai in 2015, he impressed me then too. I always felt he could dominate at any level. He played an important role in Ranji Trophy. We couldn't win the final. He always gave the impression he could dominate any bowler at any level,' Pandit reckons.

The environment that Dahiya had spoken of was finally there. Now, it was about ironing out the chinks in his game.

'During my tenure with Mumbai, I told him about that one shot he should avoid playing in day's cricket. It was the reverse sweep. I stopped him. He is a much better player. Throwing his wicket for one boundary didn't make sense. He was convinced,' Pandit recounts.

'Your wicket is not cheap,' Pandit would drill into his head.

The results with the bat were not just a result of the pep talks. A lot of grind went into it in the off season prior to the month the Ranji Trophy got underway in 2015.

Pandit narrates one of his most gratifying moments working with Surya:

'I used to work a lot with him in the off season. The ball pitching on middle and leg stump, he would play towards mid-wicket and square-leg and I kept saying the ball should be driven back to the bowler. He also realised it.

'The result was there while he was batting against Saurashtra in the Ranji Trophy final that season. He had taken Saurashtra's lead seamer Jaydev Unadkat head on. He hit five–six boundaries straight back past him and admired each of them. Surya nodded his head each time like he was telling the world that he had perfected a shot he wanted to play for long.'

One could sense the changes in Suryakumar Yadav's game. Pandit lists three critical points that brought about the positive changes.

He realised the importance of his presence in the team.

He started changing with the responsibilities given to him.

He realised he could play for India and started working tirelessly on his fitness.

Shouldering responsibility was identified as the critical factor behind the turnaround.

'He always had the nature to lead a team. He would come forward and take initiative. He was always holding the team together. He started believing in himself. Once he got opportunity in the U-23 India team, he felt he could play for India. He had now calmed down. He was given the responsibility to lead the Mumbai batting unit and talk about how to approach a game.'

The sensitive part in his development was done. He was now in a good space. It was time to translate that into major contributions.

## Beating frustration and going to the next level

The cobwebs in his mind were dusted off. There was consistency in his batting too. But there was nothing that would make the world sit up and take notice.

Suryakumar Yadav was an integral part of the Mumbai set-up. That's where the story ended for him.

In the two Ranji Trophy seasons in 2016–17 and 2017–18, Surya scored 715 runs in 11 matches and 460 runs in seven matches respectively. His average lurked around 39 and 40. He had below average Vijay Hazare Trophies too.

It is said that any decent batsman, who has been playing domestic cricket for five–six years, will inevitably score around 500 runs a season. But that doesn't set him apart.

To put things into perspective, Mumbai cricket was witnessing the emergence two batting stars in Prithvi Shaw and Shreyas Iyer during the same period.

The fancy cameos were not going to take him anywhere. That double hundred in his third First-Class now seemed a lifetime ago.

'You need to have the big scores. There's no two ways about it. For that, one needs the in-born quality of patience. With Surya's approach, it's difficult to score a big 200 or 300. He might do it once in a while but that won't be enough to go up a level,' Pandit opines.

Pandit got working on him again.

'Surya understood that if he had to play for country, he had to have big and consistent scores. Whenever we talked, I told him it may take time,' Pandit gives a peek into the conversations he would have with Surya.

'There's no doubt you are dominating the attacks and you are scoring a couple of hundreds. But the big innings are not there. You have to work on that because you may be a good player in Mumbai but you have to compete with ten other batsmen in the country,' Pandit would say to Surya.

Pandit knew Surya was running out of time to make it to the big league. He was already twenty-seven. It's the age when selectors tend to look away from you if you are not even in the India 'A' scheme of things. Surya was given a clear picture of where he stood by Pandit.

'It became a competition against other 10–12 batsmen in the country. The vision was to play for India but not with average performances. He had to have big performances and knock the door so that the selection committee would think of him. I always told him there are fifteen other players like you in the country. You had to beat them with performances.'

Amidst all the agony and despair, Surya found stability in his life when he married Devisha in July of 2016.

'He was unsettled before his marriage. Once he got married everything started falling into place for him. He calmed down and there was composure in his life,' Aswalkar says with conviction.

The Surya of 2017 was a patient and composed character.

It reflected in the Syed Mushtaq Ali tournament in 2017–18. He plundered 217 runs at a strike rate of 188 in eight matches. His enterprising batting in the middle-order had the IPL scouts very interested.

His performances in the Syed Mushtaq Ali Trophy attracted handsome bids during the subsequent IPL auctions. Suryakumar Yadav was bought for Rs 3.2 crore by the Mumbai Indians.

He was back at Wankhede, his home ground, for the IPL. It would become his comfort zone and the launch pad he yearned for years.

The Mumbai Indians wasted no time in playing their big buy of the season. Surya too was off the block straightaway. A 43 off 29 against the Chennai Super Kings in the opening game of the tournament was enough to declare he meant business.

Surya was not going to get settled in the middle-order though. The Mumbai Indians line-up was thin on experience in the middle-order. They had Ishan Kishan, Surya, Hardik Pandya as their numbers 3, 4 and 5, followed by Kieron Pollard and Krunal Pandya.

The Mumbai Indians skipper Rohit Sharma decided he had to bat at No. 4. Surya had to give up his preferred batting position.

The Mumbai Indians management came to him with an offer of opening the batting–something he had never done in his career.

Surya was in a fix. Giving up his batting number was not a big issue. But switching to something he had never done at a stage of his career when he could barely afford anymore failures was never going to be an easy call.

'Surya called me one night and said Mumbai Indians coach Mahela Jayawardene wanted him to open the batting,' Aswalkar recalls.

'*Kya karna hain,* sir (What should I do, sir)?' Surya asked Aswalkar.

'*Agar saamne se tere ko bola gaya hain toh haan bol de* (If they have come to you then you should agree to do what they ask you to do). At the higher level of cricket, if the captain wants to bat at your position and you refuse to open then you won't find a place in the team,' Aswalkar advised.

Sure enough, Surya was opening in the third game of the tournament against Delhi Daredevils at Wankhede. It was his den and he roared. A 53 off 32 balls was testimony of his adaptability.

The Mumbai Indians didn't make it to the last four that year but Surya finished as their highest run-scorer. He had piled up 512 runs in 14 matches while striking at 133.33.

Surya had tasted blood.

Red-ball cricket, however, still didn't seem to agree with him. He had another average Ranji Trophy season with Mumbai in 2018–19. But he was growing into this ominous white-ball player at the same time – 241 runs at an average of 48.20 and a strike rate of 105 in the Vijay Hazare Trophy and 360 runs while averaging 51.42 and striking at 145.16 in Syed Mushtaq Ali were only raising his stocks.

It was World Cup year in 2019. Rohit Sharma decided to open the batting for the Mumbai Indians in the IPL. Obviously, he didn't want to be out of touch while opening the batting in the World Cup in a couple of months.

Surya was back in the middle-order. He had proven he could shoulder the responsibility now. And he did – 424 runs in 16 matches with a strike rate of 130.86 ensured he closed out games for the Mumbai Indians and was pivotal in the team regaining the IPL trophy.

The Mumbai Indians were becoming the powerhouse in the IPL, and Surya was one of their heavy machineries.

Once the 2019 World Cup was done, Indian cricket had hit the reset button. It was time to rebuild the pool of players.

Surya now believed he was ready to make the grade. Instead, the selectors ignored him even for the India 'A' team which was touring the West Indies in July 2019.

India played series after series and Surya's name didn't feature in any of the teams.

But he had decided to make things hard for the selectors. Surya churned out performances with a vengeance. His numbers in the domestic season read:

**Vijay Hazre Trophy:** 4 innings, 226 runs; Average: 113, strike rate: 154.79.

**Syed Mushtaq Ali Trophy:** 10 innings, 392 runs; Average 56, strike rate: 168.96

**Ranji Trophy:** 10 innings, 508 runs; Average: 56.44, strike rate: 95.13, 2 hundreds and 2 fifties.

There was a definite buzz about Surya. Harbhajan Singh came out in his support and suggested he be selected for India's T20 team immediately in the winter of 2019.

The selectors finally picked him for the India 'A' for a tour of New Zealand in January 2020. Surya came back scoring just 60 runs in three one-day matches.

At twenty-nine, frustration and anxiety were bound to creep in.

'Frustration *bahut zyada thha* (He was very frustrated). You won't believe, he used to come to the ground every day and talked to me a lot. It was like we went back to caring for a little kid,' Aswalkar recalls the tough times.

'*Tera kaam hain khelna. Jinko dekhna hain woh dekhenge* (Your job is to play. Someone will notice you). Sometimes you have to work extra to achieve something. You ought to struggle,' Aswalkar would tell Surya.

Aswalkar was glad that Surya kept scoring runs and ensured nobody could drop him. '*Tera* bat *bol raha hain* (Your bat is doing the talking),' the coach would keep telling him on a loop.

'Selection *nahin ho raha hain, koi puchh nahin raha hain. Yeh* chapter *sabki zindagi mein aata hain* (Every cricketer goes through this phase when he feels no one's noticing him and he isn't getting selected in spite of his performances). You don't utter anything about anyone in front of anyone. If you learn that then it will be easier for you,' was Aswalkar's suggestion to Surya.

The image of Surya reassuring the Mumbai Indians dressing room after finishing off a tricky chase against the Royal Challengers Bangalore in Abu Dhabi in IPL 2020 is one of the highlights of the tournament.

That unbeaten 79 from his blade came a couple of days after he was ignored for the tour of Australia in November–December. Surya finished with 480 crucial runs as the Mumbai Indians retained the IPL title.

The national selectors couldn't find a place for him since there was Manish Pandey and Shreyas Iyer who were already performing for India in white-ball cricket.

India coach Ravi Shastri took to Twitter and declared that Surya's time would come soon.

Playing for the Mumbai Indians was the only cushion he had to absorb the shocks. He had his wife in the UAE during the IPL. He later revealed that he went for a walk with his wife to calm down after the Indian team was announced in October. Rohit Sharma and Zaheer Khan were right by his side to help him overcome this phase.

'The Mumbai Indians environment helped him a lot. The likes of Hardik, Krunal and Ishan Kishan could understand him and were more like him,' Aswalkar claims.

The raging debate over Surya's non-inclusion was because his batsmanship in the IPL 2020 was breath-taking. His crisp shots over and through covers and his ability to find the mid-wicket boundary with as much ease as he would do it on both sides – behind the wicket – proved he had developed a scary range of shots.

It happened during the lockdown.

'He changed his routine in the lockdown. The Covid cases were on the rise in the colony. If he trained then other people started saying why they were not allowed to go out. So, he stopped training for a while. He would come to the BARC Colony ground in the afternoons when the pitches would dry out and become tough for shot-making. Also, practising in the heat would enhance his endurance. He knew they were going to play in the UAE,' Aswalkar recounts.

'He improved his off-side game. Once he did it, his game started looking different. If you look to play through the off-side, the bat automatically starts coming down straighter and you don't need to play across the line,' the coach points out.

Surya's moment came in March 2021. At the age of thirty, Surya took the field for India for the first time in a T20I against England in Ahmedabad on 14 March. He didn't get to bat.

In the next match, he walked out to bat at No. 3. Jofra Archer tried to rattle him with a fast bouncer. Surya got inside the line of the bouncer and disdainfully hooked it for six.

All the years of agony culminated in a memorable moment. Suryakumar Yadav had hit the first ball he faced in international cricket for a six. Surya wasn't done yet. He finished with 57 off 31 balls. India defended 185 with England falling eight short. Surya was the player of the match for his debut innings.

Surya followed it up with another imperious 17-ball 32 before he was controversially given out caught at fine-leg. Suryakumar Yadav had become the talk of the town.

'He should have played for India earlier. He is three–four years late. In the one-on-one discussions, I always said that he was capable of playing for India. He transformed immediately when he realised he was capable of playing for the country,' Pandit says of the moment that turned things around for Surya.

'As a person he is still same as he was twelve years ago. *Bas thanda ho gaya thha* (he had just calmed down) once he realised how he wanted to go about his career,' Aswalkar sums up.

Suryakumar's journey is testimony of how perseverance can do wonders. All those years spent in agony and despair culminated in a dream debut. But those years have made sure Surya is far from satiated.

Surya, in most ways, has been an un-Mumbai batsman. Looking at the broader picture, though, his perseverance through his career would make any quintessential *khadoos* Mumbai batsman proud.

# CHAPTER 6

# ISHAN KISHAN: POCKET DYNAMITE

## *Initiation in Patna*

For decades, just like in Rajasthan, cricket in eastern India too strove to be taken seriously at a national level. The smattering of representations largely came from Bengal. Pankaj Roy would be the biggest name coming from the zone until Sourav Ganguly arrived. Debasis Mohanty and Shiv Sunder Das put Odisha on the map in the late '90s and early 2000s.

Bihar produced cricketers who would become respected names in domestic cricket but none would go on to become national news. It took the brute force and raw talent of MS Dhoni to break the glass ceiling. Ranchi became a tourist destination once Dhoni took the cricketing world by storm with a whirlwind 148 against Pakistan in an ODI in Visakhapatnam in April 2005.

In one go, Bihar and Jharkhand had something to flaunt about in front of the cricketing world.

Yet, carving a career out of cricket in Bihar would get tougher by the day. Bihar's cricket association had problems of its own and there was also this issue of officials not being able to arrive at a consensus regarding important decisions. There were factions fighting amongst themselves. Corruption charges were levelled. Hence Jamshedpur and Ranchi in Jharkhand became the destination for professional cricket in the region. Jharkhand State Cricket Association (JSCA) earned affiliation in place of Bihar.

Pranav Pandey hadn't anticipated how difficult it would get for his two sons Raj Kishan and Ishan Kishan to pursue cricket as a career in Patna.

Raj, four years elder to Ishan, was enrolled in an academy at Moin-ul-Haq Cricket Stadium in Bihar's capital. A seven-year-old Ishan would accompany him to the ground. The game became irresistible for Ishan. He pleaded with his father that he too wanted to play.

Uttam Mazumdar, who was the head coach of the academy, felt he was too young to start playing. After much insistence from Raj, Mazumdar threw a few balls to Ishan. The bat swing and the natural flair impressed the coach. There was something special to work with here.

'Ishan was so small that we couldn't even find batting pads in his size. After looking around for some time, we found a pair of really small pads and a bat. Then he started going to the academy,' Pranav recalls.

The Bihar association was already derecognised by BCCI by then. After playing most of his domestic cricket matches for Bihar, Dhoni had made it to the Indian team while playing for Jharkhand.

If there was any recognised competitive cricket played in Bihar, it was the tournaments organised by the School Games Federation of India (SGFI).

A year later, Raj had the first crack at the U-16 Bihar team that would play in the SGFI tournament.

'Raj used to go for the U-16 trials. Ishan insisted he wanted to go for the trials too. He was just an eight-year old. It was unrealistic that he would be picked for the U-16 teams,' Pranav says.

The confidence came from the fact that Ishan had always played against senior boys.

Pranav fondly narrates a local match that got him believing in his younger son's abilities. 'Once during a school tournament, he went out to open the batting. There was a bowler who was nearly six-feet tall and Ishan was just a little kid. *Humko laga aaj isska sar phat jaega ya koi chot lagegi* (I felt that he will either get hit in the head or get hurt in some way),' he recalls.

'I asked the coach if he will be able to manage while opening the batting.'

'*Dekhte rahiye. Khelega bhi aur marega bhi* (You keep watching. Not only will he play but he will dominate too),' pat came the coach's response to reassure the nervous father.

'Ishan *ne kaafi pitai ki* (Ishan really hammered the bowling). The crowd went berserk,' Pranav proudly says.

Back to the U-16 Bihar SGFI trials. Ishan went for the trials and came back with his name in the squad.

'He was hitting the drives so well that the selectors picked him at that tender age. The selectors were particularly impressed by two or three consecutive drives,' Pranav says.

Ishan travelled with the Bihar U-16 team for the SGFI tournament.

'The selectors had made it clear to him *woh jaa toh raha hain par mauka milega nahin* (he may be with the team but he won't get an opportunity to play). But it didn't matter much. He was very young,' Pranav recalls.

Ishan was coming up well. He became Mazumdar's favourite ward in four years. Mazumdar devoted all his energy on Ishan.

The first bump came in 2009 when Mazumdar had to move

to Noida to be by his ailing father's side.

'After Mazumdar sir left, one coach from Sports Authority of India (SAI) came to Patna on a posting. His name was Ajit Mishra and he was from Odisha. He groomed Ishan really well,' Pranav says.

Ishan had turned thirteen and he was already a buzz in Bihar's cricketing circle. For all the talent this kid had, there were barely any opportunities to get into the system of Indian cricket.

It was time to find a way and take a big call.

## Moving to Ranchi and becoming U-19 India captain

If Ishan had to grow as a professional cricketer, he had to move out of Bihar and ply his trade in Jharkhand.

'Ishan's performances in Patna were all magnificent. People started asking me why I was wasting time here. We never know when Bihar cricket will be re-recognised. The senior cricketers in Patna prodded us to go to Ranchi,' Pranav says.

Playing for Steel Authority of India Limited (SAIL) in Ranchi was seen as the best option.

'I didn't know anyone in SAIL. The idea came from a few senior players in Patna. When Ishan was scoring runs in Patna, they suggested we should shift Ishan to Ranchi. Nobody knew us there. The senior player spoke to somebody in SAIL. SAIL needed a wicketkeeper. Ishan was a little kid yet he was selected,' Pranav recounts the toughest decision he had to take with Ishan.

A thirteen-year-old Ishan was now living all by himself. Ishan shared a small apartment with four–five cricketers. It was provided by SAIL.

'They used to cook and do the chores themselves. Ishan couldn't cook. His duty was to fill the water bottles and do the dishes,' Pranav says.

Ishan would come to Patna for two months a year during the monsoons when it's the off-season for cricket. He would catch up with his studies, go to his native place and visit his grandmother. Pranav and his wife would rarely make two-day visits to Ranchi.

His schooling had become an issue with this arrangement. Ishan was studying in Delhi Public School in Patna. When he reached Class IX, there were questions about his attendance. He was already playing U-16 cricket for Jharkhand. It became a tricky situation.

'The principal gave him two choices: either play cricket or concentrate on studies,' Pranav recalls.

'We decided *dekhte hain, ek chance lete hain* (Let's see by taking a chance). He was already representing the state at the U-16 level. We decided to pursue cricket. Ishan was moved to Ashwini Public School in Patna. He would study at home and just turn up for the exams in Patna.'

Ishan was in a zone. His goal was clear to him. There couldn't be any compromises on the sacrifices. He never got sucked into the popular culture of *khep* cricket either.

Jharkhand cricket, still in its nascent stages, went through an overhaul and Ishan was catapulted to playing with the big boys in the senior Jharkhand team for the Vijay Hazare Trophy in 2013–14 at the age of fifteen.

Pranav recalls when he was first selected for Jharkhand, Ishan didn't give away much even as rest of the family was thrilled to bits.

'Papa, important *yeh nahin ki* selection *ho gaya hain.* Important *yeh hain ki wahan pe jaake jagah banake rakhe* (Father, it's not important that I am selected. What's more important is that I hold on to my place when I join the team),' a composed Ishan explained to his family.

'He didn't get carried away. There was this air of maturity

about him,' Pranav states.

Ishan was unfortunately run out for 44 off 75 balls on his Jharkhand debut against Odisha in March 2014. He played another match in the tournament and added another 21 runs to his tally.

The following season, he made his First-Class debut in a Ranji Trophy match against Assam in Guwahati. Ishan made an impression straightaway, scoring 60 in his first innings.

Jharkhand were clubbed in a group which played for promotion in Ranji Trophy. Ishan made the most of the bowling attacks he was facing. In six matches that season, Ishan had scored 451 runs for Jharkhand.

He was a prodigy. Hailing from a developing cricket state such as Jharkhand never amplified his reputation as it does for boys from cities like Mumbai, Chennai, Delhi and Bengaluru.

Ishan was shortlisted in coach Rahul Dravid's first India U-19 team. Ishan and Rishabh Pant were vying for a place as the lead wicketkeeper in the team which was supposed to travel to Bangladesh for the U-19 World Cup in January 2016.

Just before Dravid would prune the list even further, Ishan turned up for Jharkhand in the Ranji Trophy in October 2015. Ishan's Ranji season didn't get off to a great start. He scored a duck in the first match of the season.

But his talent could never be subdued for long. In the second match of the season, Jharkhand travelled to Rajkot to play Saurashtra. An underprepared pitch was waiting for them. Ishan put the pressure right back on the bowlers. He scored 87 high-quality runs off 69 balls in a session of bold counter-attacking batting on a raging turner.

In the first tournament that the India U-19 team played under Dravid, Ishan could just manage 30 runs in three matches against Bangladesh and Afghanistan in Kolkata. Rishabh was adjudged the player of the series and it seemed Rishabh had pulled away a fair distance from Ishan in the race.

A maiden First-Class century against Goa in the Ranji Trophy seemed to have brought him back to form. Converting the domestic form into performances in U-19 cricket surprisingly was taking too long.

On a tour of Sri Lanka with the India U-19s, Ishan and Rishabh were captaining in alternate matches. While Rishabh flourished, Ishan mustered 83 runs in five matches.

Dravid, however, had enough faith in him. Not only was Ishan selected for the U-19 World Cup a month later, he was named the captain of the team! This piece of news was least expected in the Pandey family in Patna.

'*Humein koi umeed nahin thhi* (We had no hope). We didn't believe he was made the captain. I had no idea this could happen,' Pranav firmly states.

It was around five in the evening when Pranav received a call from one of his friends.

'*Aapke ladke ka kya naam hain jo* cricket *khelta hain* (What's the name of your son which plays cricket)?' the friend enquired.

'Ishan,' Pranav promptly replied.

'*Arey ussko toh* India U-19 *ka* captain *bana diya gaya hain* (He has been named the captain of India's U-19 team),' the friend broke the news.

Pranav was still unsure. He enquired how did his friend know that for sure.

'He sent me the screenshot of BCCI's tweet. I looked up and confirmed the news,' the proud father says, grinning from ear-to-ear.

A wicketkeeper from Jharkhand who hits the ball hard – the parallels with MS Dhoni were quickly drawn across the country. That he played the Vijay Hazare Trophy under Dhoni that season was like flirting with destiny.

For Ishan, though, playing with Dhoni a month ahead of the U-19 World Cup was nothing but acquiring as much knowledge from the master strategist of Indian cricket.

'I was the junior-most player in the Jharkhand team. I was standing at the boundary and observing what he was doing and why. What field he was setting for which bowler. When a wicket used to fall, he used to tell me that 'I placed this fielder because of Varun's (Aaron) pace'. He would tell me what kind of field I could set if I had a really fast bowler in the team,' Ishan would humbly say.

'We don't talk much about cricket at home because he is consumed by cricket anyway. It didn't make sense to talk about cricket when he got some time off. We never ask him how his game was going. We only offered him moral support. He did everything else by himself. We didn't even know where he played, who he met and what kind of discussions he would have with Dravid or Dhoni,' Pranav says, while talking about the day when the big comparisons became the talk of the town.

The Pandey household tried its best to cancel out the noise around Ishan.

At seventeen years of age, he was competing with his deputy Rishabh for the title of heir apparent to MS Dhoni.

## The torrid U-19 World Cup and the fight to regain ground

The confidence in the millennial Indian cricketers is startling. Ishan reached Bangladesh with a hairdo that resembled Virat Kohli at the time. A whirlwind 160 in the warm-up game against Canada raised the expectations.

As the tournament wore on, though, his struggles to score runs for India U-19s looked unending. He struggled to get going while Rishabh, Sarfaraz Khan, Armaan Jaffer and Anmolpreet Singh carried the batting on their shoulders.

Ishan did show some of his spark when he scored 52 against Nepal with his opening partner Rishabh going berserk from the other end with a 78 off 24 balls. Ishan scored 21 runs on either side of that knock of 52 even as India made the final.

During a training session in Fatullah a couple of days ahead of their quarterfinal against Namibia, coach Rahul Dravid ripped into him.

Ishan kept trying to slog his way out of poor form and missed every time. Dravid halted the nets and thundered: 'Ishan, come out of the nets.'

He then turned to Rishabh and said: 'Take Ishan aside and talk to him. Make him understand that hitting is not all about slogging.'

Rishabh put his arms around his shoulder and took him for a stroll. Within minutes, Ishan was up and running, diving around and egging his team on during the fielding drills.

That was the kind of team bonding that Dravid had taught the boys.

The pressure on him was obvious. Ishan didn't let his poor form affect his conduct though. He would hold his own in front of the media and not give a glimpse of the battles he was fighting in his mind.

There was the IPL auction on the day of the quarterfinal though. Something to look forward too.

'We don't have to think about it now. *Iske baad* IPL *hi toh khelna hain*, I hope (Anyway, we will have to play after this),' Ishan said during a casual chat on the eve of the quarterfinal and the auction.

'I have stopped taking calls during this tournament. I can't let distractions come in my way here. There were people calling me, mostly friends and relatives, to ask what my chances in the IPL were. I needed to keep that aside,' he asserted.

India U-19 brushed aside Namibia and, by the time the match was over, Ishan had won a Rs 35-lakh contract from Gujarat Lions.

The glee on his face that evening was infectious.

Going by the bundle of joy that Ishan was, it seemed as if a high school boy had cracked an entrance exam even before the board results were out.

'An IPL contract means a lot to a player. It gives a lot of happiness. You get confidence from it that you have to prove yourself in the World Cup so that people think that you've been picked for the right reasons,' a visibly elated Ishan had said. 'I've played four matches here but haven't done well in three of those. For now, I won't keep my body language loose and focus as much as I can,' he then claimed.

The pressure seemed to have evaporated from his system. But the runs were yet to come. When Alzarri Joseph trapped him LBW for four in the final in Dhaka, the way Ishan flung his head back told a story of despair.

India U-19s collapsed and couldn't stop West Indies U-19 from chasing down the 146-run target. The Dhaka sky was gloomy all day but it couldn't match Ishan's mood. You could see the hurt in his eyes. It was heart-wrenching to see a seventeen-year-old crestfallen and yet facing the media.

'He was so young that he couldn't absorb the hype around him. When he came back from the U-19 World Cup, we tried to counsel him. We needed to start working hard again,' Pranav says.

India 'A' and U-19 fielding coach Abhay Sharma offered a peek into a pep talk given to Ishan at the time.

'Once I had posed a question to both Rishabh and Ishan. I asked them who kept wickets in the greatest number of ODIs for India after MS Dhoni. They were surprised to know it was Rahul Dravid. They started laughing. I told Ishan if Dravid could keep wickets in so many matches for India when he was not even a wicketkeeper then he should realise where he could reach because he was a genuine wicketkeeper. Don't undermine yourself and keep working on your game,' Abhay reminisces.

'There are some players who take time to mature. You have to have discussions with players as per their IQ. It doesn't help if you do the big talk and the kid struggles to understand it. At this level, it's more about your mindset than skills,' Abhay stresses.

It was time to flush the U-19 World Cup out of the system. Twenty-seven runs in five games in his maiden IPL season had pushed him down the pecking order of up-and-coming cricketers.

Domestic cricket and its unrelenting grind awaited Ishan.

The season didn't start well for him though. Scores of 4 and 0 while opening the batting to start the Ranji Trophy campaign against Karnataka threatened to tarnish his reputation at a higher level of cricket. Déjà vu!

He didn't have much time. He decided to relinquish his preferred opening slot. He was now batting at No. 6 in the next match against Ranji giants Karnataka. A counterattacking unbeaten 159 off 211 balls shot him back in the limelight.

Later in the season, he squared off with one of his best mates and competitor Rishabh Pant during a match against Delhi. Jharkhand had the first go with the bat. Coming out to bat at 80/4, he tore apart the Delhi attack. He finished with 273 off 336 balls. Rishabh, in reply, smacked two centuries in the match and one of them became the fastest in the history of Ranji Trophy.

There's a funny story about the century Rishabh scored in the second innings of that match. The fastest first-class century against his name fails to quench his thirst even as he has happy about flirting with records.

'I knew Ishan (Kishan) had hit 14 sixes and set the record for most sixes in a Ranji innings in that match. I wanted to eclipse it. I fell after hitting 13,' Rishabh quipped after the match.

It was as if the superheroes from the Marvel world collided and shook the cricketing scene in India.

Ishan finished with 799 runs from 10 games while Rishabh had scored 972 in eight. Rishabh had edged ahead.

Ishan had done enough to be in the national selectors' scheme of things. India 'A' tours and Duleep Trophies was part of his calendars.

Inconsistency became his bane. Often there would be sparks of brilliance before bursting into flames.

Anyway, he was still one of the exciting wicketkeeping prospects in Indian cricket.

## The Mumbai Indians schooling and making the grade

His hitting ability and flair were hard to ignore. In 2018, the Mumbai Indians were on the lookout for a young Indian impact wicketkeeper-batsman. Delhi Daredevils would pay handsome amounts to retain Rishabh Pant and Sanju Samson was part of the Rajasthan Royals family.

The scouts felt there was enough in Ishan to work with and handsome deal of Rs 5.5 crore came to the nineteen-year-old. Short boundaries and a true pitch at Wankhede Stadium were assumed to work in Ishan's favour. Yet, he blew hot and cold.

The strike-rate was up there but his innings were too short for a top-order batsman.

It was difficult to justify the amount spent on him with 275 runs in 14 games. The Mumbai Indians couldn't even qualify for the play-offs. They were back to headhunting for a reliable and impactful wicketkeeper. Thus, they arrived at Quinton de Kock.

A month before the IPL in 2019, Netflix released a documentary on Mumbai Indians' campaign in the previous season. In the first episode, it was shown that Ishan's lifestyle and discipline were far from satisfactory for a professional franchise such as the Mumbai Indians.

Staying up late into the night, gaming, partying and not being able to keep up with the fitness standards, all of these had become an issue for Ishan. The management of the Mumbai Indians worked overtime to get him on track. But they were not going to leave him in the lurch.

Even as the Mumbai Indians' machinery got down to working on Ishan, de Kock assumed the role of the first wicketkeeper. Ishan did get seven games as a batsman in the season but could muster 101 runs and his strike-rate plummeted to 101.

Inconsistency had taken over his cricket even in the domestic scene. The domestic seasons were interspersed by a few breath-taking knocks, but he was in no way setting domestic cricket on fire. He did just enough to stay in the scheme of things and travel with India 'A' teams.

Rishabh Pant, Washington Sundar and Khaleel Ahmed, his teammates from the India U-19 team, had all started playing for India by 2018. He wasn't even halfway there.

He would put up a jovial face when you met him during domestic matches. He would say his biggest competition is himself. He couldn't have wasted time thinking about slipping down the pecking order.

'Even if he got frustrated, he never expressed it in front of us. We have always seen him confident,' Pranav would say.

The Mumbai Indians coach, former Sri Lanka captain, Mahela Jayawardene turned into a hard taskmaster after his first season with the franchise ended in disappointment in 2018.

In an interview to Cricbuzz in April 2021, Jayawardene bared himself on Ishan.

Here's the excerpt from the interview:

*'We had to train him with all his bad habits off the field too. Bad as in not partying but that he was gaming a lot. Keeping Ishan focussed, as a coaching group, is a constant effort. I tried to give him that kind of instruction and clarity. I felt that the more he thinks, the more he gets into trouble. Like his state coach was saying, sometimes he tends to make easy situations tough because he sometimes overthinks unnecessarily.'*

The pandemic struck, the lockdown happened, and a new-look Ishan turned up in the UAE when the IPL started in September 2020.

Leaner and hungrier from the outset, Ishan finally took a high-profile tournament by storm.

Benched in the first two games of the tournament, Ishan got off to a flying start when he was played against the Royal Challengers Bangalore. Batting at No. 4, he hammered 99 off 58 balls to help the Mumbai Indians match the 201 by the Royal Challengers Bangalore.

Ishan was now a key member in the heavyweight Mumbai Indians batting line-up. With consistency in his game, he was now a reliable cog which helped the team become the first one to win consecutive IPLs. What propelled him into reckoning for the Indian team were 516 runs in 14 games at a strike rate of 145.76.

He would not get tired of crediting Hardik Pandya, Krunal Pandya and Suryakumar Yadav for his turnaround. These three pushed him hard and drilled it into his mind that if he didn't improve his fitness and off-side stroke play, he had no chance of making it big.

Not for nothing that his father would say, 'The Mumbai Indians changed Ishan as a person and even his game changed.'

Four months later, when Indian cricket was flaunting the depth in its pool of resources following the historic tour of Australia, Ishan earned his maiden call-up for the five-match T20Is against England at revamped Motera Stadium in Ahmedabad.

On 14 March 2021, he was thrown into the deep in the second game of the series.

Opening the innings, chasing 165, Ishan unassumingly flicked a thunderbolt from Jofra Archer for a boundary off the first ball he faced in international cricket.

In the 10th over of the chase, Ishan slog-swept leg-spinner Adil Rashid into the stands to bring up his fifty on international debut. He finished with 56 off 32 balls to set up a comfortable win.

It was a manic night across Bihar and Jharkhand as Ishan went on a rampage. There were people in Patna taking offence when broadcasters introduced Ishan as a cricketer from Jharkhand.

The proud dad now would slyly say: '*Ab toh woh desh ka bachcha hain na* (Now, he is the son of India).'

The excitement that night hit the roof. Everyone in Ishan's family was dazed. Ishan couldn't speak to them for more than 30 seconds. It needed time to sink in.

Another four months later, he repeated the show on his ODI debut against Sri Lanka in Colombo. With a lot of 23 players in the UK for the inaugural World Test Championship final against New Zealand and a five-Test series against England, Shikhar Dhawan was leading a young team blended with some experienced white-ball players.

While chasing 263 in the first ODI of the tour, Ishan walked out to bat in the sixth over of the chase. The first ball he faced, he skipped down the track to off-spinner Dhananjaya de Silva and hit him over the long-off fence for a six.

After nine overs of high-octane batting, he pulled off-spinner Charith Asalanka for a boundary over mid-wicket to bring up his fifty in 33 balls. His 59 off 42 again set up an easy win for India.

He would later proudly claim that he had announced in the dressing room that he would hit the first ball for six no matter where the ball was pitched.

It's this unwavering self-confidence that has seen him make it to this level. Five years of a bumpy ride, hitting the toughs for most part of it, had now culminated in positioning right next to his best mate from the U-19 days, Rishabh Pant who had already become a hot property in international cricket.

Mates and competitor from their teens, Ishan and Rishabh now earned another chance to win a World Cup again. This time playing for India at the T20 World Cup 2021.

The fame, the money and the pressure of high-performance sport can be overwhelming for anyone, let alone a boy in his early 20s.

'I don't know much about fame. But I handle his money. He doesn't have any idea about the money that comes in. He likes buying clothes and shoes. He asks for pocket money and I transfer it into his account which is a different one from the one where all his money comes in,' Pranav claims.

Ishan has seen through the rough times. It's time to build and not commit the same mistakes off the field as he earlier did.

'There's a bit of relief and satisfaction in us that he is now an India cricketer, but Ishan realises that the responsibility increases once you have represented the country,' the father states with pride.

On to the next phase of Ishan Kishan's career!

## *CHAPTER 7*

# SHREYAS IYER: SWAGGER IS HIS GAME

### *The initiation*

The hustle in Mumbai cricket is eccentric in nature. The sport has long ceased to be a mere form of recreation for kids in the city. As you take a tour around the fabled *maidan*s in the city, you notice that the number of aspiring cricketers jostling to make the grade is daunting. The rich history and pride of Mumbai cricket make it even more frightening. You ought to hustle to survive in the ultra-competitive world of Mumbai cricket.

The sight of kids, barely able to make sense of the world, running rugged to become cricketers, is routine. If you walk through the grounds, the number of soft stories from financially challenged households is hair-raising. There's no way one can differentiate between an affluent kid and an impoverished one once they hit the ground. Cut-throat competition is the name of the game.

Shreyas' journey in cricket is a departure from a regular budding cricketer in the city. There has been no overbearing drama to take up the sport and pursue it. His father Santosh was a businessman who ensured an easy-going, hassle-free middle-class life for his family.

Cricket was merely an option to be explored for Shreyas. Santosh had enrolled his son at the Indian Gymkhana to learn the basics of cricket. Santosh could see his son had a ball sense and natural flair when the father and son played at home.

An adolescent Shreyas was inclined towards football. Scan his social media page and you will know how invested he is in watching world football. The busy, hectic schedule of an Indian cricketer has no bearing on his love for following football.

Shreyas' exploits for Indian Gymkhana convinced Santosh that his son could build a future in cricket. He was sent to Don Bosco School since it had a bigger presence in Mumbai's hallowed school cricket. Santosh was now taking active interest in Shreyas' game.

It was time to move to a reputed academy. The Shivaji Park Gymkhana Cricket Academy was the preferred one. Shivaji Park has been the nodal point for breeding Mumbai cricketers. This is the very turf where Ramakant Achrekar bred a host of India and Mumbai legends. Sachin Tendulkar took his baby steps in cricket here. Vinod Kambli, Pravin Amre, Chandrakant Pandit and Ajit Agarkar are few of the other big names to have learnt their skills here before going on to represent India.

Shreyas first turned up at the Shivaji Park Gymkhana for trials when he was eleven years old. Padmakar Shivalkar, a Mumbai legend and considered one of the best left-arm spinners who could never play for India, was in charge.

Former India batsman Pravin Amre, one of the best technical coaches in India, remembers the first interaction with Shreyas. 'There were 400 boys for trials that day. Paddy sir (Shivalkar) was there too. Shreyas was asked to come a year later,' Amre reveals.

A twelve-year-old Shreyas came back the next year and this time Amre was in charge of the nets and trials. 'I noticed something different about him. He was picking the length up very quickly and was middling everything. I realised I could work with him,' Amre says.

Here began a relationship between a coach and a player that was going to see Shreyas through a lot of critical junctures in his cricketing career.

## Fighting for acceptance in junior cricket

Shreyas Iyer always had a unique technique. An upright stance, bat almost flailing in his back lift, pronounced fidgety movements in the crease before the bowler was into his delivery stride – young Iyer defied the batting manual in every way.

If you get the pulse of cricket in Mumbai, you will understand that the batting coaching manual is sacred. Mumbai cricket prides itself in producing heavy-scoring batsmen. There's no wiggle room when it comes to working on batting technique.

The 'Bombay school of batting' is as much a culture as an emotion. It's an aura. It is credited for the prolific lineage of batsmen that has ruled cricket for generations. '*Khadoos*' (dogged, mean and insatiable) is the word that is famously used to typify a successful Mumbai batsman. An impeccable textbook technique is non-negotiable.

Amre doesn't beat around the bush. Shreyas was no extraordinary talent when he came to him. 'There were 400 boys in the trial. He was good enough to be selected. But he didn't stand out. He had the potential. But he certainly wasn't the best of that lot,' Amre says.

Junior cricket, especially school cricket, in Mumbai, is serious business. Score piles of runs at that level and it becomes a springboard that shoots you into the limelight of the system.

Shreyas was good. He was consistent but the numbers were not extraordinary. Amre recalls Shreyas making it into the Mumbai U-16 team within two years after joining him.

If you ask Shreyas, he will tell you how he fancied himself as a leg-spinner in his teens. He was rejected by the Mumbai selectors when he first went for the U-16 trials. The next year, he was picked on his batting abilities.

'The standard of batting in Mumbai is very high. The competition among batsmen is very intense. During his U-16 days, I would say Shreyas was among the top fifteen batsmen in his batch in Mumbai but he was far from being even in the top three,' Amre concedes.

To put Amre's observation into perspective, there were Sarfaraz Khan and Armaan Jaffer setting the school cricket scene on fire. When Shreyas was fifteen, a twelve-year-old Sarfaraz had recorded the highest score in Harris Shield U-16 cricket with an innings of 439. Next year, again a twelve-year-old Armaan scored 498 to own a record in U-14 Giles Shield Cricket. An eleven-year-old Prithvi Shaw was scoring centuries for fun and consistently notching up scores between the range of 150 and 300.

Shreyas Iyer was just another name in Mumbai's junior cricket circles. He was never the headline event.

Things got difficult for Shreyas in his U-16 days. The runs dried up and his attitude and technique were also questioned. The stalwarts of Mumbai cricket, tasked to oversee the grass roots, had little faith in his abilities.

'Shreyas has an unconventional technique. He is not the typical *khadoos* Mumbai batsman. He is different. He is always on the attack. He didn't have a power game but always found a way to keep scoring freely. His way of batting didn't please the caretakers of Mumbai cricket. There was so much resistance against him,' Amre recalls.

It didn't help that Shreyas would get out after scoring pretty 30s, 40s or even 70s. The 'Bombay school of cricket' frowns upon batsmen who get out after getting set. 'Prizing your wicket' is the core mantra of batting.

If that were not enough, Iyer senior was told by a selector that Shreyas had lost focus and there were issues with his attitude. The innate swag in Shreyas' demeanour was held against him.

'Shreyas is a very confident and sharp boy. He speaks well. But I always fear he will be misunderstood,' Amra mentions.

As things got tough for teenager Shreyas, the Iyer household was on tenterhooks. There were instances when the boy would break down at home.

Santosh Iyer intervened and took Shreyas to a sports psychologist. In an interview to *Cricbuzz* in April 2020, Santosh bared the vulnerable phase in Shreyas' life.

Iyer senior's revelation went like: 'When one coach told me that your son has talent, but he has lost focus along the way, I got a little worried. I thought he has either fallen in love or got into bad company. Eventually, I was told that there was nothing to worry. Like most other cricketers, Shreyas was simply going through a rough patch. And sure enough, he soon recovered his form and has never looked back.'

This was also the time Amre had to get involved and took special care of his favourite ward.

'There was so much talk about his technique and the way he approached his cricket. One day Shreyas and I got together and decided we will not listen to these negative comments. We will work hard on his strengths and find a way to score big runs,' Amre says.

Shreyas had gone through two torrid years in U-16 cricket. That's when Mumbai Cricket Association appointed Vinod Raghavan as the coach of the U-16 Mumbai team.

The performance at the trials that year too could be, at best, described as one which flattered to deceive. Then Mumbai selector Chandrakant Pandit, known to be a hard taskmaster, wasn't impressed. On the other hand, Raghavan was convinced Shreyas had the potential to become a very successful cricketer. It was only a matter of pulling him out of the bad patch.

Raghavan implored to Pandit to retain Shreyas in the squad. Raghavan even went on to ask Shreyas to lead the team in matches during the pre-season camps when the first line of players was missing.

Unlike all the batting prodigies, Shreyas was not a part of the BCCI's system. He couldn't be a part of U-16 National Cricket Academy programmes. The resistance against Shreyas continued even after his last season with U-16.

He missed out on selection in the Mumbai U-19 team. But this is where Shreyas started to bloom.

In Amre's words: 'Shreyas never had a prolific career in school cricket. But he started scoring runs heavily in club cricket and inter-collegiate tournaments. He finished his school and joined RA Podar College of Commerce and Economics. There he started winning matches single-handedly.'

Shreyas had a huge impact on RA Podar College. His all-round performance helped them win the Saqib Rizvi Memorial Cricket Trophy organised by Junior Colleges Sports Association of Mumbai in 2012.

The college website flaunts a news clip from *The Times of India* under the headline 'Shreyas helps Podar win title' which read: 'Leg-spinner Shreyas Iyer took 6 wickets as RA Podar College won the inter-college tournament for the Saqib Rizvi Memorial Cricket Trophy. Iyer, who scored 67 in the first innings, took 6/13 and helped bowl out Ruparel for 110. Podar registered a 241-run win in the final which was played over two days.'

Shreyas had started pushing himself now. He earned a selection in the U-19 Mumbai team later in 2012 and never looked back. Three marauding hundreds in seven matches of the U-19 Cooch Behar Trophy took him to the NCA. Performing well under the supervision of India U-19 coach Bharat Arun (who would go on to be India's bowling coach) meant a place in the India U-19 team was there for the taking.

## U-19 World Cup heartbreak and the turnaround for Mumbai

In all fairness, Shreyas Iyer was not setting the junior cricket scene on fire. He was a part of the U-19 India team leading to the World Cup in the UAE in February 2014 but was never the showstopper. He struggled in a tri-series in Australia in July 2013, scoring just seven runs in three games.

When coach Bharat Arun was about to finalise his team for the World Cup during a quadrangular series in India in September that year, a timely century ensured Shreyas made the cut.

It was a U-19 India team that had Sanju Samson and Sarfaraz Khan in it and Vijay Zol, already a U-19 World Cup winner two years ago, was tasked to lead the side. The hard-hitting Deepak Hooda and Kuldeep Yadav's mysterious left-arm spin were the exciting prospects from that batch. Sanju Samson was already a revelation for the Rajasthan Royals during the Champions League T20 in 2013 and Sarfaraz was grabbing headlines right through his junior cricket career. Shreyas Iyer was just, in essence, making the number in that U-19 World Cup squad.

Expectedly, Shreyas didn't find his name in the starting XI. He was played in just one match and that was against Papua New Guinea and was dropped for the quarterfinal against England. Shreyas looked on from the dugout as his mates failed and crashed out of the tournament.

The large, imposing empty stands at the Dubai International Stadium stared at him as Shreyas felt empty in the stomach.

India U-19s were made to play a couple of more games for the fifth spot in the tournament. Shreyas turned up like he meant business while the rest of his mates were still coping with the quarterfinal loss, cracked a couple of crucial half-centuries and ensured the team didn't have to endure further humiliation while in Dubai.

As much as Shreyas was upset about what happened in the UAE, Amre saw signs of change in his approach.

'He was very upset that he didn't get to play all the matches in the U-19 World Cup. When I spoke to him, he said he really felt he could have made a difference if he was given a chance. Shreyas insisted he could have helped India U-19 progress further in the tournament. That was heartening for me. As a coach, it gave me immense satisfaction to see my student starting to believe he could make some difference. I could see something had changed in him,' Amre remembers.

There were no IPL deals for him on the table. He did make his debut for Mumbai in Syed Mushtaq Ali Tournament in March 2014 but that too ended in disappointment. Sixteen runs in three games weren't going to take him anywhere.

It was time to hit the reset button.

'Shreyas started working very hard. He became a fitness freak after that U-19 World Cup. The hunger was like never before. He looks a bit laidback and that is mistaken as laziness. I would say he is more like Rohit Sharma who seems to be an easy-going person, but is very serious about his cricket,' Amre says.

He now wanted to test himself in alien conditions. So, it was decided that he spent his summer in England, playing for Trent Bridge cricket team in local leagues, that year.

Shreyas lived by himself and trained there at the club before getting his opportunity. In three innings, he scored 297 runs. Shreyas was growing in confidence and had become aware of his game.

Shreyas, while recounting his stint at Trent Bridge in an interview to the *Times of India*, claimed that experience turned him around as a person and cricketer. He narrates: 'I got the motivation from the 2014 U-19 World Cup. We lost the quarterfinals against England. And I wasn't playing that game. And I thought that if I played, I could have helped my team to win. I told myself that no matter what, I am going to become a very good player and I want to play for India one day. When I went to England, it taught me how you got to take responsibility because I was staying by myself and doing all the chores by myself. So I understood how to stay alone and it literally taught me how difficult life is without family. I became more responsible in terms of my decision making and my act towards others.'

He may have had found his zone but there were hurdles lined up for him back home. Missing out on a domestic season would have been detrimental to his growth as a player.

Pravin Amre was given the responsibility to coach the Mumbai team for the 2014–15 domestic season. The season was due to start with the Vijay Hazare Trophy.

Amre convinced the selectors to pick Shreyas in the team and his ward didn't disappoint. Shreyas finished as the second highest run-scorer for Mumbai behind Wasim Jaffer. He had scored 273 runs in six matches at an average of 54.60 and strike rate of 92.85.

The Ranji Trophy was next.

The forces in Mumbai cricket still resisted Shreyas' inclusion in the team. Amre says: 'I don't want to name people but there were some legendary cricketers in Mumbai who didn't believe

Shreyas could succeed at the First-Class level. There were so many objections against Shreyas. His unconventional technique again became the bone of contention. But I had made up my mind that till the time I was there, I had to play Shreyas in the Mumbai Ranji team. Otherwise it would have been difficult for him.'

Amre got his way and Shreyas was in the Ranji Trophy team. Both Amre and Shreyas were under immense pressure after the first week of Ranji Trophy season.

Mumbai had slumped to a shock defeat against Jammu and Kashmir in the opening match of the season. That had ruffled a few feathers in Mumbai cricket. It had dented their pride and Mumbai's rich history of being domestic giants was under threat.

'What made things worse was the fact that we lost the match at our home ground, Wankhede. Shreyas failed in that match (he scored seven and one). I won't lie but I got worried. There were so many questions raised by all the stalwarts of Mumbai cricket,' Amre recounts those tricky days.

The discerning eyes were about to burn down both Amre and Shreyas now.

The Mumbai team travelled to Delhi to play Railways next. The Mumbai batting collapsed to 101. Shreyas managed just 11. Unseasonal rains helped Mumbai escape with a draw. Amre and Shreyas were feeling the heat in peak Delhi winter.

The duo could sense they had just one more match to turn things around or else both would have to leave the Mumbai dressing room.

Things did turn around when the Mumbai team reached Kanpur the following week to play Uttar Pradesh. Mumbai were 58/5 when Shreyas Iyer walked out to bat. He launched a counterattack that would become a trademark of his game in the future. The 78-ball 75, along with Shardul Thakur's 87 off

100 balls, against the likes of Praveen Kumar, Ankit Rajpoot and Piyush Chawla had dimmed UP's spirits in the match.

Mumbai eventually won the match by 8 wickets. Shreyas had bought himself and his coach some breathing space.

'I vividly remember the sigh of relief we heaved when Shreyas performed. I hadn't spoken much with Shreyas leading up to that game. I knew he was under pressure and I didn't want to clutter his mind,' Amre would say.

With the Mumbai top-order out of sorts, Shreyas Iyer was batting at No. 3 against Bengal at the Eden Gardens next week. Not only did he avert another batting collapse, he put the Bengal bowlers to the sword as he brought up his maiden First-Class hundred. His 153 off 175 balls had taken Mumbai's campaign out of choppy waters.

It was time to roll.

He was back in Mumbai after a month. Shreyas then produced another match-saving unbeaten 142 against Madhya Pradesh in the first match of 2015. Mumbai cricket had found a new batting star in the new year.

Shreyas would go on to score another five half-centuries as Mumbai's campaign ended in a semi-final defeat against eventual champions Karnataka.

With 809 runs in 10 matches at an average of 50.56 and strike rate of 75.89, Shreyas Iyer was now the mainstay of Mumbai's batting.

## Finding IPL home in Delhi and the Ranji rage

When the IPL auctions arrived in February 2015, the dynamics in team composition started to see a transition. Franchises were now keen on having more Indian domestic talent in their ranks. On the back of a successful Ranji season, twenty-year-old Shreyas Iyer had become hot property.

As his name was called for bids, the Mumbai Indians and Kolkata Knight Riders got into an intense bidding war. Pravin Amre, now a part of the Delhi Daredevils (now Delhi Capitals) coaching staff, watched on as Daredevils swooped in and bought his ward for Rs 2.6 crore.

Shreyas Iyer had arrived in mainstream cricket!

In a way, Shreyas was a trendsetter for young uncapped players.

'I must say that Mr Kiran Gandhi (the owner of Daredevils) was very supportive. He had given me the licence to buy Shreyas. He trusted my judgement,' Amre says.

Sunil Valson, a member of the 1983 World Cup-winning team, has been an integral part of the Daredevils management since its inception. He notes what transpired on that auction day.

'The scouts had an eye on him. We at Daredevils realised that you don't necessarily need just slam-bang batting in T20 cricket. You need someone who can bat the innings, steady the ship and also accelerate. So, with Shreyas scoring heavily at a very good strike rate in Ranji Trophy, he fit the bill. It's not that he came out of the blue,' Valson says.

The money was in the bag. The headlines were about Shreyas. He was not used to this kind of attention.

No Indian cricketer of his age had seen that much money at the time. Keeping him grounded was going to be the next task.

Amre had a job on his hands here. 'I told him that the price tag is irrelevant here. He needed to build his career. Work on his game and make most of the opportunity that he is getting at Daredevils. His father also played a part.'

Valson offers his insight. 'Price tag brings an extra burden for no fault of the player. That's the dynamics of the auction. On that day, there were two other teams who thought they needed him. There was enough money in play when his name arrived. And when the player goes for such a huge amount, he is bound to feel the pressure. But you can't afford to get bogged down at this level. These Under-19 boys mature well these days. I must say his parents guided him really well. They really showed how one should handle such a situation. Nowadays, parents are very aware and understand the equations when their kids start making money from cricket. It wasn't the case in our days.'

The other factor, according to Valson, that defined Shreyas' rise was the way he presented himself. 'The first impression that I got of Shreyas was that he was very sharp. There was hunger and you could sense fire in the belly. He is someone who is very easy to get along with. He has very high family values. You could make out. He was refined, educated and very articulate. I am not saying that cricketers must be as articulate, but it does help. He carried himself really well,' Valson spoke of his observations.

The Daredevils management, writhing from the scars of tumultuous fortunes in the preceding seasons, had punted on this rather unheralded young boy.

Gary Kirsten, still basking in the glory of coaching India to a World Cup title in 2011, was the head coach of Daredevils and needed proof of Shreyas' abilities.

After failing while batting at No. 4 in the opening match of the season, Shreyas was moved up the order.

Amre was at work again. 'Finding a batting position in the playing XI for Shreyas was tough. The Daredevils team had big names like Yuvraj Singh, JP Duminy, Quinton de Kock, Albie Morkel, Angelo Mathews and Manoj Tiwary. All, except de Kock, were middle-order batsmen. So, I had to convince Gary that we could open with Shreyas. I had made it clear to Shreyas that if he wanted game time then he had to open. He embraced it.'

The move worked. Shreyas provided a brisk and steady start,

scored 40 off 30 balls to lay a solid foundation for Daredevils to post 184/3 against the Rajasthan Royals. Royals chased down the target off the last ball of the match. But Daredevils had found a solution to one of the many problems in their ranks.

Two matches later, he hit a 60 off 40 balls to set up a win against the Sunrisers Hyderabad. And then literally shred the Mumbai Indians attack into pieces with another match-winning 83 off 56. Midway through the tournament, Shreyas was the reliable man in the till-then ailing batting line-up.

In an interview to the author, then Sri Lanka captain Angelo Mathews had stated: 'Shreyas Iyer is an Indian player who has impressed me the most. He can play fearless cricket against international bowlers. He caught my eye straight away.'

Valson was amazed at seeing his transformation. 'We knew he could hit big. But for someone who could steady an innings to go on to be the accelerator of the best quality is amazing.'

In a team of international batting superstars, young Shreyas emerged as the highest run-getter for them. He had conjured 439 runs in 14 matches at an average of 33.76 while striking at 128.36 even as his team finished seventh in points table. He was named the emerging player of the IPL.

Twenty-year-old Shreyas Iyer was the silver lining in the dwindling fortunes of Delhi Daredevils. His debut IPL season marked the beginning of his love affair with Daredevils.

He had now caught the eye of the national selectors. He was picked for India 'A' for a series against Australia 'A'.

Rahul Dravid had just assumed charge as the coach of India's developmental sides India 'A' and U-19s.

Shreyas scored 122 runs in two unofficial Tests. Dravid was now watching.

As the 2015–16 Ranji Trophy season came around, the

spotlight was following Shreyas Iyer. The failure in the opening match against Andhra was an anomaly.

The Punjab team that went visiting Mumbai in the second week of October discovered a batting beast in Shreyas Iyer. Coming out to bat at 25/1 in the seventh over in reply to Punjab's 154, he devoured the Punjab attack.

Around 62.2 overs later, when Shreyas was walking back to the pavilion, Mumbai were 338/4.

The scoresheet read: Shreyas Iyer caught Sidharth Kaul bowled Yuvraj Singh 200 (176 balls, 25x4s, 5x6s).

He would unleash his fury to every opponent in that season. Shreyas Iyer was at the forefront as Mumbai raced towards their 41st Ranji Trophy title.

Two centuries and four half-centuries from Shreyas' blade in the league stages helped Mumbai make it to the quarterfinals.

Shreyas hit the reset button and then again picked up his pace in the knockouts.

Scores of 45 and 81 against Jharkhand in the quarterfinal followed by 90 and 58 against Madhya Pradesh in the semi-final took Mumbai to the final against Saurashtra.

This was the biggest game that Shreyas had played in his career. The pitch in Pune unusually assisted seam bowlers. A Saurashtra team, chasing a maiden Ranji title with Cheteshwar Pujara in the line-up, were skittled out for 235 in the first innings.

Shreyas, batting at No. 3, walked out to bat in the first over of the reply. Like he had done right through the season, he launched a counterattack. Chewing a game, moving around the turf without a care in the world, Shreyas Iyer single-handedly out-batted Saurashtra.

As he brought up his hundred, he had knocked the wind out

of Saurashtra.

With all eyes in Indian cricket firmly fixed on him, Shreyas Iyer's 117 off 142 balls ensured Mumbai had won the Ranji Trophy for the 41st time. Shreyas had amassed 1321 runs in 11 games, almost 500 runs more than the next highest run-getter in the season. The average of 73.38 spoke of his consistency while the strike rate of 92.70 screamed his authority and domination. He had aggregated the most runs in a season in the history of Ranji Trophy till then.

Shreyas lifting the trophy with Pravin Amre as the coach of Mumbai team was his way of paying back his coach. Amre proudly witnessed his favourite ward blossom into a run machine.

'I can't describe the feeling. When he became the highest scorer in Ranji Trophy season and won the title for Mumbai, all those big names who doubted his technique and resisted his inclusion in the Mumbai team were now on their feet, applauding Shreyas. That was such a gratifying moment for me,' Amre was overwhelmed while recounting that moment.

Making it to the Indian team looked like a matter of time now!

## Reality check and the turnaround

Shreyas Iyer's success in 2015 had set the template for Delhi Daredevils to rebuild as a team – 'Invest in youth' was the strategy.

As they hit the auction table in 2016, Rishabh Pant was picked up for Rs 1.9 crore. The Rajasthan Royals were suspended for two years for their alleged involvement in spot-fixing and illegal betting. Daredevils decided to draw the cream from the Royals, who had been fairly consistent in the IPL till 2015.

Rahul Dravid, fresh from coaching the India U-19 team in the U-19 World Cup team, had moved to Daredevils from Royals. Sanju Samson, a find at Royals in the previous two seasons, joined him. Karun Nair, having impressed Dravid at Karnataka and India 'A', also found a place in the Daredevils line-up. Then there was the debatable bid of Rs 9 crore for Pawan Negi. Mahipal Lomror and Khaleel Ahmed were the other boys straight out of the U-19 World Cup.

The Daredevils' set-up was in for an overhaul. Dravid was at the forefront of it.

Shreyas had to earn his place again. Scores of 0, 3, 0 and 19 in the first four matches of the tournament brought back the question marks over his technique all over again.

Dravid found a flaw in his technique that indicated he would struggle against international quality bowling. It was his exaggerated shuffle as the bowlers ran into bowl and the loose hands going towards the ball. The assumption was that any moving ball at sheer pace would have been trouble.

Shreyas got another two matches in the tournament and could muster another 11 runs in them.

'I remember we were in Raipur in the finishing stages of the tournament. I was going for a walk very early in the morning and I saw Shreyas sitting in the hotel lobby at 6.30 in the morning. We got chatting and he talked about how low he was at that time. We had a long chat and I got him to believe this is just a phase in his career. It will pass. He didn't need to overthink,' Valson recalls.

Weeks after the IPL in 2016, a second-string Indian team was supposed to tour Zimbabwe for a T20I series with MS Dhoni leading the team. The dreadful IPL season had undone the two superlative Ranji Trophy seasons.

Shreyas had missed the bus as rookies like Yuzvendra Chahal, Jasprit Bumrah, Rishi Dhawan, Faiz Fazal, Barinder Sran, KL Rahul and Mandeep Singh all got an opportunity to play under the captaincy of MS Dhoni on that tour.

The selectors sent him to Australia with the India 'A' team the following month. Shreyas didn't really go berserk on that tour but he was slowly regaining the confidence of Dravid – 165 runs with a highest score of 62 in five one-day matches in challenging conditions.

'Rahul (Dravid) had called me up from Australia for some work regarding Daredevils. Then he talked about Shreyas' progress. He said Shreyas looked top notch. And that was conveyed to Shreyas as well. Such praise coming from a legend like Rahul can do wonders to a player's confidence,' Valson remembers.

Back to the rebuilding phase.

The runs didn't really dry up. They weren't just coming in heaps as they did in the preceding two years.

Defending champions Mumbai finished runners-up. Shreyas had a quiet season compared to his lofty standards in Ranji Trophy cricket. Yet, he finished as Mumbai's highest run-getter with 725 runs. He had reached a stage in his career where he had got the measure of the standard of bowling in domestic cricket.

The form never nosedived. His consistency and a double hundred for India 'A' in a warm-up match against the touring Australian team brought him within touching distance of the India cap in March 2017.

India captain Virat Kohli was ruled out of the series-deciding fourth Test in Dharamsala due to a shoulder injury. Shreyas was flown over. Kohli and then Team India coach Anil Kumble observed him bat in the nets for a good one hour.

Stand-in skipper Ajinkya Rahane decided to go with an extra spinner in Kuldeep Yadav instead of replacing Kohli with a frontline batsman. The wait got a bit longer.

When the IPL 2017 came, Shreyas, Rishabh Pant and Sanju Samson combined to form the batting core for the perennially struggling Daredevils who again finished sixth in the table. Shreyas had scored 338 runs while Rishabh and Sanju had scored 366 and 386 respectively.

Sunil Valson says this was the time when these young boys were liberated. 'Shreyas had already seen two unsuccessful years at the franchise. These boys realised they had nothing to lose. They decided to play fearless cricket and not worry about the pressures from the franchise. They knew if they performed, they would be noticed and could grow as players.'

Shreyas had regained his rhythm. A superlative hundred against a touring New Zealand 'A' side, followed by his quintessential dominating 138 against Tamil Nadu in Ranji Trophy was now enough for the national selectors.

On 1 November 2017, the India cap was handed to him at Feroz Shah Kotla in Delhi for a T20I match against New Zealand. He got a run of six T20Is (against New Zealand and Sri Lanka) and scored 83 runs in five innings before earning the ODI cap on 10 December in Dharamsala against Sri Lanka.

Scores of 88 and 65 in the series suggested a long run with the Indian team was in the offing.

The grind, in no way, was over for Shreyas. The year 2018 was going to accentuate it!

## IPL captaincy and the never-ending grind

The promising start to his international career booked him a spot in India's ODI team touring South Africa in February 2018. Little did he know the three opportunities (out of the seven games) were going to be his last for eighteen months.

Back in India for the IPL, Daredevils had decided to bring in an experienced IPL skipper in Gautam Gambhir who had won two titles for the Kolkata Knight Riders. Gambhir's IPL career was into its last lap and it was meant to end with the team where he started the journey. Ricky Ponting had joined as head coach.

Before the season got underway, an excited Shreyas said: 'When Ricky speaks to the team, it gives goose bumps. He doesn't just talk about process. He talks about winning matches.'

Nothing changed for Daredevils though. Six matches into the tournament, turbulence hit the Daredevils camp. They could win just one match.

A press conference was called at the Feroz Shah Kotla with the captain and coach addressing it.

Gambhir dropped a bombshell.

'Looking at where we are in the points table as a leader of the ship, I've decided to step down. I have announced Shreyas Iyer as the next captain and this is the right way forward.' That was the last that people saw of Gambhir in IPL cricket.

The prelude to Shreyas assuming captaincy is fascinating. There was an instance before the season when he contemplated moving out of Daredevils. The rough experience of 2016 and an average season in 2017 had him thinking about better opportunities.

When the retentions happened for 2018, he was valued under Rishabh Pant and Chris Morris.

Sunil Valson narrates the phase. 'There are times when players start expecting more when retention comes. It's not that Shreyas made an issue. There were franchises going around to get the youngsters at Daredevils. Shreyas mentioned it once or twice. His father used to be in touch. He is a top guy. I sat him down with his father and explained to him that he might end up losing money in auction if the bidding doesn't go your way.

'If he went to Mumbai Indians, he would be one in many

Indian youngsters there. Here, we had invested in him and saw a leader in him. He understood that he would be secure and play all matches and grow. That will be good for his international career.'

Handing over the captaincy to him at that point wasn't easy. Shreyas was having a quiet tournament and Rishabh Pant was evolving fast and was the only performer in the first six matches. But Shreyas had a better record as an India player.

Pravin Amre explains the move. 'He was around with the team for four seasons. He had seen the transition and understood the culture. I recommended to owner Kiran Gandhi that we needed to invest in a young leader who would carry the team for years. Ricky, too, agreed.'

This was the same season when Rishabh had exploded as a cricketer and scored 684 runs in the season. Shreyas was the next highest run-scorer for Daredevils that season with 411 runs. Even as Daredevils finished last in the season, one could sense the house was finally being set in order with Shreyas and Pant playing lead roles.

As the IPL ended in 2018, India had entered the World Cup year which was scheduled to happen in England in 2019. A place in the middle-order was up for grabs.

The Indian team got on the road but Shreyas was left craving for an opportunity.

The No. 4 spot in the batting line-up would become the most-debated topic in the country for a year. Ambati Rayudu, Dinesh Karthik, Manish Pandey and Rishabh Pant were all tested in one international series after the other. And here was Shreyas Iyer who was hopping cities and countries, playing for India 'A' and domestic cricket.

The performances never tapered. Airports became his second home.

In October of 2018, Shreyas single-handedly won a Duleep Trophy final for India 'B' with a sublime 114-ball 148.

No exaggerated celebrations, he walked off the field as if it was just another day in office. He was unphased, bordering on being numb, by whatever was happening around him.

'I have stopped thinking about selections. Earlier, the selection process used to play with my mind. I didn't react when I was selected. I know I am in the scheme of things. It doesn't matter even if it's on and off,' he claimed after the match.

He then offered a peek into his mindset while dealing with this unending grind. 'I realised it's not just me but there are many others who are not being selected. I saw their frustration. Even in other sports like football there have been players who do well for their clubs but are not picked for the World Cup.'

Amre says: 'He used to get very upset during that phase. He was on the road continuously, but it wasn't translating into rewards. We talked about it and decided that it was the only option we had. We can't be thinking about selections.'

Abhay Sharma, fielding coach of the India 'A' team, would say someone like Shreyas had accepted the tricky situation very well. 'Shreyas was not a rookie who was coming from India U-19s. For such players, the pressure is huge. He knows there's pressure coming from fresh U-19 batches and then there's no space in the senior India team. You are basically sandwiched. But he received the situation really well. He was receptive and mingled with the boys in India 'A' teams. He understood he could never let his performances dip.'

The IPL 2019 came. Delhi Daredevils were now Delhi Capitals. He was now leading veteran India cricketers like Shikhar Dhawan, Ishant Sharma and Ravichandran Ashwin.

He led the team to the play-offs after seven years, finished with 463 runs but the call-up for the India team never came.

Rishabh and Dhawan were part of India's World Cup campaign and Shreyas kept waiting.

## Cementing a place in Team India

The indecision surrounding the No. 4 spot came back to haunt Team India big time in the 2019 World Cup. India could never recover from the top-order collapse in the semi-final against New Zealand. There was no player who had got a relatively long run at that position. The team paid for it.

Indian cricket was in 'rebuild mode'. Shreyas Iyer was now an integral part of the plan. And he was on the flight to West Indies for the first series after the World Cup. Rishabh Pant was identified to bat at No. 4 followed by Shreyas at No. 5.

Two mature, finely paced knocks of 71 and 65 caught the eye of captain Virat Kohli who was scoring two hundreds at the other end. Kohli had found the missing link in his middle-order. His power game had gone up several notches.

Shreyas followed it up with a couple of half-centuries in the next two ODIs that India played against West Indies in India. There was the consistency that Kohli would forever harp on.

Shreyas Iyer was a regular feature in India's playing XI in ODIs and T20Is. It was obvious to the naked eye that he was in absolute control of his game.

The tour to New Zealand in January 2020 was going to establish him as the reliable middle-order batsman Indian cricket has been searching for since Yuvraj Singh and Suresh Raina. A maiden century in the first ODI followed by a couple of half-centuries. India lost the series 0–3 but Shreyas Iyer came back as the latest superstar of Indian cricket.

When cricket resumed after the Covid-19 pandemic-induced lockdown in September in 2020, Shreyas gave a lowdown, in an interview to the *Times of India*, on his evolution as a batsman.

*'There were a few ups and downs, but I am glad that happened at an early stage because it taught me a lot of things as an individual. And I learned a lot from my failures.*

*'No player is consistent right through his career. I still remember that phase where I wasn't. I was scoring runs but in bits and pieces. My average didn't drop for sure. But I wasn't satisfied from within. But now when I look at myself, I know I've been performing in every game.*

*'A few years ago, I made a certain pattern about my batting. I know when to take singles and when to change my game. Looking at greats like Virat Kohli, Rohit Sharma, MS Dhoni, I picked up a few qualities from all of them and try to replicate in my game.*

*'I was comfortable leading Delhi Capitals also (he wasn't a regular in Indian team then) because I had the two great minds in my team, Sourav Ganguly and Ricky Ponting. They were making my job pretty much easy. But this time, being consistent in the Indian team, it gives me a lot of pride and also responsibility as a player to be captaining such an amazing team. It has given me a sense of belief that I can really dominate at this position and also win everyone's heart at the same time.'*

The maturity, which came from his run as captain of the Delhi Capitals, reflected in his game. He breached the 500 run-mark in the IPL for the first time in the tournament played in the UAE in 2020. The Delhi Capitals finished runners-up. That was the first time this franchise made it to the IPL final.

Shreyas Iyer was the face of the Delhi Capitals. His 'no-look six' (a shot where he doesn't watch the ball after striking it) had become his signature.

There was a small hiccup awaiting him in Australia in November of 2020. He struggled against the short balls directed at him on the fast and bouncy pitches of Australia.

Questions over his technique against top-quality fast bowling were back. This time he had a reply ready.

Upon his return from Australia, he wasted little time and headed to Amre.

'Clearing his mind of all doubts was the first task. I had gone through the same thing when I was typecast while playing for India. I didn't want Shreyas to be doubting himself,' Amre reckons.

In the first T20I against England in Ahmedabad, he walked out to bat with the scoreboard reading 20/3. Jofra Archer and Mark Wood were bowling thunderbolts at over 150 kmph. In a batting line-up which had Shikhar Dhawan, Virat Kohli and KL Rahul, Shreyas was the lone man standing tall to the quick, nasty short balls from the English pacer.

He sashayed around the crease and kept hitting over point. He kept doing it throughout the series and English pacers had no answer to it. Amre recalls that knock of 67 off 48 in the first T20I as Shreyas' best.

Amre concisely sums up the performance of his favourite ward: 'That's the best I have seen him batting. He played the short balls well. That was his reply to his critics. He was driving so well down the ground. He had worked so hard on his power game and that 'no-look six' was a result of months of hard work as he needed to have that other element in his game. The best thing about Shreyas is that he always found a way to score runs.'

Shreyas' grind against perceptions culminated when he reached Kanpur again on 25 November 2021. It was Dravid, who had doubts about his technique five years earlier, who was in charge of the Indian team as the head coach. Dravid got Sunil Gavaskar to present Shreyas his Test cap on the morning of the match against New Zealand.

Shreyas literally turned back the clock, played a similarly counterattacking knock like he did against UP at the same venue seven years earlier, bailed India out of a hole, scored a century on debut, followed it up with half-century in the second innings and announced he was ready to play an integral part in Indian middle order across formats.

Shreyas Iyer has never had a smooth journey. He was never the quintessential 'gifted' cricketer. But as Amre says, he always finds a way!

# CHAPTER 8

# WASHINGTON SUNDAR: THE DARK HORSE

## *A name for a cricketer's aspirations*

Washington Sundar. Unusual will be an understatement while describing the name of a boy born into a Hindu family in Chennai. It raises an eyebrow when you hear it for the first time. In a usual world, the boy would be explaining his name to people for a major part of his life. Instead, by the time he was sixteen, Washington had ensured the world, beyond his neighbourhood and school, knew his name.

Washington was a public figure at the age of sixteen. We'll come to that later.

First, let's get the story behind his name out of the way. M. Sundar, his father, was a committed cricketer from a very humble background. He even got very close to becoming a First-Class cricketer for Tamil Nadu. He was in the list of probables for Tamil Nadu's Ranji Trophy team from 1993–96.

A couple of streets from his residence in Triplicane lived an ex-army man named PD Washington. Sundar wanted to stick to cricket but he didn't have the financial cushion to sustain a career in cricket. PD Washington was his mentor here.

From buying him uniforms and books, to paying his school fee and taking him around to grounds to play cricket, PD Washington did everything that a young Sundar needed to give some shape to his life. Sundar played most of his cricket at the Marina Cricket Ground and he would invariably find his mentor watching him play from the other side of the boundary.

Sundar had decided that if ever he had a son, he would name him Washington Jr. Sundar was first blessed with a daughter Shailaja.

Eight years on, when Sundar's wife was expecting the second time, PD Washington had passed away. A few months later, after a complicated delivery, Sundar was blessed with a son.

It was a no-brainer. Sundar named his son Washington. 'Mr PD Washington is my godfather,' Washington would say. Sundar had ensured that Washington knew who this person was and why he owed his life to him. He went on to have a major influence on how Washington carried himself.

Sundar's aspiration of raising a cricketer first came through Shailaja. Sundar ran a home-run academy and his daughter started making rapid strides. She was the first person from the Shailaja family to represent Tamil Nadu. She played for U-19s, Tamil Nadu senior team and the South Zone team.

Shailaja would be the guiding 'big brother' to Washington in his growing-up years.

'I don't ask her about cricket, but she tells me at times what I should be doing (like big sister bully),' Washington would later say with a smile. 'I never talk much about my cricket, but my mother and sister tell me more about the game because they are more interested in following my cricket. It's annoying, but nice.'

'My father saw some kind of talent in me when I was six–seven years old. I used to accompany him for cricket matches (Sundar kept playing division matches) and I used to see him play. He used to feed me balls, and I used to bat,' Washington recounts his early days.

Whenever Sundar got him to knock a few tennis balls between sessions during his games, people would gather to watch him. Toddler Washington had a languid bat swing and the natural elegance of a left-handed batsman made him a treat to watch. Washington would keep knocking tennis balls at home too.

In such circumstances, it's convenient to assume cricket was forced on Washington. But everything happened rather organically for him.

'To be frank, I didn't think about anything. I always loved playing cricket, morning, evening. Since I like this game, I always play,' Washington would promptly dispel all aspersions.

Cricket was in his blood. It was time to nurture his talent!

## Growing up fast, making rapid strides

Sundar had taken it upon himself to tap the talent of his son and polish it. Shailaja and Washington went through the paces at his academy. Shailaja, a batter and a leg-spinner herself, would bowl to her brother and often get him out in the initial days.

Sundar had to be the hard taskmaster. Staying idle during practice was a strict no. For all his distinct talent with the bat, Washington was made to practice every discipline in cricket. Even before he turned ten, Washington was trying everything in the nets. He was bowling off-spin, leg-spin, medium pace and even keeping wickets.

Off-spin was decided to be his secondary skill after batting. Sundar observed he had the natural loop and dip. The accuracy seemed innate. At the age of ten, Washington was playing with the U-14s in academy matches in and around Chennai. The runs flowed from his bat and the consistency with the ball added a dimension to his cricket.

While young Washington was still raw and at a nascent stage of learning the trade, Sundar was in no mood to waste time on him. Washington went through a drastic growth spurt by the time he turned twelve. From a distance, he looked like a sixteen- or seventeen-year-old.

Age-group cricket was not the solitary ambition now. The father believed his son had it in him to play with the men.

Thus came the first major point in his life. The only way Sundar could see Washington play in competitive men's cricket in Chennai was if a stalwart in the Chennai circles saw him practice with men. In 2012, Washington was twelve when Sundar sent him to the MRF Pace Foundation to practice.

Till not so long ago, the MRF Foundation, based in the campus of Madras Christian College Higher Secondary School in Chetpet, was the dream destination to train and learn for fast bowlers across the country. It was founded in 1987 in collaboration with former Australia fast bowler Dennis Lillee, one of the most fearsome pacers in his day in the 1970s and the '80s. Through this foundation, Lillee had developed a programme for a country starved of fast bowlers. Having a National Cricket Academy (NCA) was not even an idea for the Board of Control for Cricket in India (BCCI).

Kapil Dev was the only Indian fast bowler to look up to well into the '90s. Hence, every aspiring fast bowler wanted to be a part of a learning experience from the best. From Javagal Srinath to Zaheer Khan to S Sreesanth, every fast bowler to have played for India till the first decade of the twenty-first century went through the programme at MRF pace academy. In essence, it was the hub for hungry fast bowlers.

Back to Washington. 'I did not go for any selection or such thing like that. My dad just asked me to go and practice at the MRF Pace Foundation,' Washington recalls.

The twelve-year-old was literally thrown into the deep end by his father. Unaware of the aura of the place, Washington walked in for practice. For the fast bowlers there, batsmen were merely a depiction of target practice.

In hindsight, batting against such strong pacers is quality practice for young batsmen.

'I was scared, to be honest. Facing bowlers with a speed of 140 kmph in the nets is different than facing them in the match. In the nets, they are not scared of bowling no-balls so they come forward and bowl,' is Washington's honest confession.

To put things into perspective, there was a certain Varun Aaron training at the foundation. At the time, Aaron was the face of a pace-bowling revolution in the country. He had made his debut for India and was earmarked as the fastest bowler in India. He was breaking the 150 kmph barrier quite often.

M Senthilnathan, an India U-19 captain in 1988 and a former Tamil Nadu cricketer, was the coach at the Pace Foundation and he kept an eye on this shy young boy batting in the nets.

'I went there and batted for two days and, on the third day, Senthil sir came and spoke to me and signed me up with Globe Trotters. I played in my first match in the TNCA 1st Division League at the age of twelve.' His initial days in men's cricket will always be etched in Washington's mind.

Young Washington, now fondly called Washi by everyone in the cricket circles, was rubbing shoulders with men who were twice his age. And since Chennai's local cricket structure is one of the strongest in the country, you have former India players playing in it.

'That was my first longer-format game (three-day) and I was under pressure. The game was against India Pistons. They had few experienced cricketers. I was not scared. Yes, there was nervousness but at Globe Trotters we had many seniors like Aniruddh Srikkanth while Sridharan Sriram led the side. When I made my debut, Varun Aaron and Venugopal Rao were still around. They helped me, guided me. I remember I opened the batting,' Washington remembers.

Washington amassed 596 runs and took 33 wickets from 11 games in that league. Not even a teenager then, Washington stood tall in a crowd of full-grown men. It was time to dream big!

The who's who of the coaching fraternity in Chennai began taking active interest in Washington now. Tamil Nadu stalwarts Divakar Vasu and M Venkataramana took him under their tutelage. Shailaja and Sundar were always in his ears to give advice. A team was being formed that would work on this boy. It was his support system now. Sundar was also travelling with his son to most matches.

Washington cruised through the U-16 level of cricket. A deluge of runs and meaningful spells with the ball in U-16 cricket took him to NCA. High-performance training happened to him at a very tender age. He was there at a younger age than most cricketers in the country.

Like he did as a twelve-year-old at the MRF Pace Foundation, Washington was not going to settle down at the U-16 level.

After two years of grooming at NCA, Washington served up a special reminder to the caretakers of cricket in India that he was ready to graduate to the higher level.

The Karnataka State Cricket Association (KSCA) organises a pre-season invitational tournament, where senior state teams from across the country come to Bengaluru to play and prepare for the domestic season. It usually happens in August–September.

In 2014, Washington was picked to play for the senior NCA

team. The special knock came at the Chinnaswamy Stadium in the final of the tournament against a Haryana team, which had 2007 World T20-winner Joginder Sharma and Harshal Patel in it. Washington was just fifteen at the time.

'Before the first day of the game, we all went to Chinnaswamy Stadium. We had some ball game to get acquainted with the ground, but did not have any practice. I was just visualising how it will be if I get a big 100 in the final. It is a big tournament for the preparations for Ranji Trophy,' Washington vividly remembers the day he thought he could break into the big league.

With a cloud cover and a seaming pitch on offer, Haryana seamers had taken 2 wickets in the first 30 minutes of the match. Washington was hanging in there. He was joined by Sudip Chatterjee, a twenty-one-year-old left-handed batsman coming through the ranks from Bengal.

By the end of the first day, Washington was batting on 152. Chatterjee had scored 162 himself.

'It was big,' Washington exclaims. NCA defeated Haryana in that final.

Former India batsman Brijesh Patel was at the stadium.

'Brijesh sir spoke to my dad. My dad doesn't tell me what others say about my innings,' Washington says. Clearly, Sundar didn't want his son to get ahead of himself even though the teenager was already on the freeway to bigger things.

Young Washington was identified and the U-19 World Cup in 2016 was close to becoming a reality.

## U-19 World Cup and transformation from opener to off-spinner

'My father has struggled a lot in his days and he wanted me to be a good cricketer. He saw my stroke play and flair and thought I could play some big level. This game is something I am passionate about. He thought someday I can make it to the Indian team, but I didn't think I would be part of Under-19 team.'

Washington Sundar, only sixteen, was mature beyond his years when he was representing India in the U-19 World Cup in Bangladesh in January–February 2016. He was shy and so quiet that you wouldn't know he is in the same room if he didn't speak.

On paper, Washington was picked as a top-order batsman. Opening the batting, he was the highest run-getter in a tri-series in Sri Lanka in December. He had scored 208 runs in the four matches he played on the sluggish pitches in Colombo.

U-19 India coach Rahul Dravid wanted to figure out the best opening pair between Washington, Rishabh Pant and Ishan Kishan. So, he rotated the players in the tournament.

Ishan and Rishabh's hard-hitting ability at the top earned them the opening positions for the U-19 World Cup. Washington was always going to be an important cog in the middle-order though.

Destiny had a different road to success in store for Washington though.

From a common man's view, it appeared that Washington's role was to bat in the middle order and chip in with some overs of off-spin. He started the tournament with a 62 against Ireland, went through a dry spell in the middle and scored a crucial 43 in the semi-final against Sri Lanka besides holding up one end with his accurate off-spin as India finished runners-up in the tournament. At best, he qualified as a part-timer.

Few knew that Dravid and his team of support staff, particularly bowling coach Paras Mhambrey, had identified something in his bowling that could make Washington an off-spinner of international quality.

There started a project of sorts to convert Washington into a frontline off-spinner. But there was a rider within the team management. Washington mustn't know about the plan.

In the previous tournament in Sri Lanka, he bowled 26 overs and got 3 wickets at an economy rate of 4.80. That's where Mhambrey and Dravid got interested in Washington's bowling.

'I was not given much bowling because there were not many left-handers in the opposition. In the tri-series in Kolkata (in November 2015), Bangladesh had three left-handers and I bowled. Against Afghanistan, they didn't have any left-handers I didn't get to bowl. Since we have two good left-arm spinners and three quicks, I get to bowl only when left-handers come,' is all Washington could make out.

'From the time I started playing cricket, I never liked only fielding. It's a boring job. So, I always like to bowl six–seven overs, so that 20 overs go off closely.' He was happy being a part-timer.

He wasn't aware about the work that went into his bowling. Three days ahead of the final against West Indies in Dhaka, Mhambrey, while having a casual chat with the author, divulged their plan around Washington.

'The first time I went and saw him was during the tri-series in Lanka. I feel that he has something. He has a little tweak in his fingers, he gets the ball to rip. Tall guy (standing at over 6 feet), gets a lot of bounce and if he gets consistent and gets his spin going, he'll be good. We're working with that, that's why you will see him bowling a lot more in the nets right now. He bats, he does his fielding – but whatever time he spends, maybe half an hour or 40 minutes, I want him to bowl because I want him to think like a bowler,' Mhambrey said at the Bangladesh's National Cricket Academy at the Sher-e-Bangla Stadium in Dhaka.

All of that had to be done very carefully. Washington was a reserved boy. It's difficult to understand what's going on in his head. One couldn't just assert himself on him. The management didn't know how he would react if he was told that his batting had now become a secondary skill.

Abhay Sharma, former Railways captain who led Railways to their maiden Ranji Trophy win, has been a part of Dravid's core team of coaches. He was there with the U-19 team as the fielding coach in Bangladesh.

'Washi was a very quiet and shy boy. He was impeccably mannered; the other boys liked to have fun, pull pranks and be expressive. You need to be careful with the boys who are quiet and don't express much. We decided to have competitions while training and make Washi a captain of one team. So, he had to talk about what he felt. We got an understanding how he actually feels about things,' Abhay recalls.

Washington, literally, had to be tricked into bowling more.

'We couldn't break the news to him that we felt he was a much better off-spinner than a batsman. We had made a rule that nobody would be idle during training. Everyone had to be involved in some activities after they were done with practising their primary skills. That way we got Washi hooked on to bowling.'

Mhambrey could see their plan taking shape leading up to the final. 'I think now he is kind of realising that he is developing into a better bowler. We put him in a situation and want him to bowl in difficult situations,' Mhambrey had opined on the eve of the final.

By the last week of the tournament, the blisters on his index and middle fingers were evidence of the grind Washington was put through.

On 14 February, the India U-19 batsmen collapsed against a pacy West Indian attack led by Alzarri Joseph. The Boys in Blue folded for just 145.

But there was much fight left in the Indian boys. Washington put the West Indian batsmen under immense pressure with his probing off-spin. The guile, turn and bounce were a lot to handle for even the likes of the free-scoring Shimron Hetmyer. Hetmyer, leading the Caribbean side, could score 23 off 53 balls.

A couple of catches went down off Washington's bowling. He went wicketless but his figures of 9–1–18–0 had applied enough pressure from his end for left-arm spinner Mayank Dagar to return figures of 3/25 from his 10 overs. India had made a match out of it. But they had too less to defend. West Indies scrambled home in the last over with 5 wickets in hand to win the U-19 World Cup.

Washington's performance with the ball in the final only substantiated the belief of the team management. He had proved he had the temperament to handle extreme pressure.

It was time to build on it. But the road ahead remained tricky.

## TN debut, IPL break and evolution of the off-spinner

For all the belief Dravid and Mhambrey had in Washington's off-spinning abilities, the real work was needed to be done after the U-19 World Cup.

'He needs to pursue this, be consistent, go out and hit the nets a lot more. Bowl a lot more,' Mhambrey was literally imploring while speaking to the media on the eve of the World Cup final.

'I feel he has the capacity to maybe get better as an all-rounder. He's a little better than what he looks. But he needs to bowl a lot more in the nets and at First-Class level to get that experience and confidence. And once he does that, he can get better. We are kind of working on that, we're pushing him.

'He has got a role model from the same state (Ravichandran Ashwin). Someone who he can follow.'

Ashwin too had played most of his junior cricket as a top-order batsman before growing into a prolific off-spinner.

You could sense how excited Mhambrey was seeing the potential of Washington. The resemblance in physique and career paths between Ashwin and Washington was uncanny.

Dravid, Mhambrey and Abhay also looked after the India 'A' teams. But since Washington didn't really set the stage on fire in the U-19 World Cup, he wasn't going to break into the 'A' team immediately.

What Mhambrey was concerned about was if his growth as an off-spinner would hit a roadblock once he made it to the Tamil Nadu team later in the year. Washington always preferred to call himself a top-order batsman.

'It's going to be a little difficult to break that thinking (considering himself an out-and-out batsman), so you kind of have to dig in and say okay it's not just batting, I need you to bowl as well. It's taken a little while but you see him bowling a lot in the nets nowadays,' Mhambrey said before leaving Bangladesh.

Later in 2016, Washington was selected for Tamil Nadu's Ranji Trophy team. At the age of seventeen, he was handed his First-Class debut in the opening game of the season against Ranji giants Mumbai in Lahli, a picturesque ground set in the middle of agricultural fields around 10 kilometres from Rohtak in Haryana. That year BCCI had decided to play Ranji Trophy matches at neutral venues.

The pitch in Lahli is considered to be a seamer's paradise. The water table at the ground is high and it aids prodigious seam and swing right through a First-Class match.

Washington was thrown into the deep end. He was opening the innings for Tamil Nadu on the first morning of the match. He hung around for 32 balls before he got out caught behind off Dhawal Kulkarni for just two. The second innings was going to be a tougher scrap. After battling for 113 balls and scoring 40 runs, Kulkarni got him in an identical manner. Tamil Nadu lost a low-scoring thriller by just 2 wickets.

That 40 remained Washington's highest score that season. He played another four Ranji Trophy matches that season and added just 45 runs to his tally after the first match. His bowling, however, was taking shape. Not used to bowling long spells, he still managed 7 wickets in his five matches at an average of 28.42.

Hrishikesh Kanitkar, a former India all-rounder, was coaching the Tamil Nadu team that year. He too had noticed the potential off-spinner in Washington.

The Tamil Nadu team persisted with Washington when they picked the team for the Vijay Hazare Trophy (50-over tournament) that season. He went down the batting order and started working harder on his off-spin. His dead accuracy coupled with variation in pace made him the go-to bowler for captain Vijay Shankar who was mentored by the veteran Dinesh Karthik from behind the stumps.

Washington mostly played in the latter half of the tournament. The Tamil Nadu team arrived in Delhi March 2017 to play the knockouts of the Vijay Hazare Trophy. He was cementing a place in the Tamil Nadu XI with his miserly spells.

In an informal interaction during a practice session at the Feroz Shah Kotla, Washington was just reminiscing the time spent in Bangladesh during the U-19 World Cup the previous year.

When the author asked him if he was aware how he subconsciously turned into a bowling all-rounder from a batting all-rounder, Washington wore a perplexed look. He probed for a bit and he was told how Dravid and Mhambrey subtly went about getting him hooked on to bowling off-spin. Eyes wide, Washington shook his head and then said with a smile: 'Glad they did it.'

Like the U-19 World Cup final, Washington bowled another frugal spell in the Vijay Hazare Trophy final against Bengal at the Feroz Shah Kotla.

Batting first, Tamil Nadu scrapped to a total of 217 thanks to Dinesh Karthik's 112 and Washington's hand of 22 coming at No. 7. While defending the target, Washington applied the choke on seasoned batsmen like Manoj Tiwary and Shreevats Goswami. Washington's figures read 8–1–17–0. The Bengal batsmen succumbed to the pressure and fell short by 37 runs.

Tamil Nadu were the champions and a seventeen-year-old Washington Sundar played a significant part by taking 4 wickets in the six matches he played at an average of 30.25 and an economy rate of 3.27, which is a rarity in modern-day cricket. He followed it up with a similar performance in the Deodhar Trophy against strong India 'A' and India 'B' sides.

A fortnight later, it was the IPL season. Washington, unlike a lot of his mates from the U-19 India team, was sitting at home without a deal. In 2017, the IPL had two new teams playing in place of the Chennai Super Kings and the Rajasthan Royals who were suspended for two years for their alleged involvement in spot-fixing. Rising Pune Supergiant and Gujarat Lions filled in.

MS Dhoni and Ravichandran Ashwin were bought by Rising Pune Supergiant (RPSG). Interestingly, the management decided to go with Steve Smith as the captain ahead of Dhoni.

A week before the tournament got underway, Ashwin was ruled out of the season because of a sports hernia.

Kanitkar was in the coaching staff of RPSG. He convinced the management to punt on Washington.

'When I took charge of Tamil Nadu in the preceding season, Lakshmipathy Balaji told me about his talent and that was it. He has a repetitive action and lands the bowl on the spot. We wanted an offie once we got to know that Ashwin was not going to play. Washington wasn't on anybody's radar. I suggested his name to Pune management,' Kanitkar was quoted by the *Times of India*.

In RPSG's fourth match of the season, Washington was named in the playing XI against the Sunrisers Hyderabad. He didn't get to bat but he made an impact right away with the ball.

Smith threw the new ball to Washington in the second over of the match. He was up against world-beaters like David Warner, Shikhar Dhawan and Kane Williamson. He held his own and came out with figures of 3–0–19–0 in what turned out to be a high-scoring game.

Soon, Washington became Smith's go-to man as RPSG made it to the final. The seventeen-year-old brought out his A game yet again in a final. This time it was the daunting Mumbai Indians which struggled to get him away in Hyderabad. With a spell of 4–0–13–0, Washington set the tone for a low-scoring humdinger. The Mumbai Indians were restricted to just 129. But the RPSG fell one short of completing a fairy tale run.

Washington didn't have any discernible variations in his armoury. It was his sharp mind and unwavering accuracy that saw him through 11 matches with an awe-inspiring economy rate of 6.16 and 8 wickets.

All those hours that Sundar had spent in making Washington bowl with the new ball and then bowling in the difficult overs in his pre-teen days was now reaping dividends while he played with the big boys.

Here was an off-spinner who had captured the pulse of T20 cricket. And there was much more to offer.

## Road to India debut

For all the work done on him from the India U-19 days, Washington was conveniently labelled as a product of the IPL post his impressive debut season. He was the talk of the town but it was imperative to have a solid domestic season to make the next level.

When New Zealand 'A' came to India in August of 2017, Washington was still not considered to be part of the India 'A' side. At that point, he could neither be qualified as a frontline off-spinner, nor were his batting performances encouraging enough.

The national selectors wanted to test him out at the First-Class level first. He was picked to play for India Red in the Duleep Trophy in September 2017.

As it turned out, the final of the tournament was lit up by two seventeen-year-olds – Prithvi Shaw and Washington Sundar. If Prithvi's captivating knock of 154 in the first innings made the headlines, Washington was coming into his own as an all-rounder.

On a rank turner of a pitch in Lucknow, Washington scored a critical 88 while batting at No. 7 to back up Prithvi's belligerence at the top of the innings. He then turned up to bowl and ran through the India Blue batting line-up to end up with figures 5/94. The maiden First-Class half-century and five-wicket haul was off his back.

But he wasn't done yet.

In the second innings of that match, he scored another vital 42 before dismantling India Blue with a spell of 6/87 to take India Red to a title. He had dismissed Suresh Raina in both innings and in contrasting ways. Raina was deceived to get beaten on the outside edge and stumped in the first innings while getting rapped on the pads off an arm ball in the second. Washington had outfoxed one of India's profound players of spin bowling.

Washington was named the player of the match. Washington Sundar, the First-Class player had arrived.

This performance pleased his mentors from the India U-19 team to no end. Abhay was at the venue as coach of one of the three teams playing the tournament.

'By that time, it was obvious Washington had understood that his bowling will be critical to his growth. He didn't fuss about batting. He always did take the initiative when it came to batting. He would slyly offer to open the batting. The confidence in his batting was intact. But he very well realised that it was his bowling which was going to take him to the higher level of cricket,' Abhay claims.

Just when Washington was firming up his chances to make the grade, news from the NCA came in. He had failed the Yo-Yo test, a test to determine a player's endurance and agility. Experts, however, reckoned that taking such an intense test was unfair after he had just played a First-Class tournament.

Weeks later, Washington registered his maiden First-Class century. The 159 came against Tripura in Agartala. In the six Ranji Trophy matches he played that season, Washington had taken 12 wickets and chipped in with 315 runs floating in the batting order.

The selectors had seen enough. It was time to blood him into the national side. The Indian team for a T20I and ODI series against Sri Lanka at home had Washington's name in it.

Washington wore the India cap for first time at the age of eighteen on 13 December 2017 when India took on Sri Lanka in an ODI in Mohali. The match saw Rohit Sharma score his third double century in ODIs and Washington's steady spell of 1/65 in 10 overs in a high-scoring game went under the radar.

Ten days later, he made his T20I debut against the same opposition. He was in his element straightaway. A spell of 1/22 in four overs at a traditionally high-scoring Wankhede Stadium showed how neat he had become in the format.

Washington Sundar's stocks was on a significant rise. The stellar performance in the following Syed Mushtaq Ali T20 tournament only corroborated it – 12 wickets in nine matches at an economy rate of 6.88 and 190 runs at a strike rate of 115 was just helping to build a solid reputation.

Four days after Tamil Nadu's campaign ended in the Syed Mushtaq Ali tournament, the Royal Challengers Bangalore had bought Washington Sundar for Rs 3.2 crore.

The past few months ensured Washington was on the plane to Sri Lanka to play the Nidahas Trophy (a T20I tri-series involving Sri Lanka and Bangladesh). India had sent a second-string team of sorts under Rohit Sharma.

That was also barely six months since Ravichandran Ashwin and Ravindra Jadeja were dropped from the white-ball scheme of things. Wrist-spinners Yuzvendra Chahal and Kuldeep Yadav were identified as the soldiers for ODIs and T20Is. They were, in fact, at the forefront of the wrist-spin wave that swept world cricket from 2017.

Washington was about to challenge that. Kuldeep was rested for the tournament and Washington found a place in the playing XI ahead of Axar Patel.

He finished the tournament as the joint highest wicket-taker along with Yuzvendra Chahal, both claiming 8 wickets each in five matches. Washington topped the charts with an astounding economy rate of 5.70.

Washington came back as the player of the series.

'Wrist spinners are magical. But I do feel finger spinners can be as effective. An off-spinner can be as effective provided he is proactive. If you can double-guess the batsman and be one-up on the mind games every ball, you can be good too,' Washington told the *Times of India* upon his return.

It was a simple philosophy but a huge statement coming from him because he was a quiet guy.

The subsequent IPL wasn't going to be smooth sailing. The Chinnaswamy Stadium, the home ground for the Royal Challengers Bangalore, is a six-hitting cauldron for bowlers. It's a six-hitting paradise for batters. He did his job in some crunch overs but finished the IPL with just 4 wickets in seven matches as his economy rate took a hit at 9.60.

It was just a learning curve!

## Of setbacks and comebacks

The below par performance in the IPL didn't have any bearing on the selection for India's subsequent tour of the UK in the summer of 2018. Washington was in the UK ready to challenge the fast-evolving concept that wrist-spinners are a better option than finger-spinners in limited-overs cricket.

India were supposed to start the tour with a T20I against Ireland in Dublin. A week ahead of the first match of the tour, Washington twisted his ankle while playing football during warm-ups at training.

His tour was over. Washington was literally bed-ridden for nearly four weeks since the incident.

The rehab happened at the NCA. Washington was back up on his feet for three Vijay Hazare Trophy games and then back in the Indian team for a T20I series against West Indies at home.

That one match against West Indies in Chennai where he took 1/33 runs was going to be his last international match for another nine months.

India travelled to Australia for a full tour which started with three T20Is in late November. Washington suffered another setback. The fitness test got in his way again in Australia.

The rigours of international cricket were real now.

He was still a nineteen-year-old. Handling him through this was going to be key again. And the onus was back on Dravid and his team.

Abhay recalls that phase: 'I remember we were with the India 'A' team in New Zealand while the Indian senior team was in Australia. Washington faced some fitness issue and he was sent from Australia to New Zealand. He was really down. You could see he wasn't in the best of shape.

'That's when Rahul, Paras and I spoke to him a lot. He is a reserved boy. He doesn't share much. But we had to put our arms around him and talk him through. We laid out the reality for him. He was told what he needed to do and that we were there for him. However much fame and money one may earn but one always remembers the people who guided him through during trying times. He is a very sincere kid and we knew he would bounce back.'

Washington went back to the drawing board. Put himself through intense fitness sessions and he was back leaner and fitter for the IPL 2019. He got just three matches in the tournament as the Royal Challengers Bangalore finished wooden-spooners.

The turnaround happened after the 2019 World Cup.

The magic of wrist-spinners Chahal and Kuldeep had started to fade. Washington Sundar was identified as the bankable bowler in T20 cricket. He was now a regular in the playing XI, and bowling in the Powerplay was his niche.

Skipper Virat Kohli's plans in T20 cricket revolved around Washington's bowling prowess. No fancy variation in repertoire, Washington was out-thinking world class batsmen with ease. His temperament rarely betrayed him.

The IPL in 2020 in the UAE elevated his stature as a T20

bowler. Eight wickets in 15 matches at an economy rate of 5.96 played a key role in the Royal Challengers Bangalore making the play-offs after four years.

The Indian team flew to Australia in November 2020. Washington wove his magic again in the T20I series.

The special phase in his career was around the corner. And it was his unexpected initiation to Test cricket.

## Emergence of a Test batting all-rounder

India coach Ravi Shastri held back all the bowlers from the white-ball squad for the four-Test series in Australia. With travel restrictions in place due to the pandemic, Shastri wanted to have as many options available as possible for unforeseen circumstances.

Shastri's hunch was right. India went to Brisbane for the last Test of the tour with the enthralling series tied at 1–1. India had lost Jasprit Bumrah, Mohammad Shami, Umesh Yadav, Ravindra Jadeja, Ravichandran Ashwin, Hanuma Vihari and KL Rahul to injuries during the tour. After being bowled out for 36 in the first Test, Virat Kohli had come back to India for the birth of his first child.

In Ashwin and Jadeja, the Indian team had lost their first-choice spinners. Kuldeep was the third specialist spinner on tour. Playing Kuldeep would not help the team maintain the balance it had struck with its combination in the previous two Test matches.

Shastri and bowling coach Bharati Arun's plan was simple. Get a like-for-like replacement for Jadeja. Kuldeep's inferior ability with the bat wouldn't help. Arun had seen Washington train hard and picking the brains of Ashwin through the tour.

The team management decided to punt with Washington. On 15 January in 2021, Washington had become a Test cricketer for India. He was filling in for Ashwin – something Mhambrey had predicted five years ago!

Washington was given the task of holding up one end, bowling tight wicket-to-wicket lines, while the pacers went for wickets. His perseverance got Steve Smith to play a false shot and he had the world's best Test batsman as his first wicket. Washington had taken 3/89 on a historically fast-bowler friendly Gabba pitch in his first outing in Test cricket.

His maiden Test innings was even more special. Coming in at No. 7 and scoreboard reading 161/5, Washington batted with the tail. With Shardul Thakur supporting at the other end, his languid stroke play fetched him 62 runs on debut as India cut the deficit to 33 runs.

When Rishabh Pant was taking India close to a historic win while chasing 328 in the last day, Washington joined him with 63 runs still remaining.

Two boys who played their U-19 cricket together five years ago were about to deal a telling blow to the famed bowling attack of Pat Cummins, Josh Hazlewood, Mitchell Starc and Nathan Lyon.

'When Washi came to bat, he said to me '*Macha* I'll go for the target',' recalls Rishabh. 'I said I want to go big too but he said I should stay since I was set.'

Washington knocked the wind out of the Australians when he hooked Cummins for a six bowing with the second new ball. Things started to fall apart for Australia from there on as Rishabh also got into the act.

'Rahul Dravid had always told these boys never take a step back and show that you are under pressure. That shot off Cummins testified it,' Abhay says.

He was batting on 22 off 28 balls when an overdose of

adrenaline got the better of him. He was bowled by Lyon while attempting a reverse-sweep with 10 runs still needed. He stood there dejected for 10 seconds and dragged himself off the field.

But Rishabh finished the match off and these boys became a part of a major chapter in India's Test history.

'I am disappointed, he didn't get a hundred,' Sundar senior's words in the media echoed the hunger in Washington.

Yet, the Test match was too special to be overshadowed by his expectations. Upon his return from Australia, Washington named his pet dog 'Gabba'!

Back in India for the four-Test series against England a fortnight later, Washington played a couple of crucial innings with the tail. The unbeaten 85 in the first Test in Chennai did not result in a win but he served up another special with Rishabh in the series-deciding fourth Test in Ahmedabad.

While Rishabh scored a superlative hundred on a tricky pitch, Washington deflated the English attack which had James Anderson and Ben Stokes with an unbeaten 96.

When Mohammad Siraj and Ishant Sharma were knocked over by Ben Stokes, the helpless expression on Washington's face touched a million hearts. The maiden Test century eluded him. But he had done enough for India to register a win by an innings.

'I don't want to think much about it. I'll surely get there (century),' is all Washington would say.

For three years, Washington has choked the world's best power-hitters in T20 cricket and now he has showed he can dominate world-class bowling attacks in challenging conditions.

Washington's temperament had always made him the dark horse in Indian cricket. He is now galloping towards dizzy heights of success!

# CHAPTER 9

# DEEPAK AND RAHUL: A DREAM FAMILY PROJECT

## *Making of a dream family project*

The Chahar family believes in destiny. They also realise that it's an unwavering passion towards the purpose of one's life that can make your destiny. For this family from a village around Agra, cricket became a purpose.

When cousins Deepak and Rahul boarded a flight to West Indies with the Indian team in August 2019, life came full circle. It was destiny that the brothers, born seven years apart, were about to represent the country in international sport.

If you trace their journey, obstinacy played a bigger part in the rise of the duo.

Cricket was never going to be a way of life for the Chahar clan if it was not for Lokendra Singh Chahar's stubbornness. Lokendra never played competitive cricket though. Working for the Indian Air Force, posted at Hanumangarh Air Force station in Rajasthan, he dared to dream to make cricket a career for his son Deepak.

'I wanted to be a cricketer. My father wanted me to be a wrestler,' Lokendra confesses. 'I participated in wrestling for three–four years. I didn't get the support that is needed to play cricket. I can't really blame my father for the decision. We lived in a village. There were no options. Wrestling was the best sport to pursue then.'

When Deepak was born in 1992, Lokendra hoped his son would take a liking to cricket. Deepak was his second-born after daughter Malti.

'Deepak was more interested in cricket than I had been,' Lokendra says.

Lokendra was not going to let Deepak's fascination for cricket fade away. 'I had decided that my son would get all the support that I didn't get when I wanted to become a cricketer as a kid,' Lokendra says rather emphatically.

'Deepak was average in studies. So, I decided *ab* cricket *hi khelenge* (it will be only cricket).'

Deepak was around twelve years old when Lokendra noticed his keen interest in the game. Deepak would largely play in the gullie*s* (bylanes). What struck Lokendra was that he stuck to bowling medium pace and he seemed to enjoy it.

Lokendra decided to enrol Deepak in an academy in Hanumangarh. The academy was around 12 kilometres away. It took him around 40 minutes to reach the academy one way.

A decision had to be made, and a bold one at that: After Deepak completed his eighth standard Lokendra decided it was time that Deepak stopped going to school and focus all his energies in his game of cricket.

Lokendra has an explanation for this: 'I observed that Deepak got just one or one and a half hours to play after school. The commute to the academy was also long and tiring. I realised he would never become a successful player if he only played one and a half hours a day.'

Quitting school wasn't the end of it. Lokander decided to take it upon himself to train his son. '*Maine* decide *kiya ab main hi* coach *karunga* Deepak *ko* (I decided that I would only coach Deepak).'

'I had a basic working knowledge of the game, but hardly any about the technicalities,' Lokendra concedes.

The admissions do not stop here.

'Nothing about Deepak is natural,' he would say.

It's difficult to fathom how a bowler with the expertise to swing the ball both ways against top-quality international batsmen had very little innate skills to work with.

Lokendra doesn't beat around the bush. He had developed a philosophy. '*Ek kaam saalon saal karte hain toh* normal *ho jaata hain* (If you keep working on developing something for years, then it comes to you naturally). Naturally talented players don't understand what exactly they are doing. They can't swing the ball both ways. If you ever see a bowler who swings it both ways that means he has worked very, very hard.'

There was passion and ambition in abundance. For technical expertise, the father-son duo began to rely on the internet. This was still the pre-smartphone era. It was, in fact, even before broadband services became a norm in India. People were still figuring out how India would get 2G; 4G was a distant dream.

Watching videos on the internet wasn't easy. But Lokendra and Deepak soldiered along. That was the only way to have access to top-notch technical expertise.

They broke down fast bowling to four essential aspects.

Lokendra narrates: 'We understood that a successful pace bowler must have four qualities. First things first, we needed to swing the ball. Then came speed. A fast bowler should bowl at

140 kmph and then come accuracy and variety. One can't afford to get stuck with, let's say, bowling just outswingers.'

Now, it was about gathering enough knowledge to possess those four qualities.

'We selected a few bowlers to follow. They were Waqar Younis, Malcolm Marshall and Dale Steyn. Steyn's outswing was magical.'

Then a plan was drawn. They were going to tick one box at a time. The first thing would be to get the ball to swing and accuracy. 'Our belief was that we could work on his speed later.'

The routine was chalked out and both set off on a mission – 500 balls were to be bowled every day. And this was besides the training Deepak had at the academy.

'I would make Deepak bowl 500 balls under the streetlights. I would catch the balls. And he bowled with leather balls. The 500 balls were divided into 250 each of outswing and inswing. He couldn't have been a one-trick pony,' the father says.

Deepak would play for Ganganagar district and make his way into the Rajasthan Under-15 team. Things looked to be going just fine when Lokendra had another big decision to make.

The Air Force was transferring Lokendra to the southern part of India. And Deepak was settling down in the Rajasthan cricket system.

'I decided to take voluntary retirement from the force. If I had been shifted to south India, it would have disrupted Deepak's growth as a cricketer. I used to coach him. I always had to monitor his progress. By that time, he had played U-15 and went to England with the Rajasthan team. If we had moved then, Deepak would have had to start from scratch all over again,' Lokendra recalls.

The senior Chahar was into full-time coaching now. He went

to Agra and started a small cricket academy in his hometown. Lokendra calls it a 'family project'. And this is where the story of Rahul Chahar begins.

Rahul is Lokendra's younger brother's son. As Deepak went through the hard yards, young Rahul too wanted a piece of that action.

'When we went to Agra, Rahul was only eight years old. He used to watch Deepak train and he was fascinated by it. Rahul used to bowl medium pace just to follow what Deepak was doing. I wasn't very serious with Rahul. Seeing the way Rahul bowled, I couldn't risk him playing cricket,' Lokendra says of his apprehension to invest in Rahul.

It was Deepak who had discovered Rahul's potential as a leg-spinner. Leg-spin is said to be the one of the toughest arts in cricket. As Rahul struggled with medium pace, an idea struck Deepak. He asked Rahul to bowl leg-spin one day when Lokendra was not around.

When Lokendra reached the practice area, Deepak animatedly said: 'Papa *isse dekho. Yeh* leg spin *theek dalta hain* (Dad, check this out. He bowls decent leg spin).'

Rahul was on trial for some time before Lokendra was convinced that the boy could be invested in.

'I found him to be good enough as a leg-spinner. He got into a good rhythm in six months. It was then decided that he may pursue cricket as a career,' Lokendra mentions.

Taking drastic decisions for your own son is bold but controlling your younger brother's son's life becomes a sensitive topic. There is a lot at stake here. Getting Rahul's father Desraj on board was the next step.

Lokendra narrates the sensitive phase. 'I had selected just two boys from our family to play cricket. There were four boys in the family. I took entire responsibility of Rahul. I told his dad that whatever happens to Rahul (good or bad), I'll be responsible.'

Like Deepak, school would now become a no-no for Rahul too. Rahul went to school till the fourth standard.

'They (Deepak and Rahul) didn't go to school. They just appeared for exams. They were not good in studies. My brother supported Rahul because he wasn't good in academics. Deepak was still OK. But Rahul was worse than him. So, there was no confusion between cricket and studies. Cricket was the only way.'

Lokendra had mapped out a career path for the two brothers. With Deepak already in the Rajasthan cricket system, working on a career in Rajasthan was thought to be a safer option for Rahul.

Rahul shifted to Bharatpur with his parents. He was now playing from Dholpur district.

## Deepak's grind: Chappell era to memorable Ranji debut

After he played U-15s for Rajasthan, Deepak wasn't selected for U-17 the next year. The competition in Indian cricket is so cut-throat that winning your place back in the system is an arduous ask. If you are out of the scheme of things once, it's difficult to get back in. It's almost an unwritten rule.

Lokendra recalls: 'Deepak performed well in U-19 district cricket. He didn't get any space in the Rajasthan team because there was one bowler who was close to India selection, one was at the National Cricket Academy and then there was another bowler coming through the ranks.'

It was also the time when Lalit Modi, the brain behind the inception of the IPL, was the strongman in Rajasthan Cricket Association and was enjoying a monopoly.

Indian cricket had not yet recovered from Greg Chappell's contentious stint as Team India coach, Modi had roped in the services of the Australian legend to oversee the ambitious Rajasthan Cricket Academy in Jaipur.

The first project Chappell initiated was to make a pool of 50 fast bowlers from U-19s, U-23s and the senior team. And it was decided that only these bowlers would play for Rajasthan across age groups.

Lokendra vividly remembers the prerequisites set by Chappell. 'Chappell's requirement was that the aspiring pacers should be more than 6 feet in height, athletic and strong. And it was said that they will look after how these bowlers would be groomed.'

Rejected for U-17s, Deepak had pinned his hopes on the trial to make it to Chappell's pool. 'Deepak was only sixteen and a half years old. You are not that tall or strong at that age. Deepak's height was 5 feet and 11 inches. He was not selected. The situation was such that if you missed the bus then there is no chance left,' Lokendra recounts how agonising the times were.

'Deepak went up to Chappell to ask them why he wasn't selected. Chappell told him off, saying he would never become a top-level cricketer. Chappell said he was only picking those he believed could go on to become big cricketers and represent India. Such a cricket great told us that Deepak couldn't play a higher level of cricket,' Lokendra says with an unusually heavy voice.

'Had Chappell stayed around for another three or four years, Deepak's career would have been over,' he states.

The situation for Deepak was grim. And then news trickled in that Chappell was stepping down from his role. In 2010, Tarak Sinha, the most revered coach in Delhi cricket, was given charge of the Rajasthan Cricket Academy. Former India pacer Manoj

Prabhakar, Sinha's first student and a swing-bowling trailblazer in India, was appointed the head coach of Rajasthan's senior state team.

In Lokendra's words, Tarak Sinha came as an angel for Deepak. Sinha decided to hunt talent from scratch. He went to each district of Rajasthan to get an idea of the talent available.

Deepak was training in Hanumangarh. According to Lokendra, Sinha didn't say much to Deepak.

He was seventeen and had not played state cricket after the U-15s. And then the turning point came.

Lokendra recalls: 'I received a call from RCA. They asked me where Deepak was. I said he was in Agra. They asked me to inform him that he was going to Australia with the Rajasthan senior team. Just imagine someone who didn't play after the U-15s was now supposed to travel with the senior state team and that too on a tour of Australia.'

Sinha was impressed by the boy's ability to swing the ball both ways and his physique. Prabhakar is a pioneer of swinging the ball both ways. In their eyes, Deepak was an exciting prospect. Sinha had also tested Deepak alongside U-19 boys.

'It was a huge promotion. Credit should go to Tarak Sir. He had said he will play all the matches in Australia.' Lokendra was now indebted to Tarak Sinha.

Deepak bowled well on that tour. He was now up against bowlers who were at India level. Deepak took 21 wickets in four matches. He shot past everyone else.

Aakash Chopra had now come to terms with the fact that playing for India was implausible for him. Delhi was also looking to rebuild with Shikhar Dhawan and an exciting teenager Unmukt Chand. So, he decided to run the last lap of his First-Class career with the Rajasthan team as a professional cricketer.

Former India all-rounder Hrishikesh Kanitkar had also joined him from Maharashtra.

Rajasthan, still considered as minnows in Indian cricket, played Buchi Babu and Moin-ud-Dowlah tournaments (two renowned pre-season tournaments in Bangalore and Hyderabad).

Chahar reminded Chopra of Prabhakar and captain Kanitkar found a lethal weapon in his artillery. Aakash had stuck his neck out, took to Twitter on 9 October 2010 and announced: 'I've spotted a young talent...Deepak Chahar in Rajasthan. Remember his name...you'd see a lot of him in the future:)'

'They say if you are destined to reach somewhere an opportunity will surely come your way. First, it was Tarak Sir and, now, Kanitkar,' Lokendra states with all humility.

Rajasthan started the Ranji Trophy in the 2010–11 season from the Plate Group. They were not part of the Ranji Trophy Super League. Only two teams from the Plate Group could qualify to the quarterfinals and be promoted to play in the Super League next season.

The headline of the opening day of that 2010–11 Ranji season came from Jaipur. Eighteen-year-old Deepak Chahar had figures of 7.3–2–10–8 against Hyderabad in the first 90 minutes of the season. There was assistance from the pitch, a nip in the air but it wasn't a minefield by any stretch of imagination. Deepak's 8/10 on debut rolled over Hyderabad for 21.

Rajasthan amassed 403 before Deepak returned to pick 4/54 in the second innings to seal a big win.

It set the tempo for a magical season for Rajasthan.

Rajasthan turned into giant-killers when they made the quarterfinals. They knocked out Mumbai and Tamil Nadu in the quarters and semis before prevailing over Baroda in the final.

Deepak's figures of 4/79 and 3/15 in the two innings of the final capped off Rajasthan's maiden Ranji Trophy title. Deepak had claimed 40 wickets in the season.

It marked the beginning of an era when every state team started to believe that they could win the premier domestic tournament.

## Rahul's rapid rise and U-19 World Cup heartbreak

Rahul Chahar's rise through the ranks in Rajasthan was less eventful. He was following the lead of his elder brother Deepak.

Deepak has been the biggest influence on Rahul. Since Deepak was already in the system, he would pick technical nuances from the various camps he would be in.

Whatever Deepak learnt or heard about leg-spin from coaches, he would come back and teach Rahul.

Like he said of Deepak's bowling, Lokendra doesn't mind conceding that Deepak wasn't naturally athletic. Both Deepak and Rahul had to go through some thankless strength-building routines.

'Deepak's fitness is not even 50 per cent natural. Deepak is athletic but not strong. Rahul was also slow and weak. Deepak *ko* fitness *karwata toh* Rahul also joined in. So, Rahul reaped the benefits at a very young age,' Lokendra claims.

Like he had decoded the prerequisites for becoming a successful seamer, Lokendra realised that a spinner can't be too slow through the air or off the pitch.

'As a spinner, you need speed. Our focus was to make him strong so that he could bowl quick leg-spin. For example, Afghanistan's star leg-spinner Rashid Khan's core is among the best in the world,' Lokendra says.

Going by Lokendra's words, Rahul's journey was relatively

comfortable. There were no issues with his selections in both district and state teams in junior cricket.

Rahul had developed varieties in his bowling from a very young age. The googly was his lethal weapon. 'He would take 4–7 wickets in every district match. *Itne* wickets *ikatthe karta thha* (he used to accumulate so many wickets) any selector would pick him without even seeing him,' Lokendra remembers.

Rahul was always a cut above the rest in age-group cricket in Rajasthan. If he picked 35 wickets in a tournament, the second highest would be 15.

'It was never that it happened just one season. He repeated it. Batsmen at the district level were bamboozled by him. They struggled to play him. He hardly had to worry about selections,' Lokendra says.

As he moved on to playing for Rajasthan in the U-16 Vijay Merchant Trophy and U-19 Cooch Behar Trophy, Rahul's growth happened exponentially.

'When you play in board tournaments, that's where your temperament and bravery is tested. He had worked so much on his fitness that he would bowl 25–30 overs without breaking a sweat. With his repertoire, if you bowl 30 overs in a match then you are bound to pick up at least 3–4 wickets. He would even take even 6 or 7 wickets in an innings,' senior Chahar would say.

By the time he had just turned seventeen, Rajasthan gave him the First-Class cap in a match against Odisha in Patiala on 5 November 2016. He didn't have much of an impact on the match but he had made a statement with his long spells.

He was so dominant in the U-19 tournaments that he was nearly at par with batsmen Prithvi Shaw and Shubman Gill.

In 2016, India U-19 coach Rahul Dravid had identified Rahul

as one of his key spinners leading to the U-19 World Cup in New Zealand in January 2018.

Abhay Sharma, India U-19 fielding coach, throws some light on Rahul's first impression at the NCA.

'One of the things we wanted to ensure while identifying a U-19 batch was that we would always keep a leg-spinner. Besides his ability to turn the ball sharply at a quick pace, the thing that struck us about Rahul was that he bowled very straight and wicket-to-wicket and he had a deadly googly. If you closely observe his forearm, it's very strong. That helped him giving the ball a real rip,' Abhay recalls.

Rahul was now meant to travel with the India U-19 team for every series.

In his first tournament for India U-19, Rahul bowled his team to a win in the 2016 U-19 Asia Cup final against Sri Lanka with a magical spell of 3/22. He then followed it up with a strong performance in England in 2017, returning the highest wicket-taker for India U-19s in one-day matches.

In between, he had made his List A debut for Rajasthan in the Vijay Hazare Trophy and had a very steady tournament. An IPL contract also came his way in 2017 to make him the third youngest Indian to get one. We will come back to it later.

It seemed nothing could go wrong for Rahul. He was speeding on a barren highway.

But there is this undeniable underlying anxiety in players coming from states which are not considered powerhouses in the country. Historically, ex-cricketers have claimed that they had to suffer because of the apathy of the power forces in Indian cricket towards 'smaller' states.

Abhay remembers how Rahul had suffered from those insecurities. 'He is a confident boy but he would always undermine himself when he first came into the U-19 team. That happens with boys from states like Rajasthan which hardly had any representation in Indian cricket. It took some time for him to understand that when you come to the NCA or India U-19 teams, all the players are seen through the same glass.'

Soon, Rahul's worst fear was about to come through. Rahul Chahar's name went missing from India's U-19 team which was supposed to fly to New Zealand for the U-19 World Cup in January 2018.

There were reports that a BCCI office-bearer had meddled with the selection and chairman of the junior selection committee Venkatesh Prasad got into a tiff with the official. The official wanted to have one representation from his home state association in Jharkhand. Prasad lost the fight and leg-spinner Pankaj Yadav was on the plane to New Zealand. Pankaj had not played a single match for India U-19 in the run-up to the World Cup.

'Rahul had to endure an incident which was worse than what Deepak had to go through. Rahul was the highest wicket-taker for India U-19s for nearly two years. He was also made to do promotional shoots with three–four-star U-19 players for the U-19 World Cup. And then he learns he was dropped overnight,' Lokendra recounts.

'His father and I went to pick up Rahul from Jaipur. He was bawling after seeing me. We stayed back that night. He was very upset. I told him that you don't have to feel so low. You have the performance. Rahul Dravid also said that you are very good. Don't worry. Everything will be all right,' Lokendra spoke like a caring uncle now.

Abhay explains the goof-up on the part of the team management that could have led to this mishap. 'Rahul was doing really well for us. He was one of the first ones in that batch who was identified. He was certain to travel to the U-19 World Cup.

He was playing a lot of cricket then. There was one tournament just before the World Cup. It was a challenger series. The team management thought he should be rested so that he could come fresh to the World Cup. And then we get to know he fell off the radar in the selection meeting.'

Rahul suffered a rude shock, but his journey would pick up pace from this disappointment.

## Deepak's road to IPL and India break

The 40 wickets in his debut Ranji Trophy season in 2010–11 shot Deepak to the limelight. An eighteen-year-old Deepak was well past Greg Chappell's denigration. The Rajasthan Royals brought him into their fold in the subsequent IPL season but Deepak didn't get a game.

There's a theory in Indian cricket. The first domestic season of a player only suggests the talent; it's the second and third season that establishes a player.

Indian cricket was about to go through a massive transition post the victorious 2011 World Cup campaign. Zaheer Khan, Ashish Nehra and Munaf Patel were entering the last phase of their careers. The Indian pace-bowling pool needed fresh faces.

Right before the 2011–12 Ranji Trophy season, he got injured. He missed the season and Rajasthan retained the Ranji title. A spate of injuries would go on to plague his career.

As Deepak missed the season in 2011–12, Lokendra and he got down to reviewing his bowling. There's one thing that then national selector Narendra Hirwani had told Lokendra during Deepak's first Ranji Trophy season in 2010–11.

'I was there during a match in Kanpur. Narendra Hirwani had told me that Deepak was a good bowler but was very slow. He couldn't have played for India with that pace,' Lokendra vividly remembers.

Hirwani's words stayed with Lokendra.

Deepak and Lokendra had embarked on this cricketing journey thinking Deepak will swing the ball both ways, have all varieties, and speed should be 140 kmph. It was time he increased his pace.

But it wasn't going to happen overnight. Neither was it easy to figure out how the desired pace could be attained.

'The problem was that the action he had, he could swing it well but couldn't bowl quick. And if he went for pace then it would impact the swing. We tried multiple actions. It was a huge risk to change the action at that stage of the career,' Lokendra says.

The quest to reinvent himself coincided with sub-par performances for Rajasthan.

In his comeback season in 2012–13, Deepak got just one wicket in two Ranji matches. Much of it could easily be attributed to the injury he sustained the previous year. He did look like striking form in the 2013–14 Ranji Trophy season, taking 21 wickets from four matches.

Things would unravel fast for him from here on.

'It wasn't just the injury. There was inconsistency in Deepak's performance. Somebody else was preferred ahead of him. That was a bad time,' the father would concede.

The performances dipped and Deepak was fast fading away from the consciousness of Indian cricket. The next two Ranji Trophy seasons would fetch him 33 wickets in 14 matches.

The father-son duo was still trying to accomplish something that they had long desired. The work on his action never stopped.

Lokendra describes the research and development that went behind reviving his son's career:

'His action was very side-on like Irfan Pathan. We tried multiple actions to balance pace and swing. Then we zeroed in upon Dale Steyn. Steyn used to swing the ball at high pace. We started trying the action of Steyn. And it seemed to work. The swing and pace were both there. His action is now largely based on Steyn's style.

'It takes you three or four years if you change the action. We had made up our minds, that no matter what, we will bowl at 140 kmph and swing the ball. That was the only chance to progress. If he got into an IPL team, there could be a chance he would have played for India within a year.'

In 2016, his first Ranji Trophy captain Hrishikesh Kanitkar was part of the coaching staff at Rising Pune Supergiant (RPSG). The RPSG were playing their first season of the IPL after they were brought in following the suspension of the Chennai Super Kings for two years due to the alleged involvement in spot-fixing. The RPSG had retained most of the core of the Chennai Super Kings with MS Dhoni as captain and Stephen Fleming as coach.

With no performance behind him, Deepak went for the trials at the RPSG. Kanitkar was always fond of Deepak. But this twenty-three-year-old Deepak was a different bowler now. He had developed a bagful of variations and the ball went briskly off the pitch. Fleming too liked what Deepak did.

RPSG picked him at his base price of Rs 10 lakh. The price mattered for little. This is where he would catch the attention of Dhoni.

Over the two years at RPSG, Deepak had just five games and a solitary wicket to show. He was a work in progress.

The focus was now on the shorter formats. Deepak turned a corner in the Syed Mushtaq Ali T20 tournament in 2017–18. With 19 wickets and an economy rate of 5.58 in nine games for

Rajasthan, Deepak was again a sensation after seven years of his stellar Ranji Trophy debut.

The Chennai Super Kings were back in business in 2018. Deepak fit the bill for Dhoni. One must remember that Dhoni's guidance as an India captain had seen Bhuvneshwar Kumar flourish. Deepak's ability to swing the ball both ways was reminiscent of Bhuvneshwar and he was consistently bowling over 135 kmph and nudging the 140s.

Deepak was bought for Rs 80 lakh. He was in a team captained by Dhoni.

Dhoni backed Deepak to the hilt with the new ball. He played him in 12 matches in the tournament. Deepak repaid Dhoni's trust by taking 10 wickets and going through the tournament at an economy rate of 7.28.

In the final against the Sunrisers Hyderabad, Deepak's spell of 0/25 in four overs proved the difference between the two sides.

The Chennai Super Kings were the IPL champions on return and Deepak was one of the major driving forces.

It was time for the big leap.

The national selectors picked him in the India 'A' team for a tour of England in another three weeks. Sixteen wickets in six List A games ensured he was in the Indian team for a T20I series in England that July.

On 8 July 2018, Deepak Chahar was walking out to represent India in an international match for the first time. It was a rude initiation. He returned figures of 1/43 in four overs as Jason Roy and Jos Buttler got stuck into him.

Two and a half months later, he received his ODI cap in a match against Afghanistan during the Asia Cup in Dubai.

The ODI debut was every bit painful as the T20I debut.

Having stepped down from the position in 2017, Dhoni was captaining the Indian team as designated captain Rohit Sharma was being rested for the game.

A burly and maverick Mohammad Shahzad went hammer and tongs from the word go. Dhoni could give Deepak just four overs which cost him 37 runs and a wicket. Dhoni relied on the other bowlers to peg Afghanistan back after Shahzad had hit a whirlwind 124 off 116 balls. Afghanistan were restricted to 252/8.

In reply, India couldn't get past the target and the match ended in a tie. Deepak learnt a bit about the thankless world of international cricket.

The selectors kept him in the scheme of things though. After another productive IPL season in 2019 (22 wickets in 17 matches at an economy of 7.47), Deepak was sent to England to help the Indian team prepare for the World Cup.

As Indian cricket hit a transition mode after the World Cup, Deepak was on the flight to West Indies. He played just the final T20I of the three-match series and shared the new ball with Bhuvneshwar. He overshadowed Bhuvneshwar with a spell of 3/4 in three overs.

Captain Virat Kohli was thrilled to have an option in his ranks to back up Bhuvneshwar. Bhuvneshwar returned home from the tour with a hamstring injury.

Over the next few months, Deepak would be the go-to bowler with the new ball in the T20Is.

In the next T20I against South Africa in Mohali, he picked up 2/22 in his four overs to set the tone for a comfortable win.

Soon after the match got over, he made a revelation about his rise. 'I know my limitation. I can bowl quick for four overs or in shorter formats. So, I conserve myself for shorter formats,' he said.

Lokendra elaborates: 'Deepak understands his body and limitations because nothing is natural about him. If bowling at over 140 kmph comes to you naturally, you can bowl 13–14 overs in a day. But if he worked on bowling long spells, he will be a 130 kmph bowler. If he bowls quicker than that, it would require more power. Chances of getting injured are more. The Indian team doesn't have a place for in-between bowlers. Either you have prodigious swing, or you stand out with pace and movement.'

On 10 November 2019 in Nagpur, Deepak Chahar became the first Indian bowler to do a hat-trick in T20I cricket. Deepak's moment of glory came in the second ball of his fourth over, when his yorker knocked over Bangladesh's Aminul Islam's off-stump. Shafiul Islam was his first victim off the last ball of his third over, while Mustafizur Rahman was his second.

Deepak had taken 6 wickets for seven runs and owned the best bowling figures in the history of T20I cricket.

Stereotyped as a bowler who could only bowl well with the new white ball, that night in Nagpur dispelled all doubts over his skills at the death.

'He didn't bowl much at the death for Chennai Super Kings because Dhoni had the roles divided and Shardul Thakur was entrusted with the job of bowling the final overs. But whenever he did go to Deepak in the final overs, he has rarely been taken to the cleaners. That hat-trick against Bangladesh proved he had become a complete bowler,' Lokendra says with a smile. He has the right to be proud.

Deepak became an integral part of India's T20 scheme. Aakash Chopra's tweet in 2010 had aged well!

## Rahul's road to success

Before Rahul was controversially dropped from India's U-19 World Cup team in 2018, he was on a roll. He made his First-

Class debut for Rajasthan in Ranji Trophy in 2016, besides becoming a regular in Rahul Dravid's India U-19 team.

After a solitary Ranji match, he represented Rajasthan in the Vijay Hazare Trophy in the same season and made an impact straight away, bowling tight spells. The purple patch had helped him quietly land an IPL contract with Rising Pune Supergiant in 2017.

The IPL break too came his way through elder brother Deepak.

'There was one year when he was on a roll and achieved a lot. He played India U-19 when he was barely seventeen. He was the highest wicket-taker in the U-19s. He was on every tour. The Ranji trophy debut happened and he became eligible for the IPL auctions. I filled up a form to enrol him for the IPL auction. Deepak was already with RPSG. Deepak had told coach Stephen Fleming to have a look at his brother in the trials. He was asked to come for the trial. Fleming liked him. And he got a contract with RPSG,' Lokendra says.

Rahul got three matches under the captaincy of Steve Smith and had decent outings with 2 wickets at an economy rate of 8.28 to show for his efforts.

It was all a learning curve and Rahul was literally racing through it before the India U-19 selection controversy happened. There were concerns about how he would pick himself up from there.

But he put all concerns to rest in the next tournament he played for Rajasthan. It was the Syed Mushtaq Ali T20 Trophy. It was the defining tournament for the Chahar brothers. Deepak was lethal with the new ball and was backed up by Rahul in the middle part of the innings in the four matches he played in the business end of the tournament in Kolkata.

Rajasthan made it to the final of the tournament and their last three opponents were Mumbai, Punjab and Delhi (the heavyweights in domestic cricket).

Rahul really turned on his magic against Punjab and Delhi. In a low-scoring match against Punjab, the eighteen-year-old was all over Yuvraj Singh. After labouring for four runs in 10 balls, Yuvraj went down the track to Rahul and was beaten by his vicious googly to be stumped by a fair distance.

That wicket reignited the zeal in Rahul. In the final against Delhi at Eden Gardens, Rahul put up another show against Gautam Gambhir who is referred to as one of the best players of spinners in contemporary cricket.

Gambhir was going great guns when Rahul was given the ball to bowl the final over of the power play. Rahul stood at the top of his run-up like he was on the prowl. He charged towards the bowling crease with such intent that his prey could barely move. Gambhir was beaten for five consecutive balls as the googlies fizzed past his outside edge. Each time he was beaten, Rahul looked him in the eye and promptly went back to his run-up. The sucker punch came off the last ball of the over. The vicious leg-break knocked over Gambhir's stumps.

Rahul Chahar had become a sensation.

The IPL auctions happened and Rahul went for a whopping Rs 1.9 crores to the Mumbai Indians after an intense bidding war with the Rajasthan Royals.

Dravid had assured Rahul that he would bag a big deal in the IPL. He wasn't off the mark.

Brothers Deepak and Rahul had bagged big deals that season. Deepak was at Rs 80 lakh. Lokendra shares a rather amusing story. He believes Deepak could have gone for a higher price if it wasn't an error in judgement on their part.

'*Humari galti thhi* (It was our fault). Deepak had filled the form for the auction as an all-rounder. But the all-rounder category came late in the day. Rahul went in as a bowler. Rahul's name came early in the auction. Deepak's came later. By the time Deepak's name was called, teams had exhausted a lot of the money. If the teams had money left, Deepak would have fetched more than Rs 2 crores,' Lokendra recalls.

'We had some idea that Rahul would draw huge bids. It was not a surprise or a fluke that he went for so much. But we expected Rs 1 crore,' Lokendra mentions.

The coaching staff with the India U-19 team couldn't have been more relieved. Abhay Sharma recalls: 'We (Dravid, Paras and I) used to be in regular touch with Rahul after the U-19 World Cup. Deepak used to be at NCA and we talked to him about Rahul and how he should be encouraged. After such an incident, boys of his age are bound to think that it's the end of the road. But Rahul is the prime example of the saying, 'You never know what God has planned for you.' God opened up a greater opportunity for him immediately. Rahul is honest and puts in a lot of effort. I can't recall an instance where he has gone for a lot of runs. He deserves every bit of the success.'

Rahul didn't get a game in the 2018 IPL campaign. Leg-spinner Mayank Markande from Punjab was preferred ahead of him.

He had got used to greater setbacks at a very early age. This was not going to bother him much. He was all about picking the greatest minds in the game at the Mumbai Indians – be it chief coach Mahela Jayawardene or Zaheer Khan.

Rahul had tasted blood in the Mumbai Indians camp.

He was about to take domestic cricket by storm later in 2018. In ten Ranji Trophy matches, he picked up 41 wickets at an average of 24.90. He followed it up with 20 wickets from nine Vijay Hazare Trophy matches with an average of 17.50 and economy of 4.28.

This was also the period when Indian cricket was drooling over wrist-spinners Yuzvendra Chahal and Kuldeep Yadav. The selectors had already picked him for Rest of India teams in the Irani Cup.

'Rahul didn't play the season after being bought for 1.9 crores. Markande and he are different bowlers. He worked really hard in the Mumbai Indians nets and the practice matches. Then the Mumbai Indians management realised he is better,' Lokander reckons.

When the 2019 IPL came around, the Mumbai Indians reposed their faith in Rahul as their lead spinner. Rahul would go on to pick up 13 wickets from 13 matches with a miserly economy rate of 6.55 as the team lifted the IPL trophy for the fourth time.

Zaheer Khan became his go-to man now.

'I go to Zaheer *bhaiyya* (Zaheer Khan) because I understand what he tells me. He understands my type of bowling and sometimes he even sits for an hour when I bowl. He took a separate session with me and told me the problems and solutions. Initially, I was bowling safe balls, I wasn't attacking, but he told me that I am an attacking bowler and can take wickets. He would ask me to go out and attack, and not to worry if I was hit for a six. He gives me confidence and tells me to bowl freely,' Rahul would say.

The stellar IPL ensured he was selected for two India 'A' series (against Sri Lanka 'A' at home and a tour to West Indies. Rahul bamboozled the batsmen in both series.

In a matter of a month from the 'A' series, both brothers were part of the Indian dressing room during a T20I series in West Indies. Rahul was identified as the back-up to Chahal and Kuldeep.

Rahul Chahar would go on to have a couple of more impressive IPLs for the Mumbai Indians and was, subsequently, breathing down Chahal's neck for a place in the Indian team.

## Life comes full circle

Deepak and Rahul, coming from remote towns from the hinterland, have defied all odds. Lokendra took on the onus of coaching them and they rarely questioned him or his motives. The brothers grew as cricketers at a time when their state association (Rajasthan Cricket Association) was suspended by the BCCI when Lalit Modi, banned by the board for alleged corruption in the IPL, was re-elected as its president.

RCA was run by an ad-hoc committee set up by BCCI. There was no one to speak for the players.

Here's how Lokendra sums up the journey: '*Yeh sapna thha dono saath mein khele* (It was a dream that both brothers should play together). When I started coaching, Rahul was not in the scene. *Maine tapasya* Deepak *ke liye ki thhi ki mera beta* Indian team *mein khele* (I had prayed and made sacrifices for Deepak so that I could see my son play for India). When Rahul joined, then it became about both of them.

'There were times when people would have been apprehensive about our mission. Confusion happens when you are good in studies and you are capable of becoming a doctor or an engineer or a civil servant or have a great career out of studies. Then you must put that on stake to play cricket.

'We knew they were not going to go any higher than becoming a sub-inspector because neither of them were good in studies. So, there was no confusion. As a back-up, we had thought of starting a business for them if cricket didn't work out.

'We had simplified everything. 'Work hard all day' was the mantra.

'When it came to fitness, it was all Deepak. I would only observe. Deepak was very passionate and used to watch videos. He had gone to the U-15 camps. He was crazy about fitness. He understood what was needed. As a thirteen-year-old, Deepak observed how trainers trained senior cricketers and he picked it up from them. He would arrange his fitness regimes and go to gyms and train accordingly. He puts fitness ahead of his cricket skills. Rahul inherited this habit from Deepak.

'In his early days, if coaches tried to tell Deepak something, he would not do it unless I was convinced.

'Battling apathy and playing from Rajasthan, which is considered a small state in terms of Indian cricket, was a universal problem for all cricketers in the state. Suppose you did well in domestic tournaments, selectors would say let them repeat it season after season. My two boys did that. They have realised they can always bounce back from adversities.

'The equation changed once the IPL arrived. It is now *janata ki awaaz* (the people's voice). If the selectors don't pick them when they are performing, they will face backlash.

'The player who went to the U-19 World Cup instead of Rahul didn't play a game in that World Cup. He doesn't even play Ranji Trophy and is nowhere close to the IPL.

'Mumbai Indians didn't play Rahul in the first season but once he got the opportunity, he ensured he performed. Now they trust him so much that they don't have a back-up.'

Lokendra is someone who coached these two kids but he himself never went to an academy, had no knowledge, trained himself and then trained the boys.

'When they toured for India together in West Indies, it was like life coming full circle for us,' he signs off.

# CHAPTER 10

# AVESH KHAN: THE GENTLE GIANT

## *The making of an accidental cricketer*

In a rather laidback city of Indore, a soft-spoken Ashique Khan was content running a small roadside paan shop. Selling candies to kids and making paan for the grown-ups was enough for Ashique to provide for his family on a daily basis.

Ashique Khan was the youngest of three brothers. His nephews and nieces were already married. There were 25 people in the house, three generations in all, living under the same roof. All Ashique aspired for was to marry off his two daughters and ensure his son Avesh, who was the second child, completed his education.

There was no time for unworldly dreams. Ashique typified a middle-class father of Indian society. The paan shop yielded enough resources to help the next generation to build a comfortable life. But it was not meant to be. One fine day the civic authorities razed the paan shop because the streets near the shop had to be widened. Ashique was almost forty then.

He promptly took up a job at a private company. The budget that his family was living on was insufficient and would not last for long. Setting up another shop would be tedious and time-consuming. That phase left a lasting impression on Avesh.

Avesh was a regular kid hanging out in the neighbourhood, playing cricket with tennis balls. It was no big deal. He was happy bowling quick to the neighbourhood kids. Ashique recalls his son always wanted to bowl.

'Everyone plays cricket with tennis balls. Even we used to play in our younger days. There's nothing special about it,' Ashique says, and he is quick to add, 'There was absolutely no plan of making Avesh a cricketer.'

Cricket in India, on either side of independence, was majorly influenced by the royals. So, the powerhouses outside Mumbai were largely in Saurashtra, Mysuru and Indore.

The Holkar dynasty in Indore was driving the cricket culture in the city. Col CK Nayudu and Col Syed Mushtaq Ali are the pillars of Indore's cricket history from the pre-independence era.

Indore's relevance in Indian cricket faded away as the game started growing pan-India. This is despite Rajsingh Dungarpur, a BCCI strongman for decades, hailing from the city.

The city did hunger for its share of role models. Narendra Hirwani and Amay Khurasiya offered some hope in the '90s followed by Naman Ojha in the second decade of the twenty-first century. But all of that was short-lived. Becoming a cricketer of international repute from Indore was reduced to a fallacy.

Ashique too had no such aspiration for his son. Living within two kilometres of the Holkar International Stadium wasn't enough to be an inspiration either. The city lacked the structure for cricket, and he was too caught up with everyday struggle.

'There was really no plan of Avesh becoming a serious cricketer. But I never stopped him from playing. *Bas kissi club mein daal diya* (It was just about enrolling him in some club),' Ashique says.

'*Mohalle mein jitney* teams *thhe, unmein khelta thha* (He

used to play for the neighbourhood teams). One day in 2007–08, Avesh came up to me and requested that he wanted to join a club,' Ashique recalls the plea of his eleven-year-old son.

Ashique never wanted to deny his son of trying his hand at something. Avesh was enrolled in a club called Indore Colts. It was around 10 kilometres away, on the other side of town, and buying a cycle to cover the distance was out of question because there was the matter of not being able to afford one.

'Initially, he would walk 1.5 kilometre to take a tempo (shared autorickshaw) to reach the club,' Ashique says. This arrangement was taking a toll on Avesh. Ashique bought him a second-hand bicycle. Avesh had to go for practice twice a day. That meant he cycled nearly 40 kilometres a day.

At the turn of the second decade of the 21st century, a real opportunity came within touching distance. In January 2011, former India opener Amay Khurasiya was roped in as in-charge of the academy of Madhya Pradesh Cricket Association (MPCA) at Holkar Stadium.

A circular went around every club in Indore. The MPCA had asked each club to send five of its best players for trials.

Avesh very casually informed his father that Indore Colts had recommended his name for the trials.

'*Haan, tu bhi chale jana* (Fine, you too should go for trials),' was Ashique's nonchalant reaction.

'The son of a friend was also a good player. The friend told me one day, '*Bhaijaan, tumhara bachcha* Avesh *ki* bowling *bahut tez hain* (Brother, your son Avesh bowls really quick).' I never took it seriously, though. I had never seen Avesh bowl,' Ashique claims.

The MPCA was looking at selecting around 30 players across age groups. About 100 players were going to be rejected. The players were up to twenty years of age. Avesh was fourteen. Former BCCI secretary Sanjay Jagdale was personally supervising the camp.

On the day of the trial, Ashique's friends insisted that he needed to watch how his son was doing at the trials. The trials were literally next door. Ashique reached the venue but couldn't see Avesh bowl.

After a while, Ashique's friend quipped: 'Let's go from here. Avesh is the best among all those we were watching.'

'What are you saying?' was Ashique's perplexed reaction as he left the venue.

Ashique waited anxiously for Avesh to come home after the first round of the trials that evening. He needed to know what exactly transpired.

'Papa, *sab log* bowling *daal rahe thhe* (Father, everyone was bowling there),' Avesh started narrating the drama of the day.

Khurasiya said curtly: '*Yeh lo* ball. *Jao daalo* (Here's the ball. Go bowl).'

'*Maine 2–3* ball *daali.* Khurasiya *sir bole hatt jao ab yahaan se* (I had barely bowled three deliveries when Khurasiya sir asked me to move away from the pack). I thought I was rejected. Tension gripped me,' Avesh told his father.

Once the session at the nets was over, Khurasiya walked up to Avesh and said: '*Tum toh bahut tez* ball *daalte ho* (You bowl really fast balls).'

After a few minutes of routine questions on his background, Khurasiya told Avesh, '*Bahut badhiya hain* (Very good).'

Avesh was selected for the academy. 'Once he came under the wings of Khurasiya sir, we started thinking he could become something. That was the turning point,' Ashique fondly states.

Getting over the conventional middle-class mindset was the next challenge for Ashique. Ignoring studies was a strict no-no. But to prioritise cricket over academics was an even greater challenge.

Ashique's generation grew up listening to the rhetoric, '*Padhoge likhoge banoge* nawab, *kheloge kudoge banoge kharaab* (You will be a king if you study hard; you will be ruined if you play all the time).'

'I told myself that was wrong. I had stopped his cricket for a year when he did poorly in his studies. Once Khurasiya sir came into the picture, I changed my thinking,' Ashique says.

There was a direction to Avesh's career now.

## The rise to India U-19s

Once Avesh came under the wings of Khurasiya, his growth graph peaked exponentially. He was tormenting batsmen across age groups and tournaments across the country.

In a matter of three years, he had aced U-16, U-19 and zonal tournaments.

The U-19 Vinoo Mankad Trophy was in Indore in 2013–14. Avesh picked up 14 wickets in four matches. Before he could make sense of what was happening around him, Avesh was representing the U-19 India team when he was barely seventeen.

He was picked for the U-19 Asia Cup in Dubai that preceded the U-19 World Cup in February 2014 at the same venue. The coach of the U-19 team, Bharat Arun, was highly impressed and gave Avesh a place in the U-19 World Cup team.

'First, he played U-16, then division league matches. I thought he would be a certified professional now. With time, our expectations and aspirations got bigger. We used to think '*Agar* India U-19 *khel gaya toh isske liye* easy *ho jayega.* Job *mil jayegi* (If he played the U-19 for India, then things would become easier for him and would help him get a job).' Once he played U-19, we thought '*Agar India khel gaya toh mazaa aa jayega* (It will be real fun if he played for India),' Ashique recalls.

'*Khelna hain toh sirf shauk ke liye nahin* (If he wanted to play, then it shouldn't be just a hobby),' was the mindset.

On 15 February 2014, a seventeen-year-old Avesh was representing India U-19 in the opening game of the U-19 World Cup against Pakistan. Avesh bowled eight overs for 50 before getting injured in the second match against Scotland. Avesh's campaign was over. India were knocked out of the tournament in the quarterfinals. But Avesh's journey had just begun.

Amid the fast-changing life, it was thought imperative that he finished his basic education.

'Amay sir *bolte thhe padhai bhi zaroori hain* (Amay sir always insisted education is also very important),' Ashique says.

'Avesh was doing his twelfth from the CBSE board. I knew he wouldn't be able to clear it because it's very tough. He was busy playing U-19 cricket too. I had to ensure he could pass twelfth comfortably. I got him a private form from MP board. And he cleared the exams,' Ashique recounts.

Once he cleared the board exams, it was back to the grind on the cricket field. The MP selectors wasted little time and handed him his First-Class cap against Railways in the 2014–15 Ranji Trophy season.

Avesh was sharing the new ball with Ishwar Pandey, who had by then played for Chennai Super Kings and been on tours with the India team. Avesh returned figures of 2/41 in 24 overs of sharp pace bowling on his debut.

Fifteen wickets in five Ranji Trophy games were enough to ensure his spot in the India U-19 team for the next U-19 World

Cup in Bangladesh in 2016. This time, he would be playing under coach Rahul Dravid.

'Papa, *kuchh mat karo. Ghar pe baitho,* namaaz *padho* (Father, you don't have to work anymore. Just be at home and offer your namaaz),' Ashique recalls Avesh telling him before leaving for the tournament.

Avesh was clocking over 140 kmph regularly in every match India U-19 played in the lead-up to the World Cup. His pace and disconcerting bounce became the talking point in that World Cup.

'*Sawaal hi nahin uthta* (The question doesn't arise),' the boy from Indore asserted when asked if he was willing to cut down on his pace for the sake of better accuracy after the first match of the U-19 World Cup.

This didn't come just from his Rahul sir (Dravid, the coach of the U-19 team); he also had strict instructions from his childhood coach Amay Khurasiya.

'Amay sir has clearly told me that steady line and length can only be effective if I can bowl quick. In this tournament I haven't hit the 140-mark yet but I will surely do,' Avesh had said during a chat at the team hotel lobby in Dhaka after the second match of the tournament.

'I work very hard on yorkers. Not many bowlers bowl that in India. Amay sir stresses on it and also the other variations. I am a swing bowler with the new ball and rely on seam movement with the older ball,' Avesh declared.

Avesh, standing at over 6 feet, lived up to his billing in the tournament, picking up 12 wickets in six matches at an economy rate of 3.48 and an average of 15.08.

The gentle giant from Indore was making the right noise. One could see he was the future of Indian fast bowling. Yet, he missed out on an IPL contract in the auctions which happened during the tournament. His teammates were all part of the IPL by the time the quarterfinal against Namibia ended in Fatullah.

Rishabh Pant was bought for Rs 1.9 crore, captain Ishan Kishan had earned Rs 35 lakh from Gujarat Lions and Sarfaraz Khan was already a buzzing talent in the IPL.

Avesh channelised his disappointment to a fiery spell against West Indies in the final. Defending just 145, he came out bowling the heavy balls. He got rid of the dangerous Gidron Pope in the third over of the chase and the subsequent war cry belied his calm demeanour and spoke of his passion. His spell of 1/29 in 10 overs dragged the final to the last over but 145 was too little to defend. The grind awaited Avesh!

## The grind to make a point

For all the excitement around him, Avesh was now subjected to the anonymity of domestic cricket post the U-19 World Cup. There was no IPL for him to stay in the public eye.

He wasted no time after returning from Bangladesh. He couldn't have afforded it!

Within four days of the World Cup, Avesh was marking his run-up for Madhya Pradesh in the CK Nayudu U-23 semi-final. 'Final *jeetna hain ab* Mumbai *ke* against (Need to win the final against Mumbai),' he said.

Madhya Pradesh fell short in the final and the grind had just begun for Avesh.

Watching his friends amidst the glitz of the IPL wasn't easy that year. '*Bura toh bahut lagta thha* (It definitely hurt a lot). I can't describe the phase that Avesh went through,' Ashique says.

Ashique, for one, knew how to deal with disappointments. Sulking is never an option. Neither is blaming someone for your own troubles.

'I believe in what is correct. I understand how much potential one has. I never believed he was a good T20 bowler. I had a feeling if he ever made his debut that would be in Tests,' Ashique says with a straight face.

'MP *walon ko utna* preference *nahin milta* (Players from MP don't get preference). When he was selected for U-19, it happened after years that a player from MP was representing India,' Ashique proudly states. There's no room for negative thoughts in that Khan household.

Avesh's form dipped. He didn't get a game for Madhya Pradesh in the 2016–17 domestic season.

For the first time in his career, he could see big speed-breakers.

Just as the dark times were about to engulf Avesh, a ray of hope came from the Royal Challengers Bangalore. Bharat Arun was now the bowling coach of both the Indian team and the Royal Challengers Bangalore. Avesh was picked up at his base price. The Royal Challengers Bangalore was meant to be a finishing school for him.

He got just one match in the 2017 IPL where he picked 1/23 in his quota of four overs. Arun was happy with his progress.

Avesh won his place back in the MP Ranji Trophy team in the 2017–18 season. Six wickets in three games weren't really a flattering return, but enough to make the national selectors and the Indian team management decide to invest in him. He was picked to play for the Board President's XI in October against a touring New Zealand side before he was flown over to South Africa as a net bowler in January 2018.

The confidence from the exposure started reflecting in his game. He came back from South Africa and had an impressive Syed Mushtaq Ali Trophy. Seven wickets at an economy rate of

6.85 in five T20 matches ensured he earned a hefty IPL contract worth Rs 70 lakh from Delhi Daredevils for the 2018 IPL season.

Things seemed to be falling into place for Avesh, finally.

Avesh's ability to bowl the heavy bowl and cramp the batsmen stood out at the Daredevils camp. Coach Ricky Ponting was thrilled to have an exciting Indian fast bowler in his ranks.

Yet, Avesh was still undeniably raw. He went at over 10 runs per over in the six matches he played and could pick up only 4 wickets.

Bowling against high-end batsmen on a big stage still didn't come to him. He needed to grow tactically.

Your performance at the IPL can either springboard you to dizzy heights of fame and success, or pull you down for good.

Having a string of poor performance on prime-time TV doesn't augur well for the self-confidence of any player, let alone an introvert like Avesh.

Before he could plunge to depression and anxiety, Ashique did what he does best. Hold up a mirror.

'There must be some deficiency in you. You couldn't make the most of your opportunities,' Ashique would tell his son.

'He is not capable of playing T20 cricket,' the father firmly believed.

'Don't take that pressure of having to do well in T20 cricket. Don't obsess over IPL. Just keep working harder. Your target should be Test cricket. *Baki sab apni jagah* (Rest will be taken care of),' Ashique's motivation speech is never sugar-coated. But it did the trick on his son.

Avesh cleared the cobwebs in his head. He went back to Khurasiya and started working on a comeback plan of sorts.

The obsession over the IPL receded. There was now a plan to prove a point in the Ranji Trophy.

'He was made to understand that the Ranji Trophy was his best chance. It's the closest to playing Test cricket,' Ashique says.

For all the natural abilities he had, the wickets weren't coming as easily now as they used to in his teens.

Picking up a total of 3–4 wickets in both innings became a norm for Avesh. That was never going to be enough to take him to the next level.

'You have to pick wickets in heaps,' the message was drilled into his mind.

'Think about getting batsmen out.'

'Don't waste your deliveries by bowling too many short balls.'

'Before the batsman gets his eye in and footwork going, you have to dismiss him.'

The template was laid out for Avesh.

'He learnt to bowl 2–3-wicket spells during the 2018–19 season. Then he started running through sides. If he got one, he would pick up another couple,' Ashique remembers.

During the 2018–19 Ranji Trophy season, Avesh was back tormenting batsmen around the country like he used to in his early days.

He reached Delhi in the last week of 2018 in red-hot form. The national selectors were now tailing him. Navdeep Saini was already a name knocking on the doors of India selection. Avesh had to do a lot to leapfrog his competitors.

On a cold winter morning, Avesh let it rip at the Feroz Shah Kotla. He knocked over the top four in the Delhi's batting line-up inside 30 minutes. Stumps were cartwheeling all over the place. The likes of Nitish Rana and Dhruv Shorey could barely get their bats down to Avesh's searing, swinging full-length deliveries.

One could hear the ball smacking wicketkeeper Naman Ojha's gloves from the adjacent practice facilities. Avesh had picked up 6/51. He had already picked 34 wickets in six matches.

'The key to my success has been workload management. The support staff is ensuring that I don't bowl too much in the nets and have kept me fresh for matches. I have always bowled fast but I had to ensure I can keep bowling all day. First-class cricket is vastly different from U-19 cricket. I know I have to keep hitting the spot at that pace,' he claimed after the intimidating spell.

He finished the season with a tally of 35 wickets from seven games. He was now a definite part of the India 'A' programme.

Avesh followed it up with another 28 wickets at an average of 19.85 in five matches in the 2019–20 Ranji Trophy season. He had cracked the code to succeed in First Class cricket.

His consistency in domestic cricketer meant he was always around the Indian team as a net bowler on tour. He was in England helping the Indian team prepare for the 2019 World Cup before travelling with the India 'A' team to West Indies a month later.

Yet, the breakthrough IPL season eluded him. It was bound to prick him. The Delhi franchise rebranded as Delhi Capitals played him in one match each in 2019 and 2020 edition.

'He was getting a lot of wickets in Ranji Trophy for two seasons. But he used to crib that he wasn't getting opportunities in IPL despite bowling well,' Ashique says.

It was time to fight the demons in his head once again!

## Finding his core during the pandemic

When the Covid-19 pandemic hit the world in March 2020, Avesh gained some perspective.

Images of hordes of stranded migrant labours moved Avesh to the core. The family had experienced uncertain times and they couldn't have just sat back and not done anything.

'We were watching TV and were deeply pained by the images that were being telecast. My father had said that the almighty has given us enough to help these helpless people. We decided to go to the highway and give them dry snacks and bottles of water which could hold them for at least a day,' Avesh says.

'The pandemic has made life so uncertain. It has taught us the value of our families and being happy in the moments we get with them,' he states.

Uncertain times had hit Indian cricket too. The BCCI waited till September to get things underway with the IPL in the UAE.

On the cricketing front, things still hadn't changed much for Avesh. He was played in just one match and he conceded 30 runs in three overs. He was now getting edgy.

He would often call his father from the UAE and say: '*Naam chalta thha. Bolte thhe kal ka* match *khelega. Par hota nahin thha* (My name would do the rounds. They said that I would play the next day's match, but it never materialised).'

'*Mujhe nahin malum udhar kaisa* bowling *kar raha hain* (I didn't know how he was bowling there),' was Ashique's reaction.

A '*Theek hain yaar* (It's alright)' was all he would say to console his worried son.

One day Ashique had a tough talk with his son. '*Woh sab chhor* (Keep all these things aside). Think about the Australia tour. That's your best chance to get a Test cap. Don't obsess about not playing much in the IPL. We want an international stamp,' Ashique told Avesh.

Avesh didn't make the cut even as a net bowler for the tour Down Under from November 2020 to January 2021. As luck would have it, almost all reserve players got a Test cap on the tour that defined the strong structure of Indian cricket.

'If he had gone, he would have had got the opportunity. He never performed well in the IPL,' Ashique rues.

But the father does cut some slack. 'To be honest, he didn't get a fair run in the T20s. He didn't get enough opportunities. It's important for confidence. If rookies don't get opportunities, it hurts their confidence,' Ashique claims.

The IPL 2020 in the UAE saved Indian cricket from accumulating  huge losses. It also ensured players had money coming into their bank accounts. But that accounts for barely 20 per cent of the uncapped domestic players in the country. Nearly, 700 cricketers were still in the lurch.

The BCCI did organise the Syed Mushtaq Ali Trophy and the Vijay Hazare Trophy. But it's the Ranji Trophy that brings nearly 60 per cent of the annual earnings for a domestic player.

'I feel for the domestic players who didn't have a Ranji Trophy to play. I had an IPL contract but there are a lot of players who don't have a job and are dependent on the bulk money that comes from Ranji Trophy. I realised that I am blessed, and I had to make the most of the opportunities I was getting,' Avesh says.

The financial significance of the Ranji Trophy aside, a full season of First-Class cricket polishes a cricketer.

Avesh realised that if he had to make better use of the opportunities, he had to alter his routine. 'Playing First-Class matches helps you to get into a rhythm. I realised I had to shed weight after the last IPL. I needed to work really hard on my fitness to bowl well consistently in this year's IPL.'

Giving up biryani was the toughest part for him. 'I hired a personal dietician. He put me on a routine. I plan everything now. I shed 6 kilograms in three months and that has helped me in my endurance. My dietician does allow me to cheat and eat biryani and the delicacies at home once in a while. He has given me a bit of liberty during Ramadan as I have been fasting for a month,' he smiles.

The Syed Mushtaq Ali Trophy in January 2021 was critical for him. In a stark departure from his plan of excelling in red-ball cricket, white-ball cricket was all he had to stay relevant in the scheme of things in Indian cricket.

The shortest format of the game was still not kind to him. Bowling at his home ground, he gave away 39 runs for one wicket in the first match of the tournament against a lowly ranked Goa team.

'Will we ever get to hear that you picked 3–4 wickets in a T20 match? Or is it that we will keep hearing about you conceding 40 runs and getting a wicket,' an agitated Ashique confronted Avesh that night after the match.

'You have played the IPL. You must have the confidence to knock over batsmen in state teams,' the father was stirring up his rather sedate twenty-four-year-old son. He wanted to be sure that if Avesh was playing cricket professionally, it had to be played seriously.

'If someone hits him a boundary off the first ball, he loses confidence,' Ashique explains Avesh's problem.

The harsh words did make a difference. Avesh finished the tournament as the third-highest wicket-taker. His 14 wickets came in just five matches at an average of 10.64 and an economy of 7.45.

'We all felt he had finally learnt the art of bowling in T20 cricket,' Ashique claims.

The confidence was restored. Avesh contemplated of moving from the Delhi Capitals and going into the auction pool again, a move fraught with risks.

A composed Ashique took over and asked: '*Tera toh* Delhi *mein hi jagah pakka nahin hain.* Auction *mein agar koi nahin kharida toh* (You don't have a final place in the DC team. What will happen if nobody bids for you in the auction)?'

Avesh insisted that most teams look for Indian pace bowlers. Someone or the other would surely be interested in buying him.

'But I told him let it be. Just keep playing for Delhi Capitals,' Ashique put his foot down.

The Delhi Capitals retained Avesh ahead of the auctions in January 2021.

The IPL was back in India. He took the field for the Delhi Capitals in April and he looked a different person just from the way he moved around the field. Leaner and agile, Avesh was hitting the mark straightaway.

The yorkers was going down right under the bat of the batsman in crucial times. Something he had aspired to do with aplomb as a U-19 cricketer for India five years earlier.

The pace was right up there with the new ball.

By the time the raging second wave of the Covid-19 pandemic in India forced the authorities to suspend the IPL in the first week of May, Avesh had picked up 14 wickets in eight matches at an economy rate of 7.70. He was now the go-to pacer for the management of the Delhi Capitals.

A week later, when he finished his evening namaaz on the last Friday of Ramadan, a phone call came to inform him that he would be travelling to England with the Indian team as a standby for a three-month tour which included the World Test Championship final against New Zealand and five Tests against England.

Travelling with the team during the pandemic is different to any tour as net bowler as the Australia tour had proved earlier in the year. Avesh was now definitely part of the top-line fast bowlers to carry Indian cricket forward.

A journey that started out as a riveting one in his teens became a story of hard grind. Avesh, however, never disappeared from the system's eyeline.

Humility is the one word that best describes Avesh. On most occasions, you would hardly know he is standing right behind you.

'*Kam bolne wala hain. Bakiyo ke samne phir bhi bol lega. Par mere saamne ek dum nahin bolega* (He speaks very little. He would still talk with others, but he rarely opens his mouth in front of me),' Ashique quips.

Avesh has faced his share of trials and tribulations in life. What he most remembers are the tough times the family faced when demonetisation happened and how it affected his father when he lost his job.

It was in good faith that Ashique had handed over his son to Amay Khurasiya. 'Amay sir once told me that all kid's parents keep asking about their ward's progress. But I never went to him,' Ashique says.

'You know better than me,' would be Ashique's response. 'You have called Avesh *beta*. I am a nobody then. Why should I even ask you? Whatever needs to be done, should be done by you.'

Ashique met Khurasiya just twice just because he was summoned by the coach. 'I have met him only twice. Because he had once asked me to come and scold Avesh. *Daatna zaroori bhi hain* (It's important to reprimand as well),' Ashique recalls. The value of education was never undermined even as cricket became the priority.

'*Padhai karwao isko* (Make sure Avesh studies),' Khurasiya told Ashique curtly.

Khurasiya insisted Avesh never gave up academics despite his rise in cricket.

Avesh completed his graduation in commerce. He would study 2–3 days a week and ensure he got passing marks.

'He got his college admission through the sports quota. He didn't have to attend college. Graduation was a must for him. He never objected. The Indian Oil Corporation (IOC) offered him a scholarship for two years when he played the U-19. Then he got a job there,' Ashique says.

'Avesh *ab* MBA *kar raha hain* (Avesh is now doing his MBA),' Ashique proudly states even as his son is on the verge of getting into the Indian team.

For all his success as a cricketer, Ashique ensured he understood the value of money. There was no room for splurging. A regular domestic cricketer earns as well as any corporate employee.

'He used to ride an Activa scooter till three years ago. We didn't even have a Vespa. It's been five years since he is playing the IPL, he has played two U-19 World Cups and five seasons of Ranji Trophy. Father and son shared one bike. We used to drop each other. I never allowed him to splurge. He got a car (i20) in 2020,' Ashique says in a rich baritone.

Avesh still lives in the same house where his father was born. He is not one to forget his roots but he is well on his way to lay a stronger foundation for the future generations.

# CHAPTER 11

# NAVDEEP SAINI: THE OUTSIDER

## *Introduction to cricket*

There's an adage in Delhi cricket circles: 'Cricketers in Delhi are not made because of the system. They are made despite the system.'

Navdeep Saini's rise through the ranks in the Indian cricket team corroborates it. But his story was never meant to go through the system. Not Delhi, for sure!

Navi, as he is fondly called by people around him, was the kid next door playing cricket just for fun in the anonymity of a semi-urban neighbourhood.

Taraori, a small village town in Haryana along National Highway 44, is very hard to pinpoint even on the state map. Ten kilometres from Taraori is Karnal district. Navdeep goes by Karnal whenever asked where he hails from.

Access to formal cricket coaching in such a remote town was next to impossible. Like any other kid in love with cricket in this country, Navdeep did dream of playing for India. But it was more of a fantasy for him.

He had no clue about the cricket ecosystem. There was hardly any cricketing role model from that part of the country. Running around and playing cricket on rough grounds around the paddy fields was the closest thing to cricketing glory for Navdeep.

His father Amarjeet Saini was employed with Haryana Roadways as a driver. Even in his wildest dreams, Amarjeet never thought his younger son Navi would be one of the fastest bowlers to have bowled in India colours.

His mother is a homemaker. She would worry about her frail son, playing around all day. She would pack an extra paratha in his tiffin box with a generous amount of ghee. Her husband would leave for work early in the morning and returned late in the evening. She was the caretaker for her sons. She struggled to understand Navi's fascination with cricket. He used to be glued to the TV to watch cricket irrespective of who was playing.

Like in most lower-middle-class Indian families, that cricket could be a career, never crossed the minds of the members of the Saini family.

Looking back, though, Amarjeet feels Navdeep had an unusual fondness for bowling for a five-year-old.

'Navi had asked me to buy him a ball when he was around five or six. I asked him if he wanted a bat like most other kids prefer. But he insisted on getting a ball. It was a plastic ball. But that was the first ball he bowled with,' Amarjeet recalls.

The field next to the local gurdwara became their venue for Sunday cricket.

## Growing-up years

Navdeep was in love with cricket. He was obsessed. He drooled over Dale Steyn and Brett Lee. He had a life-size poster of Zaheer Khan in his room. But there was no direction.

Local cricket tournaments with tennis balls were his hunting ground. Well into his teens, he would skip school excursions just to play in local tournaments.

Navi's interest in cricket baffled Amarjeet and it became difficult for him to digest that his son invested so much time in cricket.

'Navi had become a nomad in his teens. He would play matches everywhere around Ambala and Patiala. There was hardly any scope or facilities for formal cricket training. So, I was sceptical about his ambitions,' Amarjeet says.

Navdeep was desperate for formal coaching, but nothing seemed to be materialising. 'There were a few cricket coaching centres, about fifteen kilometres from my village. But we couldn't afford them. So, I kept playing tennis-ball cricket,' Navdeep says.

Not that Amarjeet didn't try to enrol Navdeep in a good academy. Yograj Singh, a former India fast bowler and the legendary Yuvraj Singh's father, ran the most prolific academy in Chandigarh, about 125 kilometres from Karnal. The distance, however, was the least of the Saini family's concerns.

Amarjeet asked around and his friends informed him that Yograj's academy was expensive and very difficult to get in. Navdeep wasn't going to let that dishearten him.

Navdeep continued to play local tournaments and revelled in intimidating batsmen and seeing stumps flying around.

The life-changing moment came in 2010. It was the first defining moment in his career. This is where things started happening for him. He was eighteen. Before that he was aimlessly playing local tennis-ball tournaments.

Indian cricket was high on the flourishing Indian Premier League (IPL) by 2010. The aspirational value of the IPL had gone through the roof in its first three seasons. Everyone wanted a slice of the glitzy experience.

Former Delhi all-rounder Sumit Narwal, a native of Karnal, decided to start the Karnal Premier League (KPL). Sumit and his brother Amit replicated the basic model of the IPL. Sumit himself had made his IPL debut that year, playing for the Rajasthan Royals.

They could get six teams after conducting trials and having the auctions. Navdeep was sold for Rs 10,000. The lanky, frail boy was the big-money player in the village!

But there was a catch. Navdeep had never played with the leather cricket ball. He was a soft-ball star in the area and hard-ball cricket wasn't going to be easy. He was not playing in anonymity anymore. There were crowds, intimidating in their own way, and a setting under flood lights just amped the game quotient.

'I touched a leather ball for the first time when the trials were organised. I was jittery. But those trials gave me a decent idea about how to bowl with the leather ball by the time the tournament started,' Navdeep looks back at what he calls the turning point of his life.

Navdeep's natural ability came through. He ripped through the defence of batsmen with such pace and frequency that it bewildered everyone watching the match.

The eighteen-year-old unassuming, wiry fellow had caught the attention of Sumit.

The system awaited his arrival!

## The controversial Ranji debut for Delhi

Sumit Narwal was just the guide needed to offer some direction to Navdeep.

Sumit was an integral part of the Delhi Ranji team from 2010–15. He would take the new ball and invariably score useful runs coming in at No. 8. He would have Navdeep tag along wherever he went. And then one day, Sumit decided to take Navdeep to the nets of the Delhi Ranji Trophy team at the Feroz Shah Kotla.

Navdeep was just another net bowler. One would barely notice him.

The air at the Kotla was intimidating for him. He was suddenly in an environment where there were three World Cup winners training alongside him.

Navdeep puts things into perspective quite well: 'I didn't have formal coaching, so access to good cricket gear was a bit tough for me. Unlike people coming through the system, I didn't have any kit sponsor. I watched these players very closely. I used to buy my cricket gear (including the clothes) with the prize money I used to get playing those domestic tennis ball tournaments.'

In the winter of 2013, Gautam Gambhir and Virender Sehwag were available for the entire domestic season. India's most prolific opening pair in Test cricket had lost its place in the Indian team.

Gambhir was made the captain of the Delhi team. He meant business. Scoring runs wasn't the only way he was going to win back his place in the Indian team. He wanted to do something special with the perennially enigmatic Delhi team to stay in the limelight. Win-at-all-cost was his mantra that season.

There was tension in the air at the Feroz Shah Kotla premises on 13 December 2013. Gambhir and the selectors – led by former India opener Chetan Chauhan – met to pick the team for the next day's match against Vidarbha. Chauhan also happened to be the vice-president of the Delhi and District Cricket Association (DDCA) at the time.

Sparks flew in the meeting. Gambhir proposed that Navdeep Saini be included in the team. His reason was simple. Gambhir had faced Navdeep in the nets for three weeks and felt this twenty-one-year-old boy could exploit the seamer-friendly pitch at the Roshanara Club ground in north Delhi.

Gambhir had gone in to the meeting anticipating some resistance. He didn't expect his proposal to be shot down outrightly, calling it 'illegal'.

Navdeep didn't play any grade or club cricket in Delhi. He was an 'outsider' for the members of the DDCA.

Gambhir, not known to hold himself back, announced that he would not play the game if his demand was not met. The selectors caved in. Navdeep Saini, an innocent boy from a small village in Haryana, was in Delhi's Ranji Trophy squad.

It was hard to assign a face to Navdeep's name before the game. He was so far from the system. But he was the buzz on the eve of the match against Maharashtra. Former India pacer Sanjeev Sharma was the assistant coach of the Delhi team then. He clarified: 'You must have seen him in the nets. He is the tall, wiry boy who bowls at a brisk pace. He bowls good in-swingers and has been troubling both Gambhir and Sehwag in the nets.'

Once the Delhi team was announced, the entire Delhi cricket fraternity protested the move. The DDCA members and former cricketers got together and deemed the move illegal and Gambhir an autocratic captain.

Former India captain and legendary left-arm spinner Bishan Singh Bedi, forever fighting to expose the malpractices of the notorious DDCA, echoed the sentiment. The sentiment was: 'Gambhir was setting a wrong precedent and undermining the system. It's unfair on the kids who have gone through the system in Delhi.'[1]

A letter signed by Bedi on the NCT (National Capital Territory) Cricket Association letterhead, of which the legendary left-arm spinner is the president, was sent to DDCA president Arun Jaitley seeking his intervention.

---

1. https://www.cricketcountry.com/news/bishan-singh-bedi-protests-against-inclusion-of-outsider-navdeep-saini-in-delhi-squad-75189)

The letter quotes Bedi: 'In today's meeting to finalise the Ranji team, an outsider, Navdeep, a fast bowler from Karnal has been selected. This boy has played no cricket in Delhi for the past year, and it is inappropriate to bring in an outsider when there are some very good boys waiting to represent Delhi.'

Navdeep was handed his First-Class debut next morning. Delhi were bowling on the first morning of the match at Roshanara Club. In Navdeep's own words, he was dazed by what was happening to him.

'Just imagine, I didn't even have proper shoes for the match. When Sumit *bhaiyya* had started taking me to the Delhi nets, I purchased a basic pair of bowling shoes with spikes. They cost me around Rs 1200. I played in my debut wearing that pair of ragged shoes. I didn't understand what high-ankle spikes are. As I gradually stayed on in the system, I learnt these things,' Navdeep recalls.

What transpired in the morning of the match was both embarrassing and sensational. One could see a hoard of DDCA members gathering by the boundary. They were wearing black armbands to protest Navdeep's selection.

Navdeep probably didn't realise he was a couple of steps away from playing for India. But as he marked his run-up, there were people, 20 feet away from him, distributing pamphlets against him just outside the boundary line.

As he went to field near the boundary line, he could hear the murmurs.

Chauhan was helpless. 'I am not against promoting young talent. But I am also the VP of this association. I can't just ignore the rules and I am answerable to members. There's a lot of pressure.'

Navdeep picked 2/18 in his first outing. The murmurs started to fade soon.

He had a rough initiation into the system. But he had the likes of Gambhir and Sehwag insulating him from the venom spewed at him.

## Tough initial years and fighting injuries

Navdeep Saini was raw. He was frail. He weighed around 60 kilograms when he was picked for Delhi. No formal training behind him, Navdeep was not ready to sustain the rigours of First-Class cricket.

Besides, Navdeep would not make eye contact with the media at domestic matches. The controversy on his debut had left scars on him. When the DDCA members were around, he would walk around apologetically.

He showed a spark on the field, though, bowling some probing spells and magic deliveries to top batsmen in domestic cricket.

For the first three seasons, Navdeep would invariably break down in the middle of the season. Every time he looked like hitting his strides and taking his game up to the next level, he would be felled by injuries.

There was a Ranji Trophy match against Rajasthan at Feroz Shah Kotla in the last week of December 2014. Navdeep had taken 7 wickets (3/31 in the first innings and 4/48 in the second) to bowl Delhi to big win in a match that was shortened due to inclement Delhi winter weather.

He had clean-bowled Robin Bist, who had batted Rajasthan to two Ranji Trophy titles in the last three years. The ball came in with the angle and straightened after pitching to open up Bist and knock over the off-stump. Bist had claimed that it was the best ball he had faced in his Ranji Trophy career.

That became Navdeep's signature delivery.

That was the first time he came out to speak to the media. '*Abhi toh seekh hi raha hoon. Lambe* spells *dalna hain.* Fitness *pe kaam kar raha hoon,*' was all Navdeep would say with a humble smile. You could sense he was in a hurry to finish the interaction.

A match later, it was announced that Navdeep had suffered a stress fracture on his back. It wasn't unexpected.

Sumit Narwal realised he needed to train with the best trainers in the business to cope with the grind of competitive cricket.

Navdeep was taken to Nasir Jamshed, a high-end fitness trainer who trains tennis players like Yuki Bhambri in south Delhi.

'I remember this frail boy coming to me. Sumit had requested me to train this boy because he had the potential to play for India,' Nasir recalls his first encounter with Navdeep.

'I had said that a lot of work was needed on him. I didn't have that much time to work on him. I could see he was from a humble background. I told them he could not afford to pay me anyway.'

Navdeep had made up his mind that Nasir was his best shot at attaining the highest level of fitness in cricket.

'Please *bhaiyya, meri madad kar do.* If you train me, I am sure I'll be playing the IPL soon. I'll give you 10 per cent of my IPL contracts,' Navdeep pleaded with Nasir. Nasir couldn't turn him away.

But travelling from Karnal to Siri Fort Complex in south Delhi on a daily basis was not a feasible option.

Navdeep put in all the money he had earned from playing for Delhi into his accommodation in Kotla Mubarakpur, a ten-minute bus ride to Siri Fort. He got a one-room apartment with bare minimum facilities.

There was a problem of drinking water. He set up a kitchen in the same room that he slept in. He slept on a mattress on the floor. But Navdeep was all set!

The training started. Gaining muscle weight was the first hurdle. Navdeep had to gain a minimum of 13 kilograms. He was put on a diet that polarised his taste. 'He was brought up on chapatis and parathas with extra ghee. This time we had to put him on a different diet,' Nasir recalls.

However, Navdeep's body wasn't responding to the diet and he would often fall sick. 'A few tests were conducted and it emerged he had an enlarged liver. Then it emerged that he was allergic to gluten. We had to put him on a diet that was gluten-free. Giving up eating rotis was very tough for him. But once he got the hang of the routine, he got addicted to fitness. All he wanted was to bowl as fast he possibly could,' Nasir says.

By the next season, Navdeep was already a different bowler. He was consistently bowling long spells and at a pace beyond 140 kmph.

In the Vijay Hazare Trophy in 2015–16, India's domestic one-day tournament, Navdeep made his first major contribution to Delhi cricket. He picked up 15 wickets in eight matches at an average of 20.33 and an economy rate 4.12. Delhi had made it to the final of the tournament.

Navdeep was finally ready for the grind!

## 2017: The breakthrough year

Navdeep Saini wasn't really setting domestic cricket on fire in the 2016–17 season. He didn't even feature in the list of top 20 wicket-takers in either of Ranji Trophy and Vijay Hazare Trophy.

But national selector Devang Gandhi saw some spark in the

boy. He followed him through the season. The disconcerting pace that Navdeep generated stood out.

'That was our first season as national selectors. Led by chairman MSK Prasad, we had decided that creating a strong pool of players should be our priority. Bowlers with raw pace was an area of which we wanted to create a big pool,' Gandhi says.

Mind you, Ishant Sharma and Mohammad Shami hadn't hit their top form at the time. Umesh Yadav was still wayward while Bhuvneshwar Kumar's pace had become a worry in Test cricket. Jasprit Bumrah was nowhere close to a becoming a Test bowler. In essence, India was yet to discover the potent pace attack that is now the envy of the world.

Navdeep was picked for the Board President's XI match against a touring Australian team which had come to India for a four-Test series in February 2017.

'It was his first representative match. I had managed to convince the other selectors about his potential. He needed to be polished. That was a great opportunity to test him out,' Gandhi recalls.

Navdeep surprised the Australians with his pace. He didn't get many wickets but he had them hopping in the crease. Steve Smith was even felled by a sharp bouncer from Navdeep.

The selectors had seen the spark and they were ready to invest in him.

Delhi Daredevils picked him at his base price of Rs 20 lakh. He didn't get a match that season.

The selectors picked him for India 'A' tour of South Africa in August that year. He picked up just 7 wickets in four innings of two unofficial Test matches.

The selectors had got feedback from India 'A' coach Rahul Dravid and Paras Mhambrey. Navdeep was identified as one for the future.

Cut to Ranji Trophy 2017–18 season.

Navdeep's Instagram page was bombarded with photos of Navdeep with a toned physique which looked as if it was chiselled out of stone. It was tough to recall that shy, frail boy who came to bowl in the nets of the Delhi state side.

He was in beast mode. The benign pitches mattered little. Navdeep was intimidating batsmen around the country with his pace and had stumps flying around more frequently.

Navdeep was at the forefront of Delhi's dominant run-in that tournament.

Then the defining match of his career happened when Delhi reached Pune to play Bengal in the Ranji Trophy semi-final at the Maharashtra Cricket Association Stadium at Gahunje. The pitch resembled the highway alongside the stadium and was deemed as a fast bowler's graveyard.

Thanks to Navdeep's spell of 3/55 in the first innings, Bengal was restricted to 286 before Delhi openers Gautam Gambhir and Kunal Chandela scored 232 for the first wicket in reply.

Bengal had Shami and Ashok Dinda in their line-up. They were rendered ineffective. Shami did finish with 6/122 but it took him 39 overs as Delhi had secured a 112-run lead.

Navdeep Saini was about to turn the match on its head. He was breathing fire on that benign pitch. He clocked over 150 kmph consistently as he bowled 12 overs on the trot. That's all he needed.

Bengal didn't know what hit them. Navdeep had taken 4/35. All his 4 wickets were bowled. Delhi had dismissed Bengal for 86 inside 25 overs and booked a spot in the Ranji Trophy final for the first time in ten years.

That spell has been referred to as one of the best spells of fierce fast bowling in Indian First-Class cricket.

Navdeep was strutting his stuff and, unlike his initial years, there was an unapologetic confidence in his demeanour.

He maintained his humility when he spoke to the media. 'My grandfather was in Subhash Chandra Bose's Indian National Army (INA). He tells me stories about facing challenges and he made me believe I could overcome any tough situation,' he said after the match.

'That spell was unbelievable. Seasoned bowlers like Shami and Dinda struggled there. But he took the pitch and conditions out of the equation. That showed he was ready for bigger things,' Gandhi says.

There was no slot in the Indian team that was flying out to South Africa next week. But the selectors decided to send him with the team as a net bowler.

'The quality of net bowlers on tours isn't really good. Here was someone who simulates the pace and bounce of Dale Steyn, Morne Morkel and Kagiso Rabada. He and the other net bowlers could be groomed,' Gandhi says about the decision.

Gambhir, however, objected to the move. He believed that it would have been better for Navdeep to be available for the Ranji Trophy final against Vidarbha.

'You have a chance to win a major trophy for Delhi. A good performance would anyway catapult you into national reckoning,' Gambhir had told Navdeep and the Delhi management communicated it to the selectors.

Navdeep did dish out another memorable spell in the final against Vidarbha on a bouncy pitch in Indore.

Delhi were all out for 296 in the first innings. Navdeep was on the loose. The balls smacked Rishabh Pant's gloves so hard that one could hear the echo resonating around the stadium. The speedometer was overworked that day.

Former India opener Wasim Jaffer, who happens to be the highest run-scorer in Ranji Trophy cricket, was standing like a monk in the way of Delhi. Navdeep had hit his rhythm. He got Jaffer to edge early on the third morning only to be dropped at second slip.

Even as Jaffer continued chipping away at Delhi's score from the other end, Navdeep had him searching for answers all morning. When Navdeep finally trapped Jaffer in front of the stumps for 78, he set off on a celebratory run spreading his arms like wings.

Navdeep Saini had taken the flight to play with the big boys.

Unfortunately, he found little support from the other bowlers and fielders. Navdeep finished with 5/135 but Vidarbha had run away with the game and clinched their maiden Ranji Trophy title.

He finished the Ranji Trophy season with 34 wickets from eight matches at an average of 22.73 and a strike rate of 48.2 balls per wicket.

Navdeep Saini was the fast-bowling find of the season.

## Big IPL deal and getting closer to international cricket

A fortnight after the Ranji Trophy final, in the third week of January 2018, the Indian team had asked the BCCI to send in a couple of fast bowlers to help them prepare for the third and final Test and the subsequent ODI series in South Africa.

India had lost the first two Test matches. The Indian batting line-up was found wanting. Virat Kohli continued to bat on a different plane but there was very little support from the other end. The quality of net bowlers given by the hosts was unsatisfactory.

The selectors responded to the call and Navdeep Saini was immediately flown out with Shardul Thakur.

'Even though the call is just for bowling in the nets of the Indian team, I feel good that my performances are recognised. This is good encouragement. Hope I can build from here,' Navdeep had stated before boarding the flight to Johannesburg.

As it turned out, he caught the attention of Kohli. Earlier in that month, former India left-arm pacer Ashish Nehra was appointed as the bowling coach of the Royal Challengers Bangalore. Nehra had retired barely two months ago and had been closely following Navdeep's progress while he was still playing for Delhi.

It may be noted that Nehra had taken 6/16 in Navdeep's Ranji Trophy debut match.

Nehra has been a big brother to Kohli right from his initial days as a domestic cricketer. Kohli trusted Nehra's judgement as the Royal Challengers Bangalore went to the IPL auction in the last week of January.

Navdeep Saini was sold for Rs 3 crore to the Royal Challengers Bangalore!

He didn't get a game in that IPL. The presence of Nehra around him was exactly what he had wanted in that scenario. Nehra took him under his wings and the entire season was about grooming him.

A couple of weeks after the 2018 IPL, Navdeep came close to an India Test cap when Afghanistan arrived in Bengaluru to play their inaugural Test match.

Mohammad Shami was going through a tough phase in his personal life and his cricket threatened to fall off the track. The selectors named Navdeep in the squad picked to play Afghanistan.

By his own admission, Navdeep thought he was named as a net bowler for half an hour after the squad was announced.

'I owe my life to Gautam (Gambhir) *bhaiyya*,' Navdeep's voice quavered as he received the news of being in the Indian Test squad.

Navdeep knew this wasn't the final destination. The journey had only begun. He was aware of how his body had betrayed him in the early half of his professional career.

The elation of a national call-up was subsumed by the anxiety of not letting down his Gautam *bhaiyya.* Taking care of his body was of paramount importance.

'I knew it was not just about playing for Delhi. I realised I had to get stronger and fitter so that I don't break down in the middle of the season. I needed to take more pressure. That's how I would be able to repay Gautam *bhaiyya*'s belief in me.'

One could feel how wave after wave of emotions swept Navdeep at that moment.

The debut didn't happen, though. It wasn't unexpected. Seasoned campaigners Ishant Sharma and Umesh Yadav were always going to be the two pacers to play in the XI.

But there was an assurance that he was in the mix and the system had taken notice of him. That it was willing to invest in him was the natural next step.

Navdeep continued to feature in every India 'A' team and was on tours to England and New Zealand that year. That resulted in him missing a lot of domestic cricket as most of the 'A' tours coincided with India's domestic calendar.

Rahul Dravid, the designated caretaker of India's supply line, is a strong advocate of persisting with a player at a higher level of cricket rather than just sending them back to the grade behind them for the sake of playing matches.

From a selector's point of view, Gandhi felt Navdeep had always shown signs of improvement. 'The National Cricket

Academy (NCA) coaching staff was very impressed with his progress. Dravid, in particular, had really good things to say about him evolving as a quality fast bowler. We could see he was improving in every series and he wasn't compromising with his pace,' Gandhi says.

Navdeep was identified as the first back-up option for the lethal pace quartet of Jasprit Bumrah, Ishant Sharma, Mohammad Shami and Umesh Yadav.

## 2019: Foraying into the Team India set-up

By the first quarter of 2019, the name Navdeep Saini had become a buzzword in Indian cricket circles. Those who follow the game, through the system, knew Navdeep was one step closer to an India cap.

In March 2019, the Royal Challengers Bangalore handed Navdeep his IPL debut. It took him an over against the Chennai Super Kings at Chepauk to shake up things. He clocked 151.4 kmph on the speed gun. The Royal Challengers Bangalore were defending just 70 on a raging turner of a pitch. Navdeep had seasoned international batsmen like Shane Watson, Ambati Rayudu and Suresh Raina as he finished a spell of 4–0–24–0 in that match.

As has the IPL done to so many cricketers, Navdeep Saini was a household name now.

Every time he ran in to bowl in that IPL season, one would have an eye on the speedometer. It was exhilarating. It was a rarity in Indian cricket. There was finally a fast bowler who was breaching the 150 kmph mark consistently and was invariably hovering around the high 140s throughout the tournament.

Kohli, Navdeep's captain at the Royal Challengers Bangalore, had called it at the top of the tournament. 'Saini is promising. He is touching 150 kmph. He is going to be a lethal weapon,'

Kohli had said after the opening game against the Chennai Super Kings.

Navdeep took 11 wickets from 13 matches at an average of 36.09 and an economy rate of 8.27 as the Royal Challengers Bangalore finished the IPL season as wooden spooners.

Kohli, about to wear the Indian captain's hat at the World Cup in England in a fortnight, had something to be excited about. Ever since Kohli assumed the captaincy of the Indian Test team in 2015, he had advocated for raw pace in his bowling line-up. Here was a fellow right in front him who could send down absolute thunderbolts tirelessly.

The Indian team decided to take four pacers as net bowlers to England for the World Cup. Navdeep, Avesh Khan, Khaleel Ahmed and Deepak Chahar were the four pacers identified to help Kohli & Co. to prepare for the showpiece event.

All four of them flew back as India's campaign got underway in Southampton. Ten days into the tournament, Bhuvneshwar Kumar suffered an injury to his hamstring. The Indian team management didn't want to rule him out. The physiotherapists got down to working overtime. But there was a fear of losing one of their premier white-ball bowlers. Shami replaced Bhuvneshwar in the playing XI but there were no reserves.

Unsure about Bhuvneshwar's recovery, Navdeep was flown back to England. He stayed there as a standby.

Bhuvneshwar recovered in the back half of the tournament and Navdeep wasn't required.

But one could sense the India cap was around the corner post the World Cup.

## The international break

India were scheduled to tour West Indies immediately after the 2019 World Cup. Jasprit Bumrah and Mohammad Shami, expectedly, sat out of the limited-overs leg of the tour. It was just the right opportunity for the Indian team management to strengthen its pool of fast bowlers.

The tour was meant to be kick off with two T20Is in Lauderhill, USA, followed by another T20I and three ODIs in the West Indies.

On 3 August 2019, Navdeep Saini was handed his India debut in Lauderhill at the age of twenty-six. Like he did in the IPL, he immediately made an impact. The prima donnas of T20 cricket from West Indies had no answer to the searing deliveries sent down by the debutant. Nicholas Pooran, Kieron Pollard and Shimron Hetmyer were Navdeep's first three victims in international cricket. And then the speedometer flirted with the 150 kmph mark before breaching it a few times in that 24-ball spell.

Navdeep returned figures of 3/17 from his four overs. West Indies could muster just 95/9 and India chased it down with 4 wickets in hand.

The Man-of-the-match award went to Navdeep and the Saini household became a celebrity corner. Taraori had arrived!

Navdeep took a total of 5 wickets in the three T20Is. Team India bowling coach Bharati Arun asked him to stay back for the two-Test series. Arun, the architect of forming a once-in-a-lifetime fast bowling attack, wanted to work with this raw talent as few of his frontline pacers had begun ageing.

In September, South Africa came to India to play three T20Is and three Tests. Lance Klusener, one of the best fast-bowling all-rounders of his time, came with the South African T20I team as batting coach.

One must know, a year ago, Klusener was with the Delhi team as the head coach for the white-ball season. He was in charge of overseeing Delhi's progress in the T20 and 50-over formats. This is where he got to know Navdeep Saini.

'I am so glad to see Navdeep Saini being recognised. You don't see many in Indian cricket who can bowl at 150 kmph,' Klusener stated during a casual chat on the side-lines of an event organised by the South African High Commission in Delhi.

Klusener had closely seen the generation of Indian cricket which was fending for itself against genuine pacers across the world. Klusener played his part too.

But he was now excited to see one of his first students from India reversing the order. 'Navdeep is an absolute gem of a human being and that added a lot of value to our Delhi team last year,' Klusener just couldn't stop gushing about Navdeep.

When asked, what clicked for Navdeep, Klusener said, 'I think he has a wonderful action which is very clean and smooth. He is superbly fit as well. But while chatting with him, I realised he is hungry to bowl consistently at 150 clicks and above,' he opined.

Over the six months after the World Cup, Navdeep had become a regular in the white-ball format.

He was in red-hot form. He had played 10 T20Is and seven ODIs before the two-Test series in New Zealand in February 2020. Ishant Sharma was fighting against time to get fit from an ankle injury. Umesh Yadav had not played much international cricket leading up to the series. Nehra was vociferous while advocating blooding Navdeep into the playing XI in the first Test match.

Eventually, Ishant got himself fit for the first Test in Wellington, picked up 5/68 and broke down again. Trailing in the series, India opted to go with the experience of Umesh in the second Test in Christchurch.

The Test cap was still eluding Navdeep!

As the Indian team returned home from New Zealand, the

Covid-19 pandemic had begun to engulf the world. Soon, the lockdown happened.

It took nearly six months for Indian cricket to resume with the IPL in the UAE. The lockdown had disrupted Navdeep's momentum.

He was still maintaining his pace on the benign pitches in Dubai, Abu Dhabi and Sharjah but he wasn't as incisive. Navdeep did bowl a couple of immaculate pressure overs but he was clearly blowing hot and cold.

Perhaps, he was searching for the length he had found before the lockdown. The 13 matches in IPL 2020 yielded just 6 wickets at an average of 63.16 and economy rate of 8.29.

The selectors still backed him for all formats for the subsequent tour of Australia.

The two ODIs in Sydney, to start the tour, dented his prospects for the rest of the tour.

The Test debut did come his way on 7 January in Syndey. An injured Ishant wasn't available for the tour. By the time the third Test got underway at the Sydney Cricket Ground, India had lost Shami and Umesh Yadav to injuries.

Stand-in skipper Ajinkya Rahane and vice-captain Rohit Sharma preferred to play Navdeep to unsettle the Australians with sheer pace.

Navdeep had an indifferent Test, picking up 4 wickets for 119 runs across two innings.

But he reached Brisbane for the final Test, knowing he had to lead a beleaguered Indian attack with Mohammad Siraj. Jasprit Bumrah, too, was ruled out due to an abdomen injury.

Navdeep looked like regaining his rhythm on the first day of the Test. He got the prolific Marnus Labuschagne to edge a rising delivery in his eighth over only to be dropped by Rahane at gully.

Navdeep had also twitched his groin in that ball. He hopped off, uncertain of coming back for the rest of the match.

But he did come back to bowl in the second innings. He ambled in and bowled five overs. Even if it looked like he wasn't putting in much of an effort, he clocked 130 kmph.

'Ajinkya *bhaiyya* asked me if I would be able to bowl with the injury, I just had to say yes. I couldn't have let the team be with one bowler short in a crucial match. I knew I might not get a stage like that again. Captain asked me if I could do it. I was in pain but said I would do with whatever I could,' Saini says when asked why he took such a decision.

'I was wondering why it was happening in such a crucial game when I got the opportunity to play after a long time,' he could barely hide the despair.

That said, he still had a little bit more to do. He walked down to the middle to accompany a rampaging Rishabh Pant who had already brought India three short of the 328-run target on a dramatic final day.

Navdeep didn't have to face a ball. But he knew he had to stretch the dodgy groin. Luckily for him, Rishabh bunted Josh Hazlewood past the mid-off fielder for a boundary.

According to Rishabh, neither of them realised the ball was headed to the fence. 'When I hit the ball, I screamed out to Saini that you have to run three. Not even two. We kept running and all of a sudden saw the mid-off fielder wasn't chasing the ball. The ball had gone to the boundary,' Rishabh recounted the winning shot.

History was made and Navdeep was in the middle of it. Ask anybody in Indian cricket circles, humility is his strongest virtue. His fiery quick deliveries belie his polite and humble demeanour. Not bad for a boy who came from a nondescript village like Taraori with no formal coaching till he was eighteen!

# *CONCLUSION*

Sourav Ganguly, after having assumed charge as president of the Board of Control for Cricket in India (BCCI), has always insisted that Indian cricket is head and shoulders above the rest of the world. The world titles may come and go but in the twenty-first year of the twenty-first century, there is barely a series, tour or tournament where the Indian team didn't go in as favourites.

He doesn't bat an eyelid before making such an audacious claim. His confidence comes from the system that produces battle-ready cricketers literally in hordes. It's been over twenty years since Indian cricket found its spark under his captaincy.

Ganguly's core idea was to go beyond the traditional power centres of cricket in India. It's taken a while. By the time he had moved on to an administrative role, he could see his vision had taken shape, thanks to the work done by the preceding administrators.

There is no ignored zone as such now. Hence, the literal overflow of talent as the years go by.

Cricket is a round-the-year industry. Opportunities come thick and fast for the ones putting in the hard yards. But the competition can make even a wait of six months seem like a lifetime.

These stories offer just an idea about how a cricketer is hardened to endure the rigours of top-flight cricket. These stories are mere examples. They maybe a template but even these players would know there's somebody hungrier than them somewhere in the country ready to make bigger sacrifices to realise the cricketing dream.

The stories will come. Indian cricket is on auto mode. There's every opportunity at your disposal provided you have the will to edge past your competitor.

In India, cricket's journey started off as a dream, then became a religion and now it has become a full-fledged industry. There's a robust structure for the next generation. One that is much better than what these twelve cricketers had evolved in. The challenges will change with the evolution of the game.

But then what is a sportsman without overcoming challenges! Indian cricket is ready to throw up many such stories in the coming years!